Sociology

Other titles by Jack Nobbs:

Social Economics (McGraw-Hill, 1969)
Economic Problems of the 1970s (Pergamon Press, 1971)
Handbook on Objective Testing – Civics, with Marion Walton (Methuen, 1971)
Objective Questions in Social Economics (Methuen, 1972)
Economics for Advanced Level (McGraw-Hill, 1973)
Economics – Exam Guide for 'A' Level (McGraw-Hill, 1973)
Daily Economics, with Paul Ames (McGraw-Hill, 1975)
Modern Society (Allen and Unwin, 1976)
Introducing Social Studies (Macmillan, 1979)
Sociology Workbook, with Robert Hine (Macmillan, 1979)
Sociology in Context (Macmillan, 1983)
Social Science for GCSE (Macmillan, 1987)

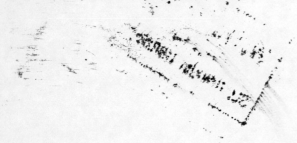

Sociology

Jack Nobbs *B.Sc. (Econ.), Dip. Soc.*
Robert Hine *BA, M.Phil.*
Margaret E. Flemming *BA, MA, Ph.D.*

Third edition
revisions by
Roger Fielding *B.Sc., M.Phil., M.Ed.*

First published 1975
Reprinted 1976 (twice), 1977, 1978
Second edition 1979
Reprinted 1980
Revised second edition 1980
Reprinted 1981
Third edition 1989

Published by
MACMILLAN EDUCATION LTD
Houndmills, Basingstoke, Hampshire RG21 2XS
and London
Companies and representatives
throughout the world

Printed in Hong Kong

British Library Cataloguing in Publication Data
Nobbs, Jack, *1923–*
Sociology.
3rd ed.
1. Great Britain. Society
I. Title   II. Hine, Robert   III. Flemming, Margaret E.
(Margaret Elizabeth)   IV. Fielding, Roger
941.085'8
ISBN 0–333–43539–7

Contents

Preface to the Third Edition

The third edition of *Sociology* has been completely revised in the light of the demands of the new GCSE examination. It covers all four English (NEA, MEG, SEG and LEAG) and the Welsh (WJEC) GCSE Examination Board syllabuses. A great advantage of this book is that it combines the expertise of four experienced teachers. In particular, Roger Fielding has brought a new insight to the text and specialised knowledge of the needs of GCSE candidates to show awareness of methods of enquiry used by sociologists and to comprehend and make use of statistical data. One of the key demands of GCSE, of course, is the requirement that students take a practical approach to their sociological studies, using both their own experience and collected evidence to explore topics and issues. This new edition has been written with these demands firmly in mind.

As Social Science Secretary to the London and East Anglian Board during 1986/87, I was a member of the committee which produced the GCSE Sociology syllabus and specimen papers. Consequently I have been able to ensure that the new edition of *Sociology* fits both the needs and the philosophy of the GCSE examination.

In 1974, Terry Schofield (Chief Examiner, GCE '0' Level Sociology for the Associated Examining Board) welcomed this book as 'interesting, stimulating and valuable' for both students and teachers. His views have been shared by many students and teachers who have used *Sociology* in the last fifteen years, confirming its value as a textbook for both classroom use and individual study. The third edition ensures that the book remains in step with social changes and also acknowledges the need for today's students of GCSE Sociology to be aware of the new examination's approach which is based upon the comprehension, application and evaluation of sociological material.

Jack Nobbs
(1988)

1 *Welcome to sociology*

►UNIT 1 What is sociology?

1.1 Models of society

Many have a notion that sociology is about people: some think that sociology is all about helping the unfortunate and doing welfare work, while others think that sociology is the same as socialism and is a means of bringing revolution to our schools and colleges. Certainly sociology is about people; but understanding some of the problems of people is only part of sociology. Sociology also leads us to look very closely at 'society' and the way 'societies' work.

ACTIVITIES 1

You have chosen to spend time studying sociology. Try to explain why you have chosen sociology and what you are expecting it to be like. Suppose you have been asked by your parents or another relative 'What's sociology, then?', and write down the sort of things you might say.

The word 'sociology' was first used by the French philosopher Auguste Comte in the late 1830s. The *Oxford Dictionary* defines sociology as 'the science of the development and nature and laws of human (esp. civilised) society; study of social problems'. We shall

go on to show what sociologists *say* and how sociology is *done* in later chapters. Here, we are looking at what sociology *is*.

Throughout the world people live in groups. The smallest grouping is usually the family, and the largest group is a nation or possibly a federation of nations, such as the United Nations. In between are a host of different groups like the ones in school, workplace, neighbourhood, village or town. We refer to all these as *social groups*. It is easy for us to think of the family as a group, but it is harder to work out precisely who belongs to a particular community.

All groups have some kind of organisation and purpose to them, and the way in which people of a group behave towards one another tells us something about the nature of the group. Sociologists look for these patterns of behaviour, and try to understand the causes which shape them.

A twentieth-century sociologist called Chris Brown has defined society as a series of relationships between people, and he says it is the nature of these relationships sociologists have to study (C.H. Brown, *Understanding Society*: John Murray, 1979). Brown says that we all have an idea of what we mean by 'society' buried deep in our consciousness, and that it has a profound influence on how we understand and interpret what happens to us and the events that take place in the world.

ACTIVITIES 2

In order to 'excavate' or dig out your own personal model or idea of society, Brown suggests drawing a picture or diagram which you think represents 'society'. Do not use words, only shapes and pictures, and do not spend more than a few minutes on this activity.

The diagram or picture you have drawn will have revealed the hidden assumptions you make which help you to make sense of the world. Brown suggests the kinds of picture people usually draw are limited to variations on a range of three or four ideas, and the most common shape chosen to represent society is a circle. The diagrams in Item 1.1 illustrate different ideas about the nature of society.

ACTIVITIES 3

Study Item 1.1 and answer the questions that follow.

1 What do you think the different circles might represent in diagrams 1a, 1b and 1c?

2 What ideas about the society would you expect people who drew diagrams like 2a, 2b and 2c to have?

3 What might the boxes in diagram 3 represent? Copy out the diagram and fill in the boxes.

4 What is prominent in all of diagrams 4a, 4b and 4c which is missing from all of the other diagrams?

5 Try to explain in words why you drew the diagram of society you did, and what your diagram reveals about the way you see society.

What makes sociology an exciting subject is that it tells us more about ourselves and the way in which we live. There are people who regard the findings of sociologists as just common sense, things which any good observer of society would have realised. The sociologist does often start with common-sense ideas – for example, that people who receive less education do not get as well-paid jobs as those who have had more education. But sociological research can show whether this is really the case, and what proportion of poorly educated people in fact have been able to get well-paid jobs. Even more important, sociologists often are able to disprove widely held wrong ideas about the society in which we live.

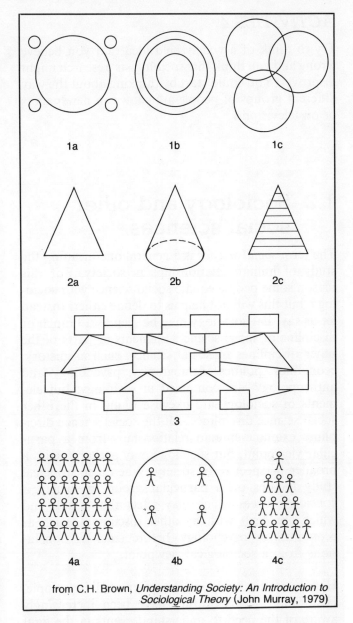

from C.H. Brown, *Understanding Society: An Introduction to Sociological Theory* (John Murray, 1979)

Item 1.1   Models of society

Another twentieth-century sociologist, Roland Meighan, has likened sociological research to a mission 'to penetrate the smoke-screen of the official versions of reality'. He goes on to say: 'The outcomes of these (sociological) missions are not guaranteed. The investigation may yield something fresh and unexpected. This may be something totally unfamiliar or it may be the familiar taking on a new meaning. Sociology may make us see in a new light the very world in which we have lived all our lives' (Roland Meighan, *The Sociology of Education*, Holt, 1981).

ACTIVITIES 4

Try to think of a widely held idea that you believe wrong and you think that sociologists' research might disprove. (You could start by thinking about the way different groups of people are shown in newspapers or on television.)

1.2 Sociology and other social sciences

The term *social science* is a general one meaning the study of human relationships in society. For this reason some people equate social science with sociology, but this will not help us to define either. Instead let us say that sociology may be seen as a branch or discipline of social science. Elements or parts of the other disciplines of social science, such as history, economics, politics, demography, psychology and anthropology, are contained in sociology; but elements of sociology are likewise found in the other social science disciplines. All the social science disciplines examine human relationships from a particular viewpoint, but sociology may perhaps claim a broader perspective of society. When a sociological study focuses on a particular group in society it considers forces which may affect that group and which are dealt with by other disciplines, such as economics or psychology, before reaching conclusions from a sociological viewpoint.

History is the study of events created by people. Historians in this century have been increasingly aware of the need to understand events in the light of social factors such as increases in population, the psychology of individuals, or the importance of social classes. There are specialised branches of history – economic history, social history, political history – but all involve human activity and human relationships in the study of the past.

Economics is concerned with getting and spending: the study of the spending and financial habits of people. The economist is concerned with the use that people make of money and capital resources. Sociologists try to establish the economic patterns of different groupings and the extent to which economic forces affect people's lives.

Politics is the study of governments and power. Sociologists study the nature and composition of groups who seek or who have attained power. Political sociologists are interested in, for example, voting behaviour.

Demography is the scientific study of population. Demographers look at changes in the population and sociologists relate these changes to society. As the size and structure of the population is important to a society, it is important to the sociologist.

Psychology is concerned with the experience and behaviour of people and how they react to certain conditions. Sociologists are usually more concerned with group psychology and social psychology.

Anthropology is one of the disciplines closest to sociology. Anthropology is the detailed study of people, most usually in pre-industrial societies. Anthropologists used to be concerned primarily with the biological changes in human development, but social anthropology today is often regarded as the same as sociology.

REVIEW

If you have studied and understood this chapter you should be able to ...

- explain in a short paragraph what sociology is about.
- draw at least two alternative models of society and explain what they show.
- outline the relationship sociology has with the other social sciences, and explain how it differs from these.

COURSEWORK SUGGESTION

Ask about ten people to draw a picture or diagram of society. Try not to give them too many clues on what to draw and see what results you get. You should then ask them why they included any of the following features in their picture:

a circles,
b stick figures,
c ladders,
d pyramids,
e triangles.

2 *Approaches to the study of sociology*

AIMS

At the end of this chapter you should be able to:

- recognise where sociologists get their data from.
- identify and use different kinds of data.
- explain and use different methods for collecting your own data.
- construct a research project of your own and carry it through to the final report.
- evaluate and criticise accounts of sociological research.

UNIT 2 Understanding data

2.1 Did you know?

Did you know that . . .

– between 1971/2 and 1983/4 there was an overall trend towards larger schools; in 1983/4, 30 per cent of public sector secondary schools in the United Kingdom had over 1000 pupils, compared with only 12 per cent in 1971/2?

– only three per cent of university first degrees awarded to women in 1983 were in engineering and technology, while 21 per cent were in language, literature and theatre studies?

– in 1985, 74 per cent of the population of Great Britain in the 25–29 age group held an educational qualification, whereas only 42 per cent of those aged between 50 and 59 did so?

Did you know that . . .

– the police recorded 3.5 million notifiable offences in England and Wales in 1984, eight per cent more than in 1983?

– cars, vans, and motorbikes are the most common targets of crime: in 1983 one in five owners had their vehicles stolen or vandalised, or property stolen from their vehicles?

– the average population in prison establishments in England and Wales in 1984 was 43 300, compared with accommodation designed for 39 200, as at the end of the year? By 1986 the average population had grown to 54 200?

Did you know that . . .

– all these facts about life in the UK are collected together in a government publication which is updated every year, *Social Trends* (HMSO)?

2.2 Sources of data

Sociologists do not always collect their own data; often they can use data collected already by other people. Such data is called *secondary data* – perhaps because it is almost second-hand. Secondary data may have been collected by people who are not sociologists at all, even by people who know nothing about sociology, Governments always collect a vast range of statistical information to help in administration, planning and policy making and there is no reason why we should not use this source of information if we are careful to understand it properly. *Social Trends* collects data from a wide range of government sources to give as complete a picture as possible of where society has got to and how it is changing. The first edition appeared in 1970. All the facts about Britain at the beginning of this unit can be found in *Social Trends 16*, the 1986 edition, or Social Trends 18, the 1988 edition. You will find the latest copy of *Social Trends* in the public library – your local library

Item 2.1   The Government Statistical Service is the greatest concentration of statistical expertise and by far the largest single provider of statistics in the UK

Item 2.2   Major surveys used in *Social Trends 18* (1988)

	Frequency	Sampling frame	Type of respondent	Location	Set sample size (most recent survey included) in *Social Trends*)	Response rate (percentages)
Census of Population	Decennial	Detailed local	Household head	UK	Full count	100
British Social Attitudes Survey	Annual	Electoral Register	Adult in household	GB	2,508 addresses	74
British Tourism Survey – Yearly*	Annual	Electoral Register	Individual adult	GB	3,500 individuals	68
Continuous household	Continuous	Rating valuation list	All adults in household	NI	4,500 addresses	73
Family Expenditure Survey	Continuous	Electoral Register	Household	UK	11,040 addresses	67
General Household Survey	Continuous	Postcode Address File	All adults in household	GB	13,248 addresses	82
International Passenger Survey	Continuous	International passengers at ports, airports, etc	Individual traveller	UK	171,000 individuals	81
Labour Force Survey	Continuous Continuous	Postcode Address File	Adult in household	UK	60,000 addresses	83
National Food Survey	Continuous	Postcode Address File	Housewife	GB	11,040 addresses	63
National Readership Survey		Electoral Register	Individual adult	GB	27,410 individuals	69
National Travel Survey	Intermittent Annual	Postcode Address File	Individual in household	GB	15,120 addresses	76
New Earnings Survey	Annual	National Insurance	Employee	GB	166,000 employees	
Survey of Personal Incomes		Inland Revenue	Tax unit	UK	68,600 tax units	95

* Previously known as the British National Travel Survey.

from *Social Trends 18* (HMSO, 1988)

will be able get it for you if they have not already got it.

Item 2.2 shows some of the major government and other surveys used to compile *Social Trends*.

We will look again at this table later in the chapter – do not worry at this stage if you do not understand all the terms in the table. The general areas covered by *Social Trends* include: population; households and families; education; employment; income and wealth; resources and expenditure; health and public safety; housing; transport; communications and the environment; leisure; participation; law enforcement and social groups. International comparisons are also included in their respective topic areas.

Item 2.3 is an example of an entry from *Social Trends*. You will see the table again in Chapter 5, on education.

ACTIVITIES 1

1 Apart from going to the library to look up statistics like these, what else might be of use to a sociologist wanting to know more about social behaviour? What other sorts of data could sociologists look at to find out about social life?

Item 2.3 Qualification levels of the population: by age, 1988

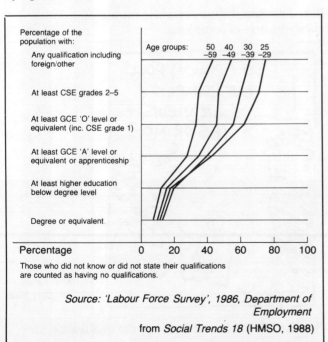

Percentage of the population with:

Source: 'Labour Force Survey', 1986, Department of Employment

from *Social Trends 18* (HMSO, 1988)

2 In what ways would watching *Grange Hill* tell a sociologist anything useful (or inaccurate) about life in schools?

3 Why do you think the government collects information like this and publishes it?

2.3 Types of data

We have already seen that some data is described as secondary data; data sociologists collect for themselves first-hand is called *primary data*. If you have talked about different ways of finding out about social life you have probably realised that sociologists can use all sorts of data to help them – books, films, diaries, conversations and observations as well as questionnaires, interviews and statistics. Sociologists call statistical data *quantitative* data because statistics try to measure the quantity of a thing. Data which does not involve statistics, numbers or measurement is called *qualitative* data because it reveals or illuminates the different qualities or characteristics of social life and social behaviour.

Key terms

- secondary data
- primary data
- quantitative data
- qualitative data

▶ UNIT 3 Collecting your own data

3.1 Asking questions

Social surveys involve the use of a questionnaire of some kind. This can take a number of forms. Either the respondents are asked a series of questions, the answers to which are filled in on a form by an interviewer, or else the respondents complete the forms themselves. Both methods have their advantages and disadvantages, depending on the kind of information you are looking for.

Questionnaires can be of the type in which the respondents are asked a set question and mark off an appropriate reply. For example, the respondents may be asked to reply to the question 'How much money do you earn before all deductions?' by ticking one of a number of boxes, as shown in Item 2.5.

This type of question is known as the *pre-coded* variety.

The respondents might instead be asked to answer a general question, such as 'What do you think of the government's economic policy?' in their own words, either by writing down their reply or dictating it to the interviewer. This is known as an *open-ended* question – one inviting the respondents to answer freely in their own way. For obvious reasons precoded questions are easier to analyse and computers may be used to do this in large surveys.

Item 2.4 Social surveys involve the use of questionnaires of some kind

How much money do you earn before all deductions?	
Under £70 per week	☐
£70 – £80 per week	☐
£80 – £90 per week	☐
£90 – £100 per week	☐
£100 – £110 per week	☐
£110 – £120 per week	☐
£120 – £130 per week	☐
Over £130 per week	☐

Item 2.5 Pre-coded questions

DO OPINION POLLS OVERSIMPLIFY YOUR VIEWS – YES OR NO?

from *Radio Times*, 15–21 February 1986

Item 2.6 It is quite difficult to write questions that yield useful responses

ACTIVITIES 2

Writing a questionnaire that all your respondents will understand in the same way is difficult. Try writing a short questionnaire, using pre-coded questions (that is, providing options and boxes to tick), about the reading habits of other students in your class; or choose another topic of interest to you.

The commonest form of investigation without an interviewer is the mail questionnaire. Respondents are sent the questionnaire through the post accompanied by a prepaid envelope for the reply. The two main advantages of the mail questionnaire are that it is cheap and results can be obtained rapidly. If funds are limited, then the differences between paying a day's wage to a trained interviewer, who may be able to see a dozen respondents, and posting out several hundred questionnaires for the same price, may be a deciding factor.

ACTIVITIES 3

You should now try to list all the things you think might be disadvantages in using mail questionnaires. Begin this exercise by imagining you are at home and a questionnaire comes through your letter box. How would you react and how would you fill it in?

Sometimes questionnaires ask a question which would be best answered by a family discussing the reply; for example, a question on family expenditure. Sociologists call this *intrahousehold consultation*. If people can reply to this sort of questionnaire at their leisure, or at least when they are all together, and not just when the interviewer calls, then they may reply more precisely, especially if they need to look up documents to give an answer. Intimate personal questions often receive a better response through an anonymous mail questionnaire than if they are asked by an interviewer.

If the interviewer is not properly trained, such things as speech, dress and manner may put off the respondent, and this does not happen with a mail questionnaire. Quite often interviewers have difficulty in making contact with selected respondents from a carefully chosen representative sample (see topic 3.2), and time may be lost before the meeting is arranged. This too will not happen with mail questionnaires.

The main disadvantage of mail questionnaires, and therefore an advantage of having trained interviewers, is that there is always a chance of the wording being confusing and the questions being misunderstood. The answers given to mail questionnaires must be taken as final, and no allowance is made for the possibility of people misunderstanding questions and being inaccurate in their replies. For this reason the choice of words, in all types of questionnaires but especially in mail questionnaires, is of the greatest importance.

Sometimes questions require a spontaneous response, before the respondent has the chance to think of a reply, and obviously this is not possible with a mail questionnaire. Other questions may be of a 'follow-up' type depending upon the answer to one particular question, such as 'Do you take part in an active sport? If "Yes", which one, and for how long each week?'. If the respondent has had the chance to read through all the questions before answering, he or she may frame the replies to match all the questions. On occasions the truthful answer can only be obtained when other members of the family are not present: people may not like to fill out the real answer to a question on how much they spend on beer each week in a intrahousehold consultation.

The usual method of using questionnaires is to have a trained interviewer. When an interviewer conducts a face-to-face interview, we call this a *formal interview*. Formal interviewing requires special skills in the interviewer. To start with, the interviewer often has to find the respondents and encourage them to answer the questions. Getting replies from reluctant respondents may be quite difficult. During a formal interview the interviewer should give an impression of neutrality, firstly so that the respondent does not give replies which he or she thinks the interviewer would like to hear, and secondly so that the respondent is not embarrassed to answer any of the questions on the questionnaire.

Checklist

Advantages of a mail questionnaire:
1 It is cheap.
2 It gets relatively rapid results.
3 It can cover a wide area.
4 It gets a good response rate.
5 There is no personal contact to distort replies.
6 It allows a considered response.

ACTIVITIES 4: Play-reading

Read the following passage and answer the questions which follow. If you are working in groups you might choose to read the passage out loud.

(A job interview for a sales rep. for Ultra Toys. Interviewer – Mr Brown. Interviewee – Mr Turner, who is desperate for the job.)

Mr Brown   Ah, come in, Mr . . . Turner isn't it? Sit down, sit down. Cigar? I don't smoke myself.

Mr Turner   No, no, I don't either.

Mr Brown   Drink? That is one of my vices, I'm afraid – the old scotch, you know.

Mr Turner   Yes, well, thank you . . . I'd like one, please.

Mr Brown   Bit early in the day for me, but I'll pour you one.

Mr Turner   Later perhaps. Yes . . . a bit later on.

Mr Brown   You drink a lot, Mr Turner?

Mr Turner   Oh no; socially, you know; hardly at all, in fact. Just to be sociable, you might say.

Mr Brown   Now then, to business. Would you say you were a confident sort of man? Could you speak easily to would–be customers, be outgoing and so forth?

Mr Turner   Oh yes, definitely, I think I'd be able to keep the conversation moving along, putting clients at their ease and making everything flow smoothly – no awkward pauses or embarrassing silences or anything like that – no, I assure you, I think my confidence in your product and in myself would reassure whoever I was dealing with and if I had to attend a party and discuss business I'm sure I'd put the right image over –.

Mr Brown   Yes – of course, do you think it's also important not to come on too strong, putting the client off? Could you be laid back if you sensed that would be the right approach?

Mr Turner   (*Pause*) Yeah.

Mr Brown   Good! Anything in your personal life that might interfere with your work?

Mr Turner   Interfere . . .? Er . . . oh! No, I'm not married or anything.

Mr Brown   No plans to start a family?

Mr Turner   Good Lord, no. Furthest thing from my mind.

Mr Brown   To be honest we were hoping our new rep. would be an imposing individual – suggest authority and dignity in the way he carried himself.

Mr Turner   Oh, I've better suits than this one. If you gave me some hints on how you wanted me to dress I'm sure I could look the part –

Mr Brown   No, I mean your height – our last salesman was six feet two inches tall. Very successful. You seem rather short, Mr Turner.

Mr Turner   I could get myself stretched, Mr Brown. There's an operation where they can cut the leg bones and fit in an extendable rod. I could be adjustable. I could wear stilts in the meantime.

Mr Brown   Well, that seems rather a lot of trouble to go to. In fact we thought perhaps a lady might suit our purpose this time. Change of image, you

Item 2.7   Informal interviews can draw out the respondent's true feelings

know. The gentle touch, etc.

Mr Turner   There's this operation you can have done. I've read about it – in a private clinic they take a sharp knife and –

Mr Brown   Thank you, Mr Turner. That will be all.

1   There are at least three questions Mr Brown asked Mr Turner which are leading questions, that is, which suggest the 'right answer' by the way they are phrased. Read the passage again and pick out the leading questions.

2   Will Mr Brown find out what he wants to know about Mr Turner? Give reasons for your answer.

3   In this passage Mr Turner was *very* anxious to say what Mr Brown wanted him to. In what ways could the same thing happen during sociological research?

4   Comment on the ways sociological researchers can avoid the problems vividly portrayed above.

Informal interviewing is more difficult than formal interviewing. The interviewer tries to get a more relaxed atmosphere in order to draw out the respondent's feelings, opinions and confidences, and yet subsequently tries to report the findings in an objective, unbiased way. Very often informal interviewing is used to follow up formal interviews after a respondent has shown some interesting characteristics which the investigators wish to look at in greater depth.

ACTIVITIES 5

It can take a lot of self-confidence to go out and do a piece of sociological research. Write down a few short open-ended questions on any topic of your choice. Practise being an interviewer by asking your questions of a student sitting near you.

Does your respondent give the answers you are expecting? Can you use the answers for your research on the topic? Do your questions really obtain the information you want?

Key terms

- questionnaire
- pre-coded questions
- open-ended questions
- interview

3.2 Taking a sample

Ideally a sociological investigation should include everyone under consideration when data is being gathered. This group is known as the *population*, but it is often impossible for a sociologist to consider everybody who should be involved in the investigation. For this reason *samples* are taken of the population. For example, if you wanted to study all the fifth-year students in your school, the population of your study would be all the fifth-year students and you might take a smaller sample from this population to interview.

Item 2.8   How would you go about taking a sample of pupils at your school?

In general, the larger the sample taken the more representative of the population it will be. A survey, no matter how large, would be biased if only motorists were asked whether the tax on petrol should be lowered, or only families with two children were asked how adequate the family allowance was. Bias can occur in many ways if the sample is not carefully thought out, so sociologists try to make their sample as representative of the population as possible.

Two factors usually limit a sample, just as they limit any investigation: time and money. The more time and money a sociologist has at his or her disposal, the more thorough the investigation can be. More time and money could mean a larger sample, and perhaps a more accurate conclusion. If we wished to investigate the problem of homelessness in Britain and had several years and plenty of money we could employ many investigators. Because resources of both time and money are usually limited, we should use them to the best advantage.

The ideal sample size is reached when there is no important advantage to be gained by increasing the size of the sample.

Methods of sampling

Random sampling is a general term meaning that each individual in the population has an equal chance of being picked out for investigation, and samples are chosen on a strictly random basis. This might involve allocating each member of the population a number and then using a computer to generate random numbers. (A random sample, however, can be taken very simply by putting every one's name on a piece of

Item 2.9   A random sample can be taken very simply by putting everyone's name on a piece of paper and picking out of a hat

paper and picking out of a hat!) An important feature of a random sample is that there should not be any chance of individual preference or personal choice affecting the sample.

ACTIVITIES 6

Imagine you are interviewing people in the street or in the school grounds. Suppose you had been told to interview anyone 'at random'. Why would your sample not really be random? What sort of people would you choose? What sort of people would you avoid?

Item 2.10   How could you interview people at random from a busy street?

Clearly, to take a random sample, in which each individual in the population has an equal chance of being picked out for the sample, you must have a full and complete *list* of your population. If you do not know who is included in the population, those people you are unaware of have no chance of being chosen. The full complete list of the population is called a *sampling frame*.

ACTIVITIES 7

1 Look again at Item 2.2 and list at least five different sampling frames that were used in the surveys listed. If you were to draw a random sample of fifth-year students at your school, what sampling frame would you use? If you have difficulty with this question look again at Item 2.8 for a clue.

2 Draw a random sample from your sociology class. List your population in order to compile your sampling frame, then pick the names out of a hat. Take a 40 per cent sample – for every ten students in the class take a sample of four students.

Sometimes a random sample takes too much time and a *systematic sample* may be used. This is not a truly random sample but can be useful in research. To take a systematic sample, you might include in your sample every fourth person from your sampling frame or population list.

In deciding whether a sample is representative or not it is important to consider *which features of the population are of particular importance*. If you are

doing research on reading habits and eyesight you will want to be representative in terms of whether people wear spectacles or not. However, if you are interested in eating habits and growth then eyesight may be irrelevant.

ACTIVITIES 8

1 What proportion of students in your sociology group (your population):
   a are girls?
   b wear glasses?
   c have dark hair?
   d are taller than five feet five inches?

2 How representative has your random sample turned out to be with reference to each of these characteristics? Are the proportions in your sample the same as the proportions in the original population?

The best method of avoiding error in most investigations is to divide the population into blocks or *strata* (layers) on a specified basis such as by income, age, sex, or education. The distribution of these subdivided groups means in effect that each stratum becomes a population on its own, and this method is termed *stratified sampling*.

In the examples we have been using, if you had been particularly interested in the eyesight of your respondents you would have divided your sampling frame into two lists – those who wore glasses and those who did not. You would then have taken your final sample in two stages, randomly sampling from

Item 2.11   Each stratum becomes a population of its own

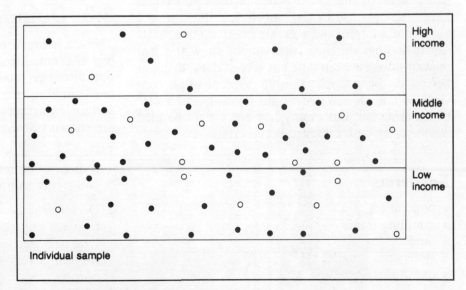

High income

Middle income

Low income

Individual sample

Item 2.12   The sampling frame is divided into four lists and the sample is taken in four stages

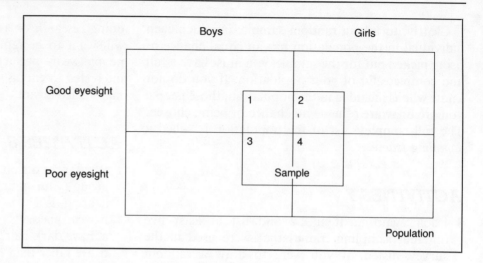

each list in turn. In this way you would have known your final sample contained the same proportion of spectacle wearers as the original population. You can *stratify* a population as often as seems necessary. For instance, if as well as eyesight the sex of your respondents was important, you would stratify your sample by both eyesight and sex.

Another non-random type of sampling is *quota sampling,* A group of investigators is given the task of finding a set number of people containing a given proportion of social characteristics – half males and half females, or one-sixth old age pensioners, etc. Commercial surveying organisations use this method of sampling.

No sociologist can afford to neglect statistics. The correct use of statistics can provide the basis for good judgement in sociology. The use of statistics can indicate whether the outcome of the investigation is likely to be significant, or whether the result could have been obtained by random chance. But statistics also require careful and accurate interpretation. Statistical findings on their own cannot show the real relationships between different sets of data. It might be found, for example, that 95 per cent of all convicted criminals are male, right-handed, and under two metres tall, but clearly not every right-handed man shorter than two metres is a criminal.

Key terms

- population
- sampling frame
- random sample
- systematic sample
- quota sample

ACTIVITIES 9

Below are four examples of sampling procedures.

Population: Voters in a small city
Sample: Every hundredth name listed in the telephone directory

Population: Students at a college or school
Sample: All students taking sociology

Population: Attenders at a league football match
Sample: Every tenth person passing through the turnstile

Population: Residents of a council housing estate
Sample: The first 100 people to be at home when you ring the door bell of every third house

How satisfactory are these sampling procedures?

3.3 Doing a survey

The whole exercise of writing a questionnaire, drawing a sample, giving out and getting back your questionnaire, analysing your data and then presenting your results is called a *social survey.* There are certain important steps to be taken in a survey. These are shown below.

1 Define the aim of your survey – what are you trying to find out and what *hypothesis* or idea are you trying to prove?

2 Decide exactly what information or data you need to reach any conclusions about your hypothesis. Don't collect information out of interest or just for fun. Every question you ask should have a purpose.

3 Write your questionnaire so that the responses you get will give you the information you need. You will need to decide whether to use pre-coded questions and boxes to tick, or open-ended questions with blank spaces to be filled in. You might use a mixture of both. Remember that pre-coded responses are easier to count up at the end but that open-ended responses may tell you things you were not expecting to find out.

4 Get a sampling frame of the population you are studying and then draw a random sample. Include as many people in your sample as you can manage but no more than you think are necessary to be representative of your population.

　If you have not got a sampling frame of your population then you cannot draw a random sample, of course, and might decide to use a quota sample instead.

5 Conduct a *pilot survey*. A pilot survey tests your questionnaire to make sure it is going to work, and may show up faults in the design of the questionnaire. For example, questions may have been included which people do not understand, or which are ambiguous. You might find people refuse to answer certain vital questions or that a questionnaire designed to take five minutes for each respondent actually takes ten minutes. You might need to rethink the time you allow for this in your full survey.

　Be careful not to give your questionnaire to anyone who is going to be in your final sample. Otherwise they will already have seen the sort of questions you intend to ask and it might affect their answers.

6 Once you have revised your questionnaire you can distribute it to the respondents included in your sample.

　You should decide whether you will post the questionnaire to your sample, or give it them and let them fill it in by themselves, or whether you will interview each respondent and fill in the questionnaire yourself according to what your respondents say.

7 When the questionnaires come back, or when you have finished interviewing your respondents, you will have lots of information to analyse and make sense of. It is at this stage that you have to use your sociological imagination. In other words, you will now have to do more than count up your replies –

Item 2.13　A questionnaire designed to take five minutes might take longer

you will have to look at your information *as a sociologist* and try to decide what it all means. If you managed to do your planning correctly your data should begin to make sense as soon as you start to count up the results.

Checklist

Doing a survey – steps to be taken:

1 Sort out your hypotheses or ideas.
2 Plan your data collection.
3 Write your questions.
4 Draw a sample.
5 Do a pilot survey.
6 Revise your methods and questions.
7 Do your survey.
8 Report on your results.

Key terms

- survey
- hypothesis
- pilot survey

3.4 Watching people

As we have said, most surveys involve a questionnaire of some kind, but important sociological research has been conducted using other kinds of data collection. There are many aspects of behaviour which could not be contained in a series of questions, no matter how well devised. Some investigators prefer to gain an impression of these, instead of seeking a mass of information that questionnaires might provide. The general name for this kind of investigation is the *observational approach*. Television documentaries, often investigation social problems, use this technique by filming the conditions under which people live, the way in which they speak and what their attitudes to things are – a qualitative rather than a quantitative approach.

There are some kinds of social activity and situations where it is best for the investigator to live among the subjects of his or her research – for example, if he or she is investigating people involved in crime. This is known as *participant observation*. The insight gained by living and working among the people being studied can be far greater than it would have been if the observer were an outsider. A deep understanding of the subject under study is possible. The participant observer must, though, be constantly aware of the need to be objective in the study – and this can prove difficult as friendships are bound to develop, and observation can cause respondents to act unnaturally. If the participant observer is not objective then he or she may well only see things in the same way as the people he or she is there to observe.

ACTIVITIES 10

Imagine you are from another planet and that you have arrived at your school. Write down what you would observe if you stood in the corridor, near a window so you could see inside a classroom and into the school grounds. *Remember* you have never seen a school before and have no idea what schools do nor whom or what they are for.

We can, finally, summarise these different approaches to social investigation in the diagram in Item 2.15.

Sociologists have to trade off the number of respondents they include in their study against closer involvement with their respondents. Clearly a sociologist might not actually meet any respondents in a mail questionnaire survey of 5000 people, but a sociologist doing a close observational study of a small group would get to know them all very well indeed.

Item 2.14 Observation can sometimes give far greater insight into what really goes on than questionnaires ever could

Item 2.15 Levels of the sociologist's involvement in different methods of social investigation

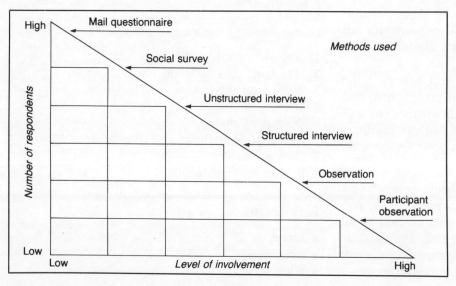

Writing up your research

4.1 Picking a problem

When picking a problem to research you should bear in mind several points:

1 The topic, as far as possible, should be of some personal interest to you. Look back over some of the work you have done and some of the topics you have studied and list the topics or ideas which particularly caught your imagination.

2 The topic you choose should allow you to use effectively and appropriately a number of the sociological research methods described in earlier sections of this chapter.

3 The research project on your chosen topic should be one you feel you can complete in the time available. It is better to set yourself a modest and manageable task and complete it well than begin a grand survey which remains unfinished.

4 Always remember your research project should be aimed at finding out facts about the topic under study, or increasing your *understanding* of an area of social life. Do not simply give your own opinions and ideas without referring to your *evidence* and *data*.

4.2 Doing sociological research

You will have to be quite organised in advance if you are to complete your own piece of research successfully. Your first job is to state the aim of your project clearly. You should write this down both for yourself and for others to see.

You should not be afraid to 'have a go'. Remember that when you do a survey you should complete a pilot survey first. This means you can correct your mistakes before it is too late. If you are going to do a small observational study you will need the confidence to start talking to people, and to direct their conversation towards the topics you are interested in exploring.

Your own coursework project will probably not go as smoothly as you would like. You will find pro-blems and difficulties. Read the extract in Item 2.16 of an account of a research project by a professional sociologist, Colin Bell – as you will see even experienced sociologists have problems.

> It would be true to say that the three of us in the field were never welded into a team; whether that was ever possible it is now impossible to say. Certainly Margaret Stacey's increasing intervention is now seen as a *consequence* of my lack of direction and co-ordination, though I saw it at the time, and certainly see it now, as one *cause* of my increasing detachment and eventual decision to take a teaching job. Anyway, by 1968 Margaret Stacey was much more heavily involved in running the project than either of us had initially anticipated. After I was at the University of Essex she took full and overt responsibility, and to that extent my departure rationalised the authority structure of the project. In the summer of 1968 Anne Murcott and Eric Bastone went to Swansea and I went to Colchester. By that time we had all had more than enough both of each other and of Banbury. This was not the happiest situation in which to start writing up a major community study, especially when one adds the data-handling problems mentioned above. That *Power, Persistence and Change* was written up at all owes more to the determination and endless energy of Margaret Stacey than to anything or anybody else. Left to ourselves I strongly suspect that we would have individually abandoned the data and the project. Yet to illustrate how bad personal relationships were at this stage, it was eighteen months after leaving the project before I was allowed to have the punch cards at Essex, largely because of the suspicion in Swansea that I would in some way 'run off' with the data and publish separately. There was also an unresolved disparity between the survey-generated data and that produced by our more general fieldwork activity. The closest approximation I know of a description of what I was doing is a phrase in William F. Whyte's *Street Corner Society* (1955). He based his sociology on 'observed interpersonal events'. I was familiar with that phrase while I was still in the field, yet I was never clear how my small-scale fieldwork observations were to fit with data from the survey.
>
> from C. Bell and H. Newby (eds.), *Doing Sociological Research* (Allen & Unwin, 1979)

Item 2.16 An account of a research project: 1

ACTIVITIES 11

In Item 2.16, Colin Bell is describing a research project he and three other sociologists (Margaret Stacey, Anne Murcott and Eric Batstone) worked on. The aim of the project was to look at social change in Banbury, a small town near Oxford. Read the passage and answer the questions that follow it.

1 List some of the problems Colin Bell found when he was doing his research. (Not all the problems are related to sociological theories and methods.)

2 What do you think Colin Bell means when he says 'there was also an unresolved disparity [gap] between the survey-generated data and that produced by our more general fieldwork activity'?

If you find yourself arguing with your classmates about your coursework project – remember it is all part of doing research!

ACTIVITIES 12

Now read the extract from Colin Bell in Item 2.17 about the problems of doing fieldwork, and answer the questions that follow it.

1 If you were to conduct a study of aspects of social life within your school or college, what difficulties would you foresee?

2 What does Colin Bell mean when he says 'fieldwork never stops' and 'doing fieldwork is like being continually on stage'?

3 Explain the difference between 'fieldworker as friend' and 'fieldworker as stranger'. Use examples given by Colin Bell and give examples of your own.

ACTIVITIES 13

Sociologists called Robert Moore and John Rex studied an area of Birmingham called Sparkbrook. Item 2.18 is Robert Moore's account of some of his experiences while doing research. Read the passage and answer the questions that follow it.

1 What does Moore mean when he says 'research ... is a way of life' and 'biography and methodology impinge upon [touch and affect] one another'?

2 Draw out the similarities between Colin Bell's and Robert Moore's experiences of research.

Later in his account Moore says the tale of his research is really just 'the everyday story of sociologists'. Now *you* should start your own study with your own piece of research.

Fieldwork bears heavily on the families of those who do it. I must emphasise again that we were all living there with our families – I, for instance, participantly observed as an expectant father in the maternity wing of Banbury's hospital. We shopped, used pubs, went to parties, movies and so on as ordinary, if hyperactive, inhabitants. The *structural* strain of fieldwork between fieldworker as friend and fieldworker as stranger resulted in great *personal* strain. We lived with this for two years at considerable personal cost. Fieldwork, let it be emphasised, never stops. We could not disentangle work from non-work. A good example of this that led to some irritation was that it was impossible to separate our everyday living expenses from those of the project; for example, when should we get a mileage allowance for running our cars, and when should we claim for entertaining in our homes an informant who may or may not also have been a friend? This was desperately important to us then; I was paid just over £1,000 a year while I was in Banbury, and the research assistants were paid £850. It may now sound very trivial, but it was the stuff of the day-to-day tensions and frequently increased our irritations with each other and the project. Doing fieldwork is like being continually on stage.

from C. Bell and H. Newby (eds), *Doing Sociological Research* (Allen & Unwin, 1979)

Item 2.17 An account of a research project: 2

I discovered that full-time research is not a job; it is a way of life, and so one's life becomes woven into the research just as much as the research becomes part of one's life. For a year I ate, breathed and slept Sparkbrook. I made new friends, made and dissolved relationships, took sides in conflicts, had problems with my landlady and went to parties. In a twelve-year retrospect it is these personal experiences that stand out and the technicalities of research that are most obscured by the passage of ideas.

To avoid sentimentality it is best only to indicate those personal experiences where biography and methodology may impinge upon one another. Some were very dramatic. For example, a building in which I was talking to an Irish political activist caught fire, and though he and I escaped a third man died. My own life was certainly saved by the failure of a fire extinguisher, which thwarted my attempt to rescue the third man; the smoke forced me back moments before an explosion destroyed the area I was trying to penetrate. This event might have brought the research to a premature end. Another time I was crouched under a hedge with bottles and bricks flying overhead as West Indians and tinkers fought a pitched battle. The police arrived in force, and I was moved on. What does the eager researcher do when moved on? I ran around the block, took my coat off and strolled innocently into the middle of the battle again.

The physical well-being of the research worker is also under threats of a different kind. For example, pints of very sweet and strong boiled tea destroy the digestion, and visiting Indian families puts one's stomach awash with it. The round of religious observances on Friday, Saturday and Sunday, interspersed with teetotal pub-crawling on Fridays and Saturdays, almost every week is physically debilitating and at times mentally numbing. Typing up notes on Monday morning becomes an ordeal. It is only in writing this that I now realise that I am owed my annual holiday from that year! How does this degree of physical involvement affect sociological judgement?

Demands on the emotions are certainly felt very acutely when one is working in the field of race relations. For example, it is very difficult to keep calm while listening to a bleary-eyed, unshaven Brummy, dribbling in his beer while holding forth on the way in which West Indians lower the tone of his locality. John Rex and I were amazed, irritated and later angered by a senior member of the local government who, in an elaborately stage-managed interview, attempted to mislead us about the local authority's race policies. But we remained polite, even deferential, throughout. The most beguiling interview was with a dim and amiable young prostitute who said as we parted that if I wanted to know any more about her work I could call at her place 'any time'.

from C. Bell and H. Newby (eds.), *Doing Sociological Research* (Allen & Unwin, 1979)

Item 2.18   Research is not a job, it's a way of life

▶ UNIT 5   Is sociology a science?

5.1 The scientific method and experiments

It is accepted that the natural sciences, such as chemistry, physics and biology, are 'scientific', but some people doubt whether the social sciences can be regarded as being scientific in the same way. Of course, it really depends upon what is meant by 'science'. The original Latin word, *scientia*, means 'knowledge', but the modern word 'science' has come to have a more specialised meaning. The careful, systematic way in which the natural scientist conducts experiments, and possibly makes predictions from the results of his or her work, is what makes that work be regarded as 'scientific'.

An experiment in the natural sciences can be repeated anywhere in the world by another natural scientist and, as long as all the conditions are the same, the same results will be obtained. One of the arguments against the social sciences being scientific is that they concern people in their human relationships, and as people vary as individuals there is no consistency of behaviour. Even if it were possible to set up experimental conditions with human beings, without putting them at risk in body or mind, it is argued that the variations between individuals (let

alone societies) would be so great as to make any results meaningless.

People who argue in this way add that even members of the same family vary, so that it would be of little use to compare findings made in a study of a British community to those made with, say, an Arab community. But this argument shows a lack of understanding of both the sociologist's aims and sociological evidence. An individual's behaviour may interest a psychiatrist or a social psychologist, but sociologists are usually looking for common patterns of behaviour found in groups, and comparisons with other groups can be sociologically significant. The surprising thing is that although we have individual personalities and different genetic constructions, we do tend to have fairly regular behaviour patterns, so that sociologists can obtain a considerable amount of information about societies and communities by observing and comparing these patterns.

Sociologists gather information in a systematic and thorough way which is quite scientific, and may include the use of statistics. But it is not always easy, possible or even desirable to design sociological

Item 2.19 Even if it were possible to set up controlled experimental conditions with human beings, the result might be meaningless

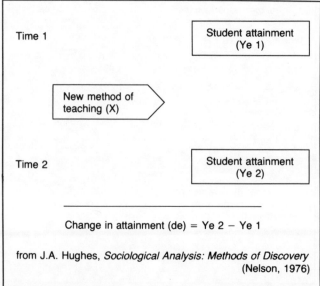

Time 1   Student attainment (Ye 1)

New method of teaching (X)

Time 2   Student attainment (Ye 2)

Change in attainment (de) = Ye 2 − Ye 1

from J.A. Hughes, *Sociological Analysis: Methods of Discovery* (Nelson, 1976)

Item 2.20 One-shot experimental design

research along the lines of the scientific experiment. Item 2.20 shows one area where it might work – the effect of teaching on student attainment. The diagram shows two groups (the experimental sample and the 'control' sample). Only the experimental sample is subjected to 'cause X'. Any change in the experimental sample that is not also present in the control sample is assumed to have been brought about by 'cause X'.

One of the tests applied to a scientific subject is whether predictions can be made about it, given certain conditions. For example, when chemists pour the right proportions of hydrochloric acid and sodium hydroxide together they can predict the result will be salt and water. As sociologists we cannot really predict with the same degree of accuracy how people will behave. But social scientists are not concerned with a hundred per cent degree of accuracy about people; totally accurate predictions about human behaviour are not necessary in social science. (In fact natural sciences do not always stand up to the same tests of one hundred per cent accuracy. Meteorology is a branch of natural science, but is the weather forecast always right?)

All disciplines of natural science and social science have their particular techniques of investigation; each is as accurate as its limitations of investigation will allow. If projections are made in the social sciences they are used only as guides towards the ways in which people *might* behave in the future, not as pointers to how they *will* behave.

Item 2.21 shows the classic design of an experiment. Experiments are, as we have seen, really the basis of the scientific method of the natural sciences.

Research using the scientific method and quantitative or statistical data begins with ideas and theories about a topic. A hypothesis is *deduced* from these theories and tested against the data collected. The hypothesis is then either proved correct or in need of modification. This is called *positivistic* research. An alternative approach to sociological research is to begin with qualitative data and, by a process of *induction*, to attempt to make sense of that data, by pointing out patterns and common themes in the data. Sociologists Glaser and Strauss argue that ideas which are developed from data like this are much more likely to make sense. They call such ideas *grounded theories* because they are grounded or based on data and the real world. Grounded theories do not force data into categories thought up by the research; rather, they use the categories which the people being studied themselves use to make sense of their experiences.

As we have seen, sociologists use all sorts of different methods (surveys, questionnaires, interviews, observation) as well as all sorts of different data (secondary, primary, quantitative, qualitative). Sociology sometimes might try to use a scientific approach; sometimes a scientific approach will not be for the best. Sociologists should always choose the best method for doing what they want to do whether that method is called 'scientific' or not.

ACTIVITIES 14

1 Does it matter whether sociology is called a science or not?

2 Why do you think sociologists have wanted to be called 'scientific'?

3 What do you think are the problems for sociologists of trying to be scientific?

REVIEW

If you have studied and understood this chapter you should be able to . . .

- explain the difference between primary data and secondary data.
- briefly describe the sources of data used in the government publication *Social Trends*.

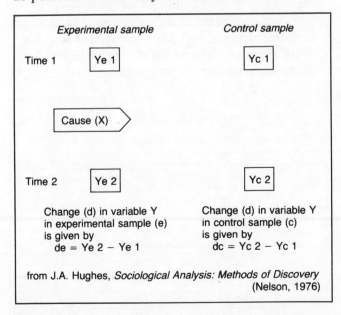

Item 2.21   Classic design of an experiment

- explain the difference between quantitative data and qualitative data.
- outline, with examples of your own, the different types of question that might be used in a questionnaire.
- compare and contrast formal and informal interviewing as methods of data collection, including in your answer a brief account of the circumstances in which each might best be used.
- explain clearly how to take a random sample, including an explanation of the procedures for stratifying the sample.
- outline the circumstances in which it may not be possible or desirable to use a random sample, including in your answer suggested alternative methods of sampling.
- using a specific example of your own, outline how you would go about conducting a social survey investigation, including careful mention of each individual stage.
- outline, in a paragraph, some of the main difficulties and problems of participant observation as a method of data collection.
- write an account of the arguments surrounding the idea that sociology is 'scientific'.

ASSESSMENT QUESTION

The question below carries 20 marks. The mark allocations to sections of the question are shown in the right hand margin.

The problem of interviewer bias in unstructured interviews is much greater. There is no fixed list of questions to work through; instead the interviewer may work through a guide which will remind him of the topic he wishes to cover. What topic he raises first, and how he leads on to the next is left entirely to him, as long as he eventually covers all the issues in the guide! Clearly the training of the interviewer is very important.

(Adapted from: *Introducing Sociology*, P Worsley et al.)

a According to the above passage, what does the interviewer use instead of a fixed list of questions? (1)

b According to the above passage, why is interviewer bias much greater in unstructured interviews? (1)

c Identify and explain **two** reasons why the interviewer would need to be trained and have knowledge of sociology. (4)

d Explain, giving examples, why a sociologist might use a postal questionnaire rather than a personal interview. (6)

e When a sociologist decided to investigate the way that husbands and wives divided tasks at home between themselves she chose the unstructured interview. Why do you think she chose this method and what are likely to be its limitations? (8)

Southern Examining Group

3 *Social differences*

AIMS

At the end of this section you should be able to:

- identify and describe the main forms of social stratification.
- identify and describe different ways of defining and categorising social class.
- show a critical awareness of the importance of gender, ethnic and regional differences as sources of social differentiation.
- outline the impact of such differences on social attitudes and life chances.
- explain the changing nature of the social class structure in the UK and the importance of the process of social mobility.
- describe recent legislation relating to social differences.
- show a critical awareness of the problems posed by the unequal distribution of income and wealth in UK society.

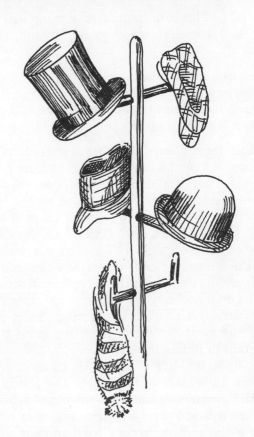

▶ UNIT 6   What is stratification?

ACTIVITIES 1

1 In thinking about social differences or '*social stratification*' ask yourself how often you put people you know into different categories – and how often you make decisions about who is 'better' than whom.

2 Choose a way of separating people into different groups and then try putting everybody in your class into two or three such groups. *Do it now*.

3 Compare the different groups which have been produced by everyone. Some of you will have listed the boys and girls separately, some may have listed people according to where they live, some even by whether they are good at sport or not!

A common characteristic of almost all societies is the way in which they divide people up and put them into different layers or strata. Throughout history strata have been recognisable: in ancient times there were slaves and freemen, in medieval society there were lords and villeins. Different divisions and strata emerge as changes take place in society, yet hierarchies continue to exist. In industrial societies such as Britain, *social class* is one of the main bases of stratification but other things, such as *sex* and *race*, are also used as a basis for discrimination between people. In Indian society the main strata are based on *caste*.

6.1 Caste

Hindu religion divides the population into five basic groups. The highest groups are known as varnas (colours) and beneath them come a group without a caste, the Harijans (Untouchables). The four varnas consist of:

Brahmans a priest caste
Kshatriyas a military caste
Vaisyas a merchant or agricultural caste
Sudras a labouring caste

Within these groups there are thousands of subdivisions: among the Brahmans there are more than 500, and there are over 200 divisions of people without caste. Caste affects the whole way of Indian life, despite laws against discrimination such as the Indian Constitution's law of 1950, which officially abolished 'untouchability'. To a large extent skin colour differentiated caste (the lighter the colouring the higher the caste), but the occupational structure of India does not truly reflect caste – for example not all Kshatriyas are soldiers, and many Sudras have made money in business. Even so, caste is still important in Indian society.

Any understanding of caste must be accompanied by some knowledge of Hinduism. The Hindu doctrine of Karma maintains that anyone who behaves well on earth will enter a higher caste after rebirth, and it is this that keeps people within their allotted caste without too much resentment. People from different castes are not permitted to marry, so membership of a particular caste is hereditary and permanent. Religious restrictions ensure that very little social contact occurs between castes. The system is, as a consequence, very rigid and unlikely to change.

ACTIVITIES 2

Find out if any of the people in your class, school or neighbourhood are Hindus. Perhaps they would not mind if you interviewed them to find out how their caste affects their lives in Britain today. We will see later whether the impact of caste is really much different from the impact social class can have on some areas of social life.

6.2 Class

ACTIVITIES 3

When people talk about social class, what kind of images come to mind? List the different social classes you can think of and list all the characteristics you think they each have. Describe a typical member of each social class.

If we talk about social class in Britain most people think of the working classes and the middle classes – some will also include the upper class or aristocracy. Social class as a sociological term and as a type of social stratification is not quite as simple as this, however. There are different ideas about what makes up and determines a social class.

Item 3.1 Can you suggest what castes these people might belong to?

The Registrar General

The Registrar General, who is in charge of the government's statistical department, divides the population into five classes based upon occupation, with a subdivision of Class 3 into manual and non-manual workers:

Class 1 capitalists, managers, scientists, professionals, (e.g. architects, doctors, lawyers, university teachers, etc.)

Class 2 lower professionals, intermediate (e.g. small shopkeepers, farmers, teachers, airline pilots, etc.)

Class 3A non-manual clerical (e.g. office workers, filing clerks, shop assistants, secretaries, etc.)

Class 3B skilled manual workers (e.g. miners, butchers, electricians, bricklayers, draughtsmen, etc.)

Class 4 semi-skilled workers (e.g. bus conductors, fishermen, postal workers, telephone operators, farm workers, packers, etc.)

Class 5 unskilled workers (e.g. labourers, messengers, cleaners, porters, kitchen hands, etc.)

Item 3.2 The Registrar General's five-point scale of occupational structure

Hall and Jones

In 1950, two sociologists called Hall and Jones devised another scheme for allocating social class based upon occupations:

The Hall-Jones scale
Class 1 professional and higher administrative
Class 2 managerial and executive
Class 3 inspectional, supervisory and other non-manual, higher grade
Class 4 inspectional, supervisory and other non-manual, lower grade
Class 5 skilled manual and routine grades of non-manual
Class 6 semi-skilled manual
Class 7 unskilled manual

Karl Marx

Karl Marx, in the middle of the nineteenth century, was one of the first writers to analyse class differences. He argued that the group which controlled and owned the means of producing food and goods was the dominant class.

In the *Communist Manifesto* (1847), written in collaboration with Friedrich Engels, Marx outlined different stages in history in which the ownership of property gave one group control over others. This applied from ancient society based on slavery, through feudal society resting upon the labour of villiens and serfs, to his own day and beyond. He believed that in the nineteenth century the *bourgeoisie*, who owned and controlled the means of production (land and factories) in the capitalist system, dominated the wage-earners or *proletariat*, the working class who 'had only their labour to sell', and worked for the bourgeoisie. Everything, Marx said, depended upon the ownership of capital (wealth) – it shaped religion, government, and even the family. In other words, economic relationships determined all other relationships.

Marx argued that there was, throughout history, a constant struggle between classes, and this *class struggle* brought about changes in society. The class struggle between the proletariat and bourgeoisie would eventually end in victory for the working class if they were to unite and overthrow the owners of capital.

Of course, many of Marx's observations started from the appalling conditions that were the results of industrialisation in the nineteenth century, when little was done to alleviate the distress of the poor. But the point he made was that class is primarily based upon economic circumstances.

Max Weber

Separated from Marx by half a century, another sociologist, Max Weber (1864–1920) saw a further development of capitalist society. Instead of the small middle class (shopkeepers and small farmers) being drawn down into the working class as Marx had predicted, Weber said the middle classes had grown in importance and number. The main reasons for this were the development of education and literacy, and the increase in working-class participation in government and politics through an extension of the right to vote. The new middle class, consisting of such people as clerks and skilled workers, had no wish to overthrow the existing social system. For their part, the working classes were organising themselves into trade unions and gaining increased benefits from raised standards of living.

Weber distinguished between class and status in advanced industrial societies. He thought the way in which the middle class had gained so much political power was not only due to their class position. The prestige and the success of the middle classes, he considered, came from their relationship with the means of production (as wage-earning employees or as a professional class) and their wealth. Status groups were stratified by Weber according to such things as education, occupation and what he termed 'styles of life', making finer distinctions between groups than Marx's single economic definition.

Changes in status are more rapid than changes in class over any given period of time; for example, the status accorded to the First Division professional footballer or to a pop star is greater now than it was thirty years ago, but there has been little fundamental change in class over the same period.

ACTIVITIES 4

Where do I fit in?

Sociologists have long been interested in the way people see their own position in society, and the position of others. When asked about class most people place themselves in a category higher than that which would be assigned them by the Registrar General. When asked, however, to rank various jobs and occupations in order of importance there is surprising agreement between people.

1 List at random around 20 jobs and occupations from all the different levels of social class groupings we have seen earlier.

2 Give this list to a selection of respondents (perhaps all the students in your sociology group could do this exercise). Ask your respondents to put the jobs in order of importance.

3 You should analyse your results and try to answer the following questions:
   a How much agreement is there among all the respondents?
   b What reasons were used for putting jobs in a particular rank in the list?
   c Why should everyone agree more or less about the order jobs should be put in?

6.3 Estate

The hierarchy in medieval England was essentially a system based upon the ownership of land, and, in the higher ranks, upon the numbers of fighting men that could be provided in times of war. Since power rested ultimately upon military force, those who possessed arms and controlled numbers of fighting men were unwilling to let their authority be weakened by any change in the system. The Church reinforced this rigid hierarchy by teaching that the social order was based on divine order.

The medieval Church too had its upper and lower ranks, which ranged from powerful archbishops to poor village priests, and it was suspicious of any ideas which appeared to threaten its own position in the social order. Anyone who challenged the feudal order or the teachings of the Church might be regarded as a heretic and liable to the most extreme penalties, even death. Thus there were two estates, the nobility and the Church.

Later a third estate developed: the townspeople increased their power from about the twelfth century onwards, until they dominated society in the late eighteenth and nineteenth centuries with the coming of industrialisation. One theory of the beginning of this rise is that because the Black Death, the plague that swept Europe between 1347 and 1350, killed a third or more of the population, the smaller numbers of agricultural workers who were left demanded higher farm wages. This in turn, according to the theory, encouraged the landowners to turn to wool production on a large scale in England. Landowners were therefore no longer dependent upon subsistence farming, and merchants and townspeople grew prosperous on the new trade.

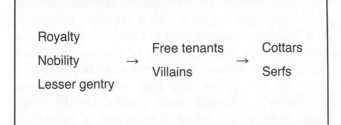

Item 3.3a The feudal hierarchy
     b Villeins harvesting corn for their lord

6.4 Gender

'Is it a boy or a girl?' The answer to this question still affects the life-chances of any infant. Whatever the biological basis of sex, the cultural definitions of gender are the result of socialisation into specific sex-roles, and sex differences are still an important source of social differentiation in all sorts of ways, which explains why you will probably find the photographs shown in Item 3.4 unusual.

Item 3.4 Women workers at traditionally male jobs

In the nineteenth century marriage was considered to be the right goal for every woman. Middle-class girls were brought up with this in mind and, once married, they passed from being under the authority of their father to being under the authority of their husband. In middle-class families it was thought to be a mark of refinement and wealth if a wife remained at home and did not involve herself in any kind of paid employment. Most married middle-class women therefore spent their time at home, either pregnant or between pregnancies and supervising the running of the household with the aid of domestic servants, nannies and governesses. In working-class families, the need for money meant that women had to try to find paid employment, but the jobs open to them were limited – domestic service, factory work, etc. They too were expected to marry and have children. One sociologist, Richard Titmus, has estimated that in 1890 typical working-class mothers married in their teens or early twenties and had an average of ten pregnancies.

The dependent role of women in society was reflected in their lack of legal rights. For example, before the Married Women's Property Act of 1882 the wife's possessions became her husband's property when she married. Divorce was virtually impossible for a woman because of the legally complicated grounds that had to be established, the cost and the scandal. Women's role in society today is still hotly debated. It is a topic to which we shall return in both this chapter and others.

ACTIVITIES 5

To provide a very simple 'test' of the importance of sex as a means of social differentiation, note the different ways boys and girls are treated at your own school under the following headings:

a in class
b discipline and rules
c sports
d subject choice

If you can, you should add some headings of your own. Compare your ideas with those of others in your class.

6.5 Race

The term *minority group* is used to refer to a group in society which, because of particular characteristics, such as having a different culture or religion or being racially separate, is sometimes placed at a disadvantage in society. This is often because the group is treated as different by other people in society and so denied the opportunities which are open to others. The term is sometimes used to apply to categories of people even though they may be neither minorities nor groups. For example, women have been called a minority group because they are discriminated against in a male-orientated society. On the other hand, some groups which are a minority, but which are privileged, such as royalty, are not termed minority groups. However, the term is perhaps most commonly applied to ethnic and racial groups.

Ethnic groups

An ethnic group is a subgroup of the larger society, with a distinct cultural tradition and a sense of common identity. For example, ethnic groups in Britain include Chinese, Jews, Indians, Irish, Maltese and West Indians. Ethnic groups may also be racial groups, but the two types of group are not necessarily identical and should not be confused.

Racial groups

Race is a classification for grouping together people in society who have a shared ancestry and the same characteristic physical features, such as shape of eyes, shape of head, skin colour or eye colour. If people have a certain set of characteristics, then we say they belong to a certain race. Race and nationality are not to be confused: race depends on physical characteristics, nationality on the person being a citzen of a certain nation, such as France or the USA. The nation itself exists because of political boundaries which separate one area of land or nation from another.

Like sex, race too is often the basis for discrimination in society, and like social class, sex and race are social differences of importance to a sociologist attempting to understand society and social interaction.

Item 3.5 Footbridge at a railway station in South Africa

Item 3.6 Racist attack on a market trader in the Midlands

ACTIVITIES 6

1 Look at Items 3.5 and 3.6 and comment on the kind of social differences you can see in the two societies.

2 What kind of attack was the one in Item 3.6?

3 What kind of person do you think did this, and why did they do it?

4 Of the two kinds of racial discrimination shown, which do you think is the harder to combat? Explain your answers.

Checklist

There are many factors upon which social differentiation can be based. These include:

1 social class
2 caste
3 gender
4 race.

ACTIVITIES 7

You should spend some time listing as many more factors as you can which can be used to single out groups of people. Your extended list, for example, might include disability and weight.

6.6 Regional differences

Where people live can make a lot of difference to their standard of living, their chances of getting a job, their attitudes and their life chances. In this section we shall look specifically at just one aspect of the regional dimension to social differences, that of housing tenure. There are considerable regional differences in housing tenure in the UK. Item 3.7 shows regional figures for the proportion of dwellings in the two main types of tenure – owner occupation (owned outright or with a mortgage) and rented from local authorities. In addition to these two types of tenure, we should add that around 11 per cent of the UK population rent their accommodation from either housing associations or private landlords.

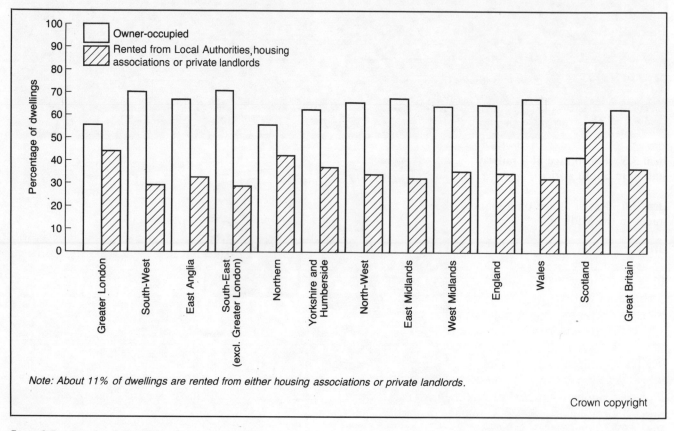

Item 3.7 Stock of dwellings by tenure, 1985

ACTIVITIES 8

Study Item 3.7 and answer the questions that follow.

1 Which region of England has the highest proportion of owner-occupied properties?

2 Which region of England has the lowest proportion of owner-occupied properties?

3 Can you think of any reasons for your findings?

4 Trace a map of the UK from an atlas and use colour coding to show regional differences in types of housing tenure.

5 Find the unemployment rates for each region. (Look in Chapter 9.) Compare regional unemployment rates with the regional differences in housing tenures shown in Item 3.7. Comment on both sets of figures.

6 The government's 1985 General Household Survey reports that owner occupation increased from 49 per cent of the total housing stock in 1971 to 59 per cent in 1984 and to 61 per cent in 1985. Comment on any other changes you can see in Item 3.8.

Tenure	1971 %	1973 %	1975 %	1977 %	1979 %	1981 %	1983 %	1985 %
Owner-occupied, owned outright	22	22	23	22	23	24	24	24
Owner-occupied, with mortgage	27	28	28	30	31	33	35	37
Rented with job or business	5	3	3	3	2	2	2	2
Rented from local authority or New Town	31	33	33	34	34	32	29	28
Rented from housing association or co-operative	1	1	1	1	2	2	2	2
Rented privately, unfurnished	12	10	8	8	6	5	5	5
Rented privately, furnished	3	3	3	2	2	2	2	2

from *OPCS: General Household Survey*

Item 3.8   Households' tenure, Britain, 1971–85

ACTIVITIES 9: *Play-reading*

Read the play-reading and answer the questions which follow.

(Phil and Steve revisit the area where they grew up. They are in their forties. It is 20 years since they left the neigbourhood – now very gentrified and upmarket.)

Phil   This area's changed a bit.

Steve   I'll say – those cars have been parked there all day and they've still got their tyres.

Phil   I mean we were over the moon to escape from this hole weren't we?

Steve   Yeah but you couldn't afford a mortgage on the outside toilet these days. Look at the pub.

Phil   I know. Full of the half-a-lager lot and I'll-have-a-ploughman's please.

Steve   Oh yes Rodney – sooopah!

Phil   I wonder what real ploughmen eat, eh Steve?

Steve   They have solicitor's lunches probably.

Phil   These cars! It's obscene what they must've cost.

Steve   I could go for this sort of life, you know, Phil. A little terraced house. Genuine gas log fire. Become posh and buy a Porsche.

Phil   What if that's something you can't afford.

Steve   I'll manage to afford it!

Phil   So you'll sell out, eh? For a jacuzzi and a flash car and holidays in untouristy places.

Steve   No, I'd still be true to my roots – I might drive an up market car, but I'd have green funny dice dangling in the back, and a Steve and Sharon sunstrip across the windscreen.

Phil   Well rather you than me. All that muesli and bread with the bits left in it would give me the runs.

1 What has happened to the area in which Phil and Steve grew up?

2 Explain in your own words the kind of attitudes they now seem to have towards the area.

3 What social class would you say Phil and Steve belong to? Give reasons for your answer.

4 What do you think Phil means when he says 'So you'll sell out, eh?'. Explain your answer with reference to the passage.

UNIT 7 Social class in the UK

7.1 How does class affect our lives?

Quite naturally we associate a person's life style with their class. A manual labourer from the East End of London will have a different way of life from a stockbroker living in a Sussex village. We would expect different patterns of behaviour from a vicar's wife and a trawlerman's wife. Although we are conscious of some of the differences of class, it may be difficult to pinpoint exactly what makes those subtle differences. Before we hear someone speak, we may try to sum them up by their age and the clothes they are wearing; hearing them speak may provide a further pointer because of accent and choice of words. If they tell us their occupation we have an even clearer picture of their social class. Why should these things be meaningful, and how much importance has class in our lives?

ACTIVITIES 10

Read the accounts in Items 3.9 and 3.10 of two fictitious couples from very different social classes.

1 Compare the two couples presented. Mention in your answer the following factors:
   a housing.
   b occupation.
   c hobbies.
   d social attitudes.

2 What does the writer mean when she says the lower middles are 'inner directed'?

3 Although the picture given of the different social classes here is exaggerated, how much truth do you think these passages contain?

The Definitely-Disgustings

Our working-class couple are MR and MRS DEFINITELY-DISGUSTING. They have two children, SHARON and DIVE, and live in council house with walls so thin you can hear the budgie pecking its seed next door. Mr Definitely-Disgusting is your manual worker, he might be a miner in the North, a car worker in the Midlands, or a casual labourer in the South. He married young, and lived for a while with his wife's parents; after a year or two he went back to going to the pub, football, and the dogs with the blokes. He detests his mother-in-law. But despite his propensity to foul language, he is extremely modest, always undressing with his back to Mrs D-D and he often does something slightly illegal, nicking a car, or knocking off a telly. He is terrified of the police, who, being lower middle, and the class just above, reserve their special venom for him. Mrs Definitely-Disgusting wears her curlers and pinny to the local shop, and spends a lot of the day with a cigarette hanging from her bottom lip gossiping and grumbling.

from Jilly Cooper, *Class: a view from middle England*: (Eyre Methuen, 1980)

Item 3.9 Mr and Mrs Definitely-Disgusting

Item 3.10   Bryan and Jen Teale: the lower middles

Bryan and Jen Teale

The Teales are probably the most pushy, the most frugal, and most respectable of all the classes, because they are so anxious to escape from the working class. The successful ones iron out their accents and become middle like Mr Heath and Mrs Thatcher, the rest stay put, as bank and insurance clerks, door-to-door salesman, lower management, police sergeants and sergeant majors. In the old days, the lower middles rose with the small business or the little shop, but the rise in rates, social security benefits and postage has scuppered all that.

The lower middles never had any servants, but as they are obsessed with cleanliness, and like everything nice, they buy a small modern house, and fill it with modern units which are easy to keep clean. Jen and Bryan have two children, WAYNE and CHRISTINE, and a very clean car.

As Jen and Bryan didn't go to boarding school, didn't make friends outside the district, and don't mix with the street, they have very few friends, keeping themselves to themselves. They tend to be very inner-directed, doing everything together, decorating the house, furnishing the car, and coaching and playing football with the children. Jen reads knitting patterns, *Woman's Own*, and *Reader's Digest* condensed books. To avoid any working-class stigma, she puts up defensive barriers: privet hedges, net curtains, talks in a 'refained' accent, raises her little finger when she drinks ... The children are always being pulled up for some real or imagined coarseness of speech. The Teales don't entertain much, only Bryan's colleagues who might be useful, and occasionally Bryan's boss.

from Jilly Cooper, *Class: a view from middle England* (Eyre Methuen, 1980)

ACTIVITIES 11

Look at Item 3.11 and answer the questions that follow it.

Item 3.11   Social class differences

1 Where do you think this photograph was taken? What is happening in this photograph?

2 List the differences you can *see* between two different types of men in the photograph. Now list the kind of differences between the two men you would *expect* to find if you were able to actually interview both men.

3 Upon what assumptions are your expectations based?

A sociologist called Ivan Reid examined the differences between the social classes in the early 1980s. He collected together a large number of statistics from surveys, censuses, opinion polls and other sources of data. His overall conclusion is that the higher up the social scale one is, the better quality and even the happier the life that will be led. To give just a few examples from his findings: middle-class and professional people tend to live longer, are healthier from birth, have happier marriages, live in better homes, visit the doctor less, retain more teeth, suffer less from almost every disease, play more sport, join more clubs, commit suicide less and smoke less. Item 3.12 shows some of these differences in the form of computer generated pictograms.

ACTIVITIES 12

Study Item 3.12 and answer the questions that follow.

1 Comment on the trends shown in each pictogram.

2 How would you attempt to explain the social class differences indicated?

Attitudes and outlook

The middle class tend to regard society as a kind of ladder which it is possible to move up rung by rung. Through such things as ability, initiative or hard work it is possible to 'get on', even though this may mean sacrifice at some stage of an individual's life. This perspective is one of *individualism*. A working-class perspective is, typically, to divide society up into 'us' and 'them' (the latter may refer to governments, landlords, bosses or virtually any official who has some kind of authority). The division is seen as more or less permanent, unless you are lucky, so for the most part you must put up with your lot and try to make the best of things as they are now, rather than worrying too much about the future. This perspective is termed *collectivist* because it is a view of society as being two collections of people, us and them.

The sociologists Goldthorpe and Lockwood studied the family life, the work and the political views of relatively well-paid car workers in Luton in the late 1960s. One of the things they were looking for was evidence of the car workers moving into the middle class and away from their working class origins. They found little evidence of this, and to help their analysis they outlined what they understood to be typical elements of both the 'middle-class perspective' and the traditional 'working class perspective'. Items 3,13 and 3.14 show Goldthorpe and Lockwood's ideas.

Item 3.12 Social class differences. The figures in each pictogram represent the *proportions* of each social class falling into the categories shown

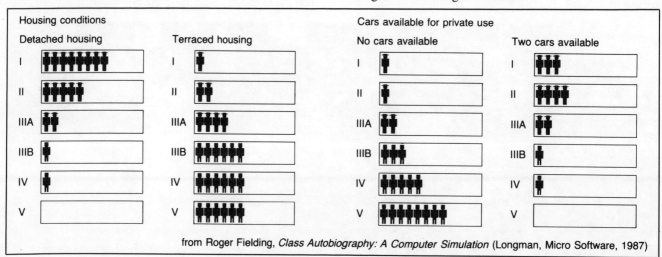

from Roger Fielding, *Class Autobiography: A Computer Simulation* (Longman, Micro Software, 1987)

ACTIVITIES 13

Read Items 3.13 and 3.14 and answer the questions that follow them.

(i) The basic conception of the social order is a hierarchical one: society is divided into a series of levels or strata differentiated in terms of the life-styles and associated prestige of their members. The structure is, however, seen as a relatively 'open' one: given ability and the appropriate moral qualities – determination, perseverance, etc. – individuals can, and do, move up the hierarchy. What a man achieves in the end depends primarily on what he 'makes of himself'. Moreover, it is felt that the individual has an obligation to assume responsibility for his own life and welfare and to *try* to 'get on in the world' as far as he can.

(ii) Consistently with the notion of a social ladder that all have opportunity to climb, wants and expectations are, from a middle-class standpoint, capable of continuous enlargement. The typical objective is to keep up a progressive improvement in consumption standards and, correspondingly, a steady ascent in terms of prestige and the quality of life-style. From the point of view of the individual or family, it is in fact a key expectation that such an advance *will* occur – that careers will progress, seniority grow, incomes rise, and so on.

(iii) The emphasis placed on 'getting on' and the expectation that over time advancement will in some degree occur together imply, on the part of the individual or family, a marked orientation towards the future. Major importance is attached to looking and planning ahead and, where necessary, to making present sacrifices in order to ensure greater advantages or benefits at a later stage. Such deferring of gratification – say, in the furtherance of a career or business undertaking – is approved of as a matter of morality as well as of expediency.

(iv) The middle-class social ethic is thus an essentially individualistic one: the prime value is that set on individual achievement. Achievement is taken as the crucial indicator of the individual's moral worth. However, achievement is also regarded as a family concern: parents feel an obilgation to try to give their children a 'better start in life' than they themselves enjoyed, and then anticipate that their offspring will in turn attain to a still higher level in the social scale. In other words, the expectation is again that advancement will be continuous – between generations as well as in the course of individual lifetimes. Indeed, through parental aspirations for children, it is possible for desires and hopes for the future to become virtually limitless.

from J.H. Goldthorpe et al., *The Affluent Worker in the Class Structure* (CUP, 1969)

Item 3.13   The middle-class perspective

(i) The basic conception of the social order is a dichotomous one: society is divided into 'us' and 'them'. 'They' are persons in positions in which they can exercise power and authority over 'us'. The division between 'us' and 'them' is seen as a virtually unbridgeable one; people are born on one side of the line or the other and very largely remain there. The social cirumstances an individual faces are thus 'given' facts of life and, apart perhaps from exceptional strokes of luck, these facts have to be accepted and 'put up with'.

(ii) Consistently with this view of social circumstances as being more or less immutable – or at any rate as being unlikely to change much for the better – wants and expectations are themselves relatively fixed. The major economic concern is with being able to *maintain* a certain standard and style of living, not with the continuous advancement of consumption norms and widening of cultural experience. In a traditionalistic context, as Max Weber has written, 'A man does not "by nature" wish to earn more and more money, but simply to live as he is accustomed to live and to earn as much as is necessary for that purpose.'

(iii) Complementary to the idea of 'putting up' with life is that of 'marking the best of it'; that is, of living in and for the present. As Hoggart observes, 'working-class life puts a premium on the taking of pleasures now, discourages planning for some future good'. This emphasis on the present and the lack of concern for 'planning ahead' are moreover encouraged by the view that there is in fact little to be done about the future, that it is not to any major extent under the individual's control. Fatalism, acceptance and an orientation to the present thus hold together as a mutually reinforcing set of attitudes.

(iv) In so far as it is felt that purposive action can be effective, the emphasis is placed on action of a *collective* kind aimed at the protection of collective interests – trade unionism being, of course, the most developed form. A prime value is that set on mutual aid and group solidarity in the face of the vicissitudes of life and the domination which 'they' seek to impose. This value in turn confirms the shared, communal nature of social life and constitutes a further restraint on attempts by individuals to make themselves 'a cut above the rest'. Such attempts, in the form, say, of conspicuous consumption or occupational advance, are likely to be interpreted by the community as threats to its solidarity, as expressions of group or class disloyalty. Even in the case of children, parental concern that they should 'do well' is confined to achievement within the context of working-class values and life-styles – as, for example, in becoming established in a 'trade' or a 'steady' job. Aspirations do not extend to levels of education and types of job which would result in children being taken away from their family and community in either a geographical or a social sense.

from J.H. Goldthorpe et al., *The Affluent Worker in the Class Structure* (CUP, 1969)

Item 3.14   The traditional working-class perspective

1 The writers say that the middle class see society as essentially 'hierarchical', and that the working class see society as essentially 'dichotomous'. Explain these ideas in your own words and try to illustrate your explanation with examples.

2 The writers also say that the middle classes are essentially 'individualistic' while working class interests are essentially 'collective'.

   Explain these ideas in your own words and try to illustrate your explanations with examples.

3 Look again at Mr and Mrs Definitely-Disgusting and the 'lower middles'. In the light of Goldthorpe and Lockwood's ideas, do you think these passages are good profiles of the social classes concerned?

7.2 The class structure of the UK

It would be wrong to assume that sociology consists of a series of separate studies of aspects of society such as the family, the educational system or the economic system. The ways in which we are brought up in the family, we learn at school and people behave towards us at work are all part of a process of experience that affects our attitudes and makes up what we are as individuals. However, we are not examining individuals, but society as a whole. If we study the ways the family is related to the educational system, how the educational system is related to the economic system, etc., we can see the structure of our social system as a whole. Attitudes are important because different attitudes produce different forms of behaviour; and one of the most basic differences of attitude found in society as a whole is that which exists between different classes. There are a host of other differences – differences by age, sex, religion, race and many more factors – but we shall look at class differences next since they underline many of the major differences in society.

Effect on the social structure

The constantly changing nature of society means that sociologists need frequently to change their theories in the light of fresh evidence. One theory is that class differences are disappearing in Britain as the better-off members of the working class are beginning to adopt middle-class life styles and values. This is known as the process of *embourgeoisement*. Some of the middle-class patterns adopted take the form of a change in family relationships and the purchase of material possessions formerly enjoyed only by the middle classes. Goldthorpe and others in their book *The Affluent Worker in the Class Structure* (Cambridge University Press, 1969) found that this was *not* the case, as we noted in the previous topic. Deliberately looking for evidence of embourgeoisement, they did find a resemblance in life styles to those of the middle class among some of the better-off working class, but in the important question of attitudes and values fundamental differences still existed between the classes. The former working-class 'us and them' perspective had been replaced by the view that social status (standing) depended upon income and spending habits.

Key terms

■ embourgeoisement: the process whereby members of the working class adopt middle class life styles and values.

Class, although not resting entirely upon economic circumstances, is, as we have seen, tied largely to the economic factor of occupation. Certainly the number of manual occupations decreases in Britain year by year and changes in the occupational structure contribute towards upward mobility. Economic change causes social change, but the important element of *behaviour* is largely shaped by the attitudes and values found in the family and among friends, and by the experience of school and work. It is here that the working class and middle class divide in their experience of life, and these divisions often remain permanently.

7.3 Social class mobility

As we have seen, estate and caste systems are rather rigid, making it difficult for people to get out of the position in society into which they are born. In the early development of industrialisation during the nineteenth century, people were no longer tied to the land and were free to seek jobs in the towns, but the harsh conditions of employment, with low wages and slum conditions (Marx referred to the industrial proletariat as 'wage slaves'), did not really entail much more freedom for most of the population. By the end of the century, however, conditions were improving and new kinds of jobs were created. Increasing educational opportunities and some political power then began to allow certain groups to better themselves.

The growth of the new middle classes at the end of the century came from the newly-educated working class. Improved economic status meant an improved social status; the possibility of changing position in the hierarchy is termed *social mobility*. When someone improves his or her position in society, this is known as *upward mobility*. A much rarer occurrence is when someone falls to a lower position in the social hierarchy and this is termed *downward mobility*. Sociologists usually measure social mobility by comparing occupations over a generation: if the son of an unskilled labourer becomes the director of a merchant bank then upward mobility has taken place (although such a rise would indeed be rare). Generally the advance of technology and economic growth mean the creation of more jobs higher up the social scale: instead of the muscle power of six unskilled labourers digging a trench, one skilled machine operator driving an excavator can do the job, and do it more efficiently. Economic growth and development has therefore meant there are more people in middle-class occupations year by year.

Education is an important factor in upward mobility, because the better an education one has, and the higher the qualifications one gains, the more likely it will be that one can get an occupation higher up the social scale. A labourer's child who gets a university place is not likely to become a labourer.

In Britain there are regional differences in the kinds of jobs open to school-leavers. In a remote valley where coal is mined, employment available to the school-leaver who is not prepared, or even unable, to move, may be restricted to mining. In a small town where there are few factories the choice is also very restricted.

Checklist

Factors which affect social mobility are:

1 occupational structure.
2 education.
3 distribution of opportunity.
4 motivation.
5 family size.
6 marriage.

The sociologist Ralph Turner considered the question of social mobility. He outlined two ideas of mobility which he termed *contest* and *sponsored* mobility. Contest mobility is the form in which eligibility for the top positions in society is dependent mainly upon the ability and effort of the individual, and institutions such as the famous public schools have little control. Sponsored mobility is the form in which recruits to the leading positions in society are chosen, not so much on individual merit, but by selection from their own class by the upper strata. In Britain both forms of mobility exist, but as we shall see in subsequent chapters, and as Turner argues, the sponsored form is more dominant.

ACTIVITIES 14

1 Explain in your own words the ideas of 'contest' and 'sponsored' mobility.

2 Give examples of your own of both kinds of social mobility.

3 Suggest which kind of mobility you believe to be dominant in Britain and attempt to give evidence to support your case.

▶ UNIT 8 Gender differences in the UK

Item 3.15 The young woman's dilemma

ACTIVITIES 15

Look at Item 3.15 and answer the questions that follow it.

1 Clearly the young lady in the cartoon is facing a career choice! What kind of options does she think she has to choose between?

2 To whom does she turn for advice?

3 Comment on the message of this cartoon paying particular attention to the example being set by the mother.

8.1 Gender differences and social change

Early socialisation is called *primary socialisation*. It is a general and broad training in and introduction into the values and habits of the society and its culture as a whole. In our society, the primary socialisation of girls encourages them to grow up thinking of themselves as less aggressive, less ambitious and less adventurous than their brothers. They might be encouraged to play with dolls and tea sets. Sociologists call this kind of socialisation *anticipatory socialisation*, because it is anticipating, or preparing girls for, the kind of roles they may well be occupying in their future. Anticipatory socialisation like this, of course, makes such future roles much more likely. Through *anticipatory socialisation* girls like those described will learn to see themselves as future wives and mothers. Socialisation therefore can lead girls to a lower level of ambition, a lesser likelihood of staying on at school, less interest in a career and a tendency to regard marriage as more desirable than an occupation or career. In society today, we continue to hold mothers most responsible for the welfare of their children. Consequently, as women rather than men remain at home to look after their young children, the course of the life-cycle becomes more important in influencing women's employment than men's.

Key terms

- primary socialisation
- anticipatory socialisation

There are a number of both formal and informal organisations in the UK today which are concerned with issues that affect women. The issues which concern these groups include: pressing for greater provision for pre-school playgroups and nursery education; women's continuing education and career opportunities; the elimination of sex stereotyping from educational materials, books, newspapers, films, plays and TV and ensuring the Equal Opportunities Commission operates to enforce the Equal Pay Act and the Sex Discrimination Act. At a more general level, these groups are interested in raising people's consciousness about the role of women in society and in ensuring that women's rights are protected.

Much has changed since the Equal Opportunities Commission came into existence ten years ago, not all of it visible to the public. But in its totality the change amounts to a record of achievement for which the Commission can fairly claim a substantial share of the credit. The transformation of the attitude of the press and mass media, from one of flippancy and trivialisation to a genuine understanding of the issues, is the most visible change. As a result, the Commission increasingly deals with a public which no longer needs to be convinced of its effectiveness but makes further demands on its resources. Ten years ago the educational establishment regarded the Sex Discrimination Act as at best marginal to its concerns. Today equality of opportunity in education between boys and girls is regarded as central part of a school's business.

from *EOC Annual Report* (1985)

Item 3.16   An extract from the Equal Opportunities Commission's Annual Report (1985)

8.2 Sex discrimination and the law

Legislation

Legal changes have affected women's role in a number of different ways:

Property   The first efforts to secure property rights for married women began in 1855. At this time, unless a woman was protected by a marriage settlement, customary among upper-class wives, then her property became her husband's at marriage. The Married Women's Property Bill of 1855 met with a great deal of opposition. The Attorney General of the time saw the Bill as a threat to the 'social and political institutions of the nation'. It was not until after the Married Women's Property Act of 1882 that a married women had the full right of independent ownership of her own property.

The Matrimonial Proceeding and Property Act of 1970 created new provisions for the distribution of property after divorce. For example, where value has been added to property during marriage, this added value belongs equally to husband and wife.

Divorce   Changes in the divorce laws have made it increasingly easy for married women to obtain a divorce. These changes have been both a cause and an effect of women working. For example, greater independence may influence divorce, but at the same time divorce might not be contemplated if women were not able to make their own way in the world.

At work   In 1919 the Sex Disqualification Act allowed right of entry of women to most professions. In 1970 the Equal Pay Act made it necessary for employers to pay women and men equal wages when they are doing the same or broadly similar work. The 1975 Sex Discrimination Act makes it illegal to discriminate against an individual on grounds of sex or marital status in employment, education, housing or other areas. The Equal Opportunities Commission was also set up at this time to support the operation of both the Equal Pay Act and the Sex Discrimination Act.

Political rights   Before 1918 it was impossible for women to vote in general elections. In 1918 women over 30 were given the vote. The voting age for women was finally equalised with that of men in 1928, when all women over 21 were able to vote. The voting age was reduced, for both sexes, to 18 in 1970.

In this unit you have been introduced to the importance of gender as a basis for social differences. In later units, on the family and work for example, you will again clearly see the importance of gender differences in society.

► UNIT 9 Ethnic groups in the UK

9.1 The ethnic groups

The Commission for Racial Equality produces statistical information on the nature of immigration to and emigration from the UK, and on the pattern of settlement of the UK's ethnic minorities. Between 1971 and 1983 more people left the UK than came in. The net loss of population during this period was 465 000, mainly as a result of emigration to Australia, Canada and New Zealand, but also to the USA, South Africa and the EEC countries.

The CRE also points out that white people form the majority of the UK's immigrant population. Nearly 3.4 million people living in the UK in 1981 were born overseas. Well over half of these (1.89 million) were white; over 607 000 were born in Ireland, 153 000 were from Australia, New Zealand and Canada, and 1.13 million from other countries including western Europe. The remaining immigrants (1.41 million) were black, and came from the New Commonwealth countries and Pakistan. (It might be a further surprise to realise that 100 000 white British people were born in the Indian subcontinent and East Africa while their parents were on overseas service.)

People migrate for a variety of reasons, including economic and political. One reason for immigration into the UK after the war was the shortage of labour for the postwar reconstruction of the economy and society. This labour shortage was met immediately after the war by workers from eastern European countries such as Poland. In the 1950s and 1960s the need began to be met by migrant workers from the West Indies, India, Pakistan and Bangladesh. Immigration into the UK in the 1980s is on the decline. Indeed, a sociologist called Castles (1984) suggests that most growth in ethnic minority populations in western Europe is now through births.

9.2 Race discrimination and the law

Just as there is an Equal Opportunities Commission fighting sex discrimination, there is also, as you have seen, a Commission for Racial Equality fighting racial discrimination.

ACTIVITIES 16

Read Item 3.17 and answer the questions that follow.

1 Explain in your own words why racial discrimination might be described as an injustice.

2 What was the general finding of the CRE survey carried out in 1985 into racial discrimination?

3 The Commission for Racial Equality says 'the statistics [on racially motivated attacks] must be treated with caution'. Why?

4 Apart from legislation, how else can society fight racial discrimination?

The Commission is in no doubt about the extent of the injustice suffered by ethnic minorities in this country and by the black community in particular. That injustice takes the form of racial discrimination. Such discrimination is unlawful but the evidence for its extent has been regularly published and is irrefutable. In 1985, the Policy Studies Institute (PSI) published a survey, funded by the Commission, of applications for employment by candidates with equivalent qualifications from a variety of ethnic backgrounds. Thirty per cent of employers were found to have discriminated against the black applicants. In this respect, matters have not improved over the past decade. The implications of the PSI survey are that tens of thousands of individual acts of direct racial discrimination are occurring every year. Only a small proportion of these are detected and dealt with. And to that one survey, the Commission can add the weight of its own evidence derived from the individual cases it deals with, the other research which it funds or conducts and the 37 reports that it has now published on formal investigations into employment, housing and other areas where discrimination occurs. To this must be added racially motivated attacks. The statistics need to be interpreted with caution but that more such attacks have been occurring is certain. The conclusion must be that the sense of injustice many within the black community feel is not based on imagined ills. It is grounded in fact.

from the *Annual Report of the Commission for Racial Equality* (1985)

Item 3.17 Racial discrimination

The Commission for Racial Equality believes that there is not enough being done to remedy the injustice of racial discrimination in the UK. They argue that there are six things which now need to be done:

1 The government and other opinion leaders in the community must express their commitment to racial equality. There is no room for neutrality.

2 Legislation must be improved, and cases of racial discrimination at tribunals heard more speedily.

3 Local and public authorities must take positive action to improve the training and employment opportunities of racial minorities.

4 The education system, in both structure and content, must reflect more appropriately the society for which the young are being prepared.

5 The government must ensure that government spending and government contracts both carry with them an insistence on equal opportunities.

6 The community must take action to allow greater participation by minorities in all aspects of this country's life.

▶ UNIT 10   Wealth and poverty

10.1 The distribution of income and wealth

A mere five per cent of the population of the UK hold over one third of the total wealth of the country, according to statistics published by the government in 1986.

In looking at the distribution of income and wealth we should first distinguish between those terms. *Income* is a *flow* received weekly or monthly. Pay, in the form of wages or salary, is the most important source of income, but Item 3.18 shows that income also comes from self-employment, rent, interest on savings, dividends on shares, pensions and social security payments.

Wealth, on the other hand, is regarded as a *stock*, held by individuals or households at any one time – in the form of houses, shares, cars, furniture, equipment and so on.

	Average income		Percentage of income paid in tax
	Before tax (£s)	After tax (£s)	
Top 1%	31,200	20,000	36
2–5%	15,100	11,700	23
6–10%	11,300	9,010	20
Top 10%	14,800	11,200	25
11–20%	8,700	7,080	19
21–30%	6,970	5,720	18
31–40%	5,700	4,710	17
41–50%	4,520	3,800	16
51–60%	3,480	3,010	14
61–70%	2,480	2,260	8
71–75%	1,660	1,600	3
Bottom 25%	NA	NA	NA

Note: Data refer to tax units, i.e. generally treat a married couple as one unit. No data are available for the 7.4m tax units (bottom 25%) whose income is not subject to tax.

from M.J. Artis ed., *Prest and Coppock's The UK Economy: 11th Edition* (Weidenfeld and Nicholson, 1986)

Item 3.18 Distribution of total income before and after income tax, 1980–81

Distribution of income

Item 3.20 shows the distribution of *household income* for 1983; that is, the income of a household where there may be more than one person receiving income.

These figures show that the top fifth (or top 20 per cent) of households account for nearly half (48 per cent) of household income before tax.

United Kingdom, 1984–85	Income before tax	
Quantile groups	Percentage share	Average income
Top 1 per cent	6.4	48,210
Next 9 per cent	23.0	19,270
Next 40 per cent	48.3	9,090
Lower 50 per cent	22.2	3,340

Source: Central Statistical Office; Inland Revenue Adapted from Social Trends 18, (HMSO, 1988)

Item 3.19 Distribution of household income before tax, 1984–85

Greater divide between the rich and poor since the advent of Thatcher

Share boom halts equality trend

by Christopher Huhne, Economics Editor

The well-established post-war trend towards greater equality in the holding of wealth in Britain has been decisively halted and may even have been reversed since Mrs Thatcher's administration came to power in 1979, according to Inland Revenue statistics published today.*

The share of the nation's total wealth owned by the most wealthy 1 per cent and 5 per cent of the adult population has stabilised or risen since 1980 on any of the three different official measures – marketable wealth, marketable wealth including state and occupational pension rights, or marketable wealth including only occupational pensions rights.

The share of the most wealthy 1 per cent in marketable wealth – homes, stocks and shares and so forth – dropped steadily until 1980 when it reached 20 per cent of total wealth, but it edged up to 21 per cent in 1981 and has stayed at that level since.

The same picture emerges looking at the richest 5 per cent whose share has stabil-ised at 39 per cent of total wealth since 1980, having previously dropped from 44 per cent in 1978, 52 per cent in 1971, and 56 per cent in 1966. The latest figures, based on probate information, refer to 1984.

If occupational pension rights are included in the definition of wealth, the share of the richest 1 per cent stabilised at 17 per cent in 1980 and has stayed there since, having previously dropped from 27 per cent in 1971. On the same definition, the share of the richest 5 per cent has stabilised at 33 per cent of total wealth.

This is in sharp contrast to the historical experience before 1979–80. Authoritative academic research from Professor Tony Atkinson and Dr Alan Harrison has shown that the trend between 1924 and 1972 was for the top 1 per cent and the top 5 per cent to lose about 4 per cent of total wealth each decade.

What appears to be happening during the Thatcher years is a mixture of three factors. First, the boom in the stock market has particularly benefited the wealthy. Secondly, house prices have risen only moderately over much of the period. Thirdly, capital taxes have become a good deal less oner-ous (with major concessions on Capital Gains Tax and Capital Tranfser Tax) even if, ironically, capital tax yields are rising too because of the share price boom.

In addition, high income earners have had substantially bigger increases in gross pay and have also enjoyed the income tax cuts, unlike most other people earning below £512. Since high earners can save more of their income, they will also have been able to build up their stock of wealth.

The figures also show that the share of total marketable wealth owned by the richest 10 per cent is 52 per cent (the same as 1980); the richest 25 per cent own 75 per cent (also the same); and the richest 50 per cent own 93 per cent. By corollary, the poorest half of the adult population of 42.7 million in 1984 owned only 7 per cent of the total marketable wealth, only a third of the amount of the richest 1 per cent.

* *Inland Revenue Statistics 1986;* HMSO, £10.50

from the *Guardian*, 28 September 1986

Item 3.20 Wealth in Britain

Distribution of wealth

ACTIVITIES 17

1 The extract in Item 3.20 comments on the holding of wealth in Britain. Read the article and, using the figures given in the third paragraph, complete a copy of Item 3.21 which shows the percentage of total personal wealth owned by the top one per cent of the population.

Year	1911-13	1924-30	1936-38	1946-48
Percentage of total personal wealth	65-70%	60%	55%	50%

Year	1951-55	1960	1966	1976	1980	1981	1986
Percentage of total personal wealth	42%	42%					

Item 3.21 Percentage of total personal wealth owned by the top one per cent of the population

2 Show these figures graphically and comment on the trends you see.

3 Imagine you are with a group of ten friends, and have a birthday cake to share. One of the group cuts the cake and takes three-quarters of it for him or herself suggesting that the remaining quarter be shared by the rest of you. What would your reaction be?

4 Imagine the same situation again. This time one of the group cuts the cake and takes a quarter for him or herself, again suggesting the remaining three quarters be divided between the remaining nine of you. While this is an improvement on the first situation, how different would your reaction be?

5 If the total wealth of the country is thought to be the 'cake', how closely do the above stories compare to the sharing of that wealth amongst the population of the UK?

Item 3.22   How do we cut the cake?

6 The author of Item 3.20 suggests that five things have halted the trend to greater equality in the holding of wealth in Britain. List, and explain in your own words, these five things. You will find them in paragraphs 7–9 of the article.

7 Read the last paragraph of the article again. Draw histograms or pie charts to show the figures given. Remember to label your figures fully and give each a title.

10.2 The redistribution of income and wealth

These figures on the distribution of income and wealth may lead us to consider how we can remove such inequalities from the social structure. Incomes are evened out to a limited extent by taxation, as the greatest burden of income tax falls on those who are most capable of bearing it. (Such a system of taxation is referred to as *progressive*.) It is also the case that poorer families receive help from the social services and from state spending on education, housing and transport subsidies.

Item 3.23 shows the distribution of 'final income' – the income a household receives *after* taxation has been paid and *including* an amount for state spending on social security benefits, education and so on.

Item 3.23   Distribution of final income to households, 1983

	Average per household	Percentage of total
Bottom fifth	3 360	7
Next fifth	4 400	12
Middle fifth	6 190	18
Next fifth	8 160	24
Top fifth	12 920	39
Total all households	7 060	100

from M.J. Artis, ed., *Prest and Coppock's The UK Economy: 11th Edition* (Weidenfeld and Nicholson Ltd., 1986)

The share of the top fifth (top 20 per cent) has fallen from 48 per cent of original income to 39 per cent of final income. The share of the bottom fifth has risen from one per cent to 70 per cent. This means that the final income of the top fifth is still over five times greater than the final income of the bottom fifth.

10.3 Poverty

We have seen that incomes are evened out to a limited extent by a progressive taxation. The Welfare State is also able to help.

The Welfare State grew out of the needs and miseries of those people in society who suffered from great poverty. From the beginnings of human life there have been some people forced to live in poverty, lacking sufficient food, clothes and shelter.

Before the state intervened it was left to voluntary groups to help the poor. Those living in squalor often combined to help themselves, and in the middle ages the monasteries helped to relieve poverty. The 1601 Poor Law placed the responsibility for relieving poverty upon local government and it was then largely the parishes who looked after the poor. In the nineteenth century practical social workers such as Lord Shaftesbury, Dr Barnardo and General William Booth of the Salvation Army accomplished much but it was clear that there could be no permanent solution to the whole problem of poverty without massive state support. The whole of society had to accept the ideals of welfare provisions. From these origins the Welfare State arose.

It was The Beveridge Report *Social Insurance and Allied Services* published in November 1942 during the Second World War which gave real impetus to the idea of 'Welfare State'. Beveridge aimed to rid society of what he called the 'five giants' of want, ignorance, squalor, idleness and disease. The Welfare State was to provide security 'from the cradle to the grave' in its provision of universal education, a national health service, national insurance and pensions. Despite this, real poverty still remains today among pensioners, single-parent families, the homeless and others.

Poverty, however, is a relative concept. Even a condemned cottage in Britain would seem like wealth to those people in Hong Kong who are dwelling in shelters made of petrol tins. People are poor because they are deprived of the opportunities, comforts and self-respect regarded as normal in the community to which they belong. It is therefore the continually moving *average standards* of that community that are the starting points for an assessment of its poverty.

ACTIVITIES 18

Study Item 3.24 and answer the questions that follow.

Item 3.24 A mother and child living in a drainpipe outside Calcutta

1 How do the conditions of the mother and child in Item 3.24 compare with the idea of 'poverty' we apply in Britain?

2 Lord Rothschild said that a rich man was 'A man who can live on the income of his income.' What do you think he meant?

REVIEW

If you have studied and understood this chapter you should be able to ...

- outline the Registrar General's classification of occupations giving examples of each class.
- explain briefly how gender can be used as a basis for social stratification. Include in your answer an account of the process of 'anticipatory socialisation'.
- give examples of the way in which social class, gender and race can all affect the life-chances of an individual.
- briefly explain the meaning of the term '*embourgoeisement*'.
- give an account of the findings of Goldthorpe and Lockwood's study of the 'affluent worker'.
- write a few sentences explaining each of the different factors which can affect social mobility.
- describe how legislation has helped improve the position of women in society.
- discuss whether legislation has helped improve the position of ethnic minorities in British society.
- distinguish between 'income' and 'wealth'.
- explain how 'progressive taxation' can help to redistribute income and wealth more equally.

COURSEWORK SUGGESTION

A study of factors reinforcing unequal gender roles looking particularly at school influences.

In this project you should try to find out whether there are any differences between boys and girls in their subject options at the end of the third year. You could do this by counting up the numbers of boys and girls in each of the option subjects in the fourth and fifth year. You could do the same with your sixth form, as well as seeing if boys are more likely to stay on than girls. You might decide to concentrate on one or two subjects specifically (such as craft, design and technology, typewriting, home economics and computing) and interview boys and girls in these options about the reasons for their choices. Alternatively you might decide to look at the patterns in as many subjects as you can and think about a range of factors which might explain the patterns you find, such as school organisation and discipline, teacher attitudes, career guidance, the media and advertising, parental and peer group pressures, etc. Remember, if you do not find very great differences between boys and girls at your school you can still produce an interesting project explaining why your school is the way it is. You might need to interview your head teacher and other teachers for this project. Prepare your questions and test them on other students in your group first.

ASSESSMENT QUESTIONS

The mark allocations to sections of the questions are shown in the right hand margin.

1 The question carries 15 marks. You are advised to spend approximately 30 minutes on this question.

a In what ways may social class affect a person's life chances? (4)

b How has Britain's class structure changed since 1945? (5)

c What are the arguments for the view that other forms of social difference are now more important than social class? (6)

Northern Examining Association

2 The question carries 15 marks.

a Describe **two** different ways in which 'social class' may be defined. (4)

b How does 'social class' differ from **one** other form of social stratification? (5)

c Explain how social class influences any **two** of the following areas:
   i voting behaviour
   ii work
   iii education
   iv leisure (6)

London & East Anglian Group for GCSE Examinations

3 Britain is often referred to as a class-bound society. But does the British public share that impression? According to our survey, the majority does. Class prejudice or discrimination is still seen to be important.

Importance of Social Class by Social Class and Party Identification (Percentages)

	TOTAL	SOCIAL CLASS						PARTY IDENTIFICATION			
		I/II	III Non-manual	III manual	IV/V	Looks after home	Other	Cons.	Alliance	Labour	Non-aligned
AFFECTS OPPORTUNITIES IN BRITAIN TODAY:	%	%	%	%	%	%	%	%	%	%	%
A great deal	25	23	27	30	33	18	34	19	24	33	22
Quite a lot	45	44	51	44	38	47	44	48	51	41	39
Not very much	25	28	29	22	22	27	12	28	22	21	27
Not at all	3	3	1	2	2	5	5	3	1	3	6
Other/Don't know	2	1	1	1	4	4	3	2	2	2	4
Not answered	*	*	*	–	1	–	2	*	*	*	1

(Adapted from: *British Social Attitudes* edited by R. Jowell and C. Airey, Gower, 1984)

a According to the above information, what percentage of social class III manual workers believe that social class affects opportunities a great deal? (1)

b According to the above information, what is the percentage of people who believe that class affects opportunities quite a lot? (1)

c According to the above information, which party supporters are most likely to believe that class affects opportunities:
(i) a great deal; (1)
(ii) not very much? (1)

d What is meant by the term social mobility? Give **two** examples of the ways it may be achieved. (4)

e The lower the social class the higher the infant mortality rate. Identify and explain **two** reasons for this. (4)

f We usually determine an individual's social class by finding out what occupation he or she has. Identify and explain **two** problems associated with determining social class in this way. (4)

g Identify and explain **two** differences between caste and class. (4)

Southern Examining Group

4 During the early years of this century a group of workers are having their lunch break. The conversation moves around to poverty.

'Poverty', continued Jack after a short silence, 'consists in a shortage of the necessities of life. When things are so scarce or so dear that people are unable to obtain sufficient of them to satisfy their basic needs. Linden is poor. His family are actually starving. There is no food in the house and the children are crying for something to eat. All last week they have been going to school hungry for they had nothing but dry bread and tea every day and this week they don't even have that.'

For Owen, poverty was more than this. 'Yes Linden is poor,' he replied, 'but poverty should not be counted only as those who are starving. People are poor when they are not able to secure for themselves all the benefits of civilisation – not just the necessities but the comforts, pleasures and refinements of life, leisure, books, theatres, pictures, music, holidays, travel, good and beautiful homes, good clothes, good and pleasant food.'

(Source: *The Ragged Trousered Philanthropist*, R. Tressell)

a From the above information, name **two** things which Owen says all people should be able to enjoy. (1)

b According to the above passage, is Linden's family situation getting better or worse? Give a reason for your answer. (1)

c The poverty described by Jack and that described by Owen are different. What **two** terms might sociologists use to describe them? Briefly explain these terms in your own words. (1)

d Explain how people can be caught in a poverty trap in Britain today. (6)

e Britain has many Welfare State services, but some poverty still exists. Discuss why this is so. (8)

Southern Examining Group

4 *The family*

AIMS

At the end of this chapter you should be able to:

- identify and describe the main types of family found in different societies.
- recognise the important social functions performed by the family for individuals and societies.
- explain the kind of alternative social arrangements to families found in societies.
- outline the impact of social class and work on family life.
- show an appreciation of the different kinds of family life enjoyed by Britain's ethnic minorities.
- show an awareness of the ways family life is changing in modern Britain, including an analysis of divorce.

▶ UNIT 11 What is a family?

Most of us have had some experience of being a member of a family group in the course of our lives. For example, we may have grown up in a group which included people we call *father, mother, brother* and *sister*. These are all terms which are primarily confined to people who are part of the family group. Also, books, magazines, films and television programmes have shown us the lives of other family groups, real or imaginary, so that we have all formed ideas about the family. In its widest sense 'family' refers to a group of people who think of themselves as belonging to a distinct group in society and who are related to one another by ties of either blood or marriage. This group is also recognised by other members of society who see these individuals as tied to one another by certain relationships.

ACTIVITIES 1

Think about all the different 'family groups' you have come across. Include those you know from personal experience, those of your friends and those you might have read about or seen on television, both in fictional stories or soap operas and in documentaries. List all the different ways a 'family group' might be made up. You should include in your list family groups with one parent, with step-parents, with grandparents, and other combinations.

As you will quickly have realised, 'the family' is by no means always made up of mother, father and two children.

Sociologists have identified two common types of family pattern, the *nuclear* family and the *extended* family.

Item 4.1 'The family' is by no means always made up of mother, father and two children

Item 4.2 Households by type, Britain, 1961–78

	Percentages	
	1961	1978
No. family		
One person		
— under retirement age	4	7
— over retirement age	7	15
Two or more people		
— one or more over retirement age	3	2
— all under retirement age	2	1
One family		
Married couple only	26	27
Married couple with 1 or 2 dependent children	30	26
Married couple with 3 or more dependent children	8	7
Married couple with independent children only	10	7
Lone parent with at least one dependent child	2	4
Lone parent with independent children only	4	3
Two or more families	3	1
Total households	100	100

from *Social Trends 10* (HMSO, 1980)

Item 4.3 Families by type and, for lone mothers, by marital status: Britain, 1981–3

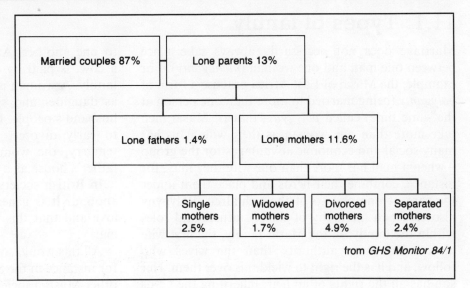

from *GHS Monitor 84/1*

The nuclear family

For a group to be called a nuclear family there must at some time be a father, mother and at least one child. This type of family structure is found in almost all societies, although the length of time in which the family remains in this form varies. The physical fact of a man and a woman producing (or adopting) a child lies at the heart of this pattern of family structure.

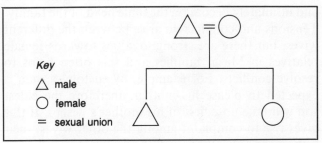

Item 4.4 Example of a nuclear family

The extended family

The extended family (sometimes also called the consanguine family) is a common family structure and includes within it the nuclear family pattern. Rosser and Harris, two sociologists, said that the extended family is 'any persistant kinship-grouping of persons related by descent, marriage or adoption, which is wider than the nuclear family, in that it characteristically spans three generations from grandparents to grandchildren'. All the members of the group do not need to live under one roof for a family group to be an extended family.

We can illustrate these two types of family pattern with the diagrams in Items 4.4 and 4.5.

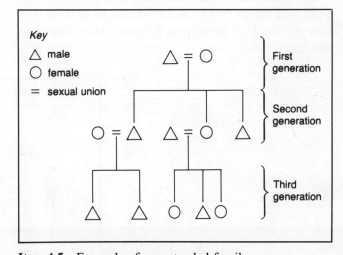

Item 4.5 Example of an extended family

Checklist

1 A nuclear family consists of a mother, father and at least one child.
2 An extended family typically extends to three generations and therefore includes grandparents.

ACTIVITIES 2

Draw a diagram of your own family. Include as many people as you think are members of your family. Label each family member and label your diagram 'nuclear' or 'extended'.

11.1 Types of family

Marriage does not necessarily always take place between one man and one woman (*monogamy*). For example, the Masai of East Africa practise a form of *polygamy* (being married to more than one person at the same time) called *polygyny*; that is, Masai men take more than one woman as their wife. This has many social and economic advantages for the group – when a man has more than one wife they may, for instance, combine their herds and place them under the care of one or two of their children. Polygyny also creates a hierarchy of social statuses and roles within the family: in the Masai family, the first wife always has more authority than the wives who follow, and has the right to wield this over them. Her son has all the rights of an heir, inheriting the herds and ultimately becoming the male head of the family. Tensions and conflicts do arise between the different wives, but there are strong loyalties towards female relatives in Masai families and this often helps to resolve conflicts. For example, by custom, a man is expected to please his mother, therefore the eldest son will take note first of his mother's wishes. If this gives rise to complaint among the other wives, their fathers and brothers will be willing to take up complaints with the head of the family.

The Sisala of Northern Ghana also practise polygyny and prefer this to be the marriage of a man to two sisters. This is because it is said that sisters do not quarrel as much as women who are strangers to one another. At marriage a *bride price*, usually a cow, is paid by the groom's family to the wife's family. A woman is expected to adjust from her role as daughter and sister to wife and mother in her husband's people. If the stress of this situation leads to early divorce, because she is not allowed to remarry, the woman will have to remain in her father's house as a daughter.

In British society, romantic ideas about marriage abound. It is generally thought that people fall in love and that this is the basis for their decision to marry.

All this would sound very strange to many people, for instance in the Sisala society, or Afghanistan and other Muslim societies, where marriage is customarily arranged by the respective parents of the couple. The social recognition given to marriage makes it more likely that the parents of children born into society will continue to remain together while they care for their offspring. In many societies, children are an economic asset. For example, in the Masai, fathers want many children, particularly boys, as they can help in looking after the herd and later go on raids to bring back more cattle to the group. In our society, children are not so economically important to the family and many married couples decide to have only one or two children. In this way marriage has become separated from the idea of having children and the happiness of husband and wife is

Item 4.6 It is generally thought that people fall in love and that this is the basis for their decision to marry

MONOGAMY	One man + One Woman	Husband + Wife	UK; Europe; USA; most western societies
POLYGYNY	One man + Several wives (simultaneously)	Husband + Wives	The Masai of East Africa; the Sisala of Northern Ghana; some Muslim societies
POLYANDRY	One woman + Several husbands This is less usual than POLYGYNY	Wife + Husbands	Marquesan Islands; Tibet
POLYGAMY	This is a category which embraces POLYGYNY and POLYANDRY. It is sometimes used as a general term to replace these.		As in second and third categories above

Item 4.7   Forms of marriage

Europeans think marriage is a private matter between two individuals marrying for love, but Hindus, Sikhs and many other people from Asia and Africa regard it differently. In these communities a marriage concerns two whole families, not just two people, and it demands much careful thought. The families must not be related, and in small villages most families are related in some way. Hindus of different castes should not marry. The families must have similar interests and not be hostile to one another. If the two fathers are competitors in business it is unlikely that they will be able to co-operate in helping their children make a success of marriage....

When Mr and Mrs Ruprai were married they had met only once before, for a few hours at a party, and they had never been alone together. When Mr Ruprai was in his early twenties his father told his brothers, a cousin and a few uncles that his son was ready to marry. One of them had a friend with a twenty-year-old daughter. After each family had found out what they could about the other, a meeting was arranged and Mr Ruprai's father took him to the girl's home. On this occasion the two young people did not see each other. However, the girl's father clearly approved of the young man and a party was arranged at which the couple could meet. The wedding took place a month later....

Kalwant had lived in Britain for seven years, had gone to an English secondary school and worked as a secretary. She had seen Rajvir at the gurdwara and when her mother asked her about marriage she said Rajvir was the sort of young man for her. He was good looking, he had many friends and he seemed kind. Kalwant knew Rajvir's sister and even she thought her brother was a reasonable young man! The families met and agreed that Kalwant and Rajvir seemed suited to one another. The young people decided to get to know one another before becoming engaged. They went for walks, met at parties and visited one another's homes. At last they became engaged.

Everyone was happy. The families had been consulted and played their traditional part. Although they agreed it was good for the young people to get to know each other before marriage they could not go along with all Western ideas. The number of divorces in Britain made them suspicious of love-marriages. The young people were happy. They had been allowed their say and had been permitted to meet and become friends.

This was not marriage Western-style or Indian-style. It was something different, and to Kalwant and Rajvir it seemed to combine the best of both worlds.

from W. Owen Cole, *A Sikh Family in Britain* (Religious and Moral Education Press, 1973)

Item 4.8   A Sikh wedding

often looked on as being just as important as raising children.

Item 4.7 shows some of the variations we find in different societies in the way they arrange their family life.

Key terms

- nuclear family
- extended family
- monogamy
- polygyny
- polyandry

ACTIVITIES 3

Read the description in Item 4.8 of the way a Sikh wedding was arranged, and answer the questions that follow it.

1 A marriage concerns two whole families, not just two people. List the ways in which you think the statement might be true, and ways in which you think marriage might be a private matter concerning only the two people involved.

2 'The number of divorces in Britain made them [Kalwant's parents] suspicious of love-marriages.' Discuss.

3 In what ways do you think arranged marriages might affect the roles adopted by husbands and wives within the marriage?

11.2   The social functions of the family

The family has two major functions: *nurture* and *socialisation*.

Nurture

A child born into society must be fed and looked after. In many societies, the parents of the child are responsible for their child's welfare and, in this way, perform a function for society in general by looking after the next generation and ensuring that it will survive.

Socialisation

As children grow up, surrounded by brothers and sisters, peer group (other children of their own age and background), parents and, sometimes, members of the extended family group, they gradually learn things about the society in which they live. For example, they will learn its language and its ideas about right and wrong. In other words, they will learn the *culture* of their society through their contact with, at first, the members of their family. The sociologist calls the way in which individuals acquire the culture of their society *socialisation*.

One particularly important element of the socialisation process is the way in which families teach children how to behave as girls and boys. Many of the differences in attitudes and behaviour we can see between girls and boys might be explained by different socialisation rather than by biological differences (see topic 8.1).

11.3 Sex role socialisation in the family

You will recall from Chapter 3, on social differences, that an important aspect of social differences relates to gender. The family plays an important role in socialising boys and girls into particular and specifically defined roles.

ACTIVITIES 4: Play-reading

Read the play-reading and answer the questions which follow.

(Parents, the Smiths, are washing up the tea things in the kitchen. They hear their son Sebastian, aged six, watching commercials on the TV in the next room. Christmas is near ...)

Mr Smith   Those commercials should be banned. We'll be bankrupt if he gets any more ideas about what he wants for Christmas.

Mrs Smith   Well, even the cheap presents have to be pushed and shoved for, you know. People who say rugby's a rough game have never been shopping in December.

(Enter Sebastian)

Sebastian   Dad? Can I have a teaset for Christmas?

Item 4.9   Children learn the culture of their society through socialisation

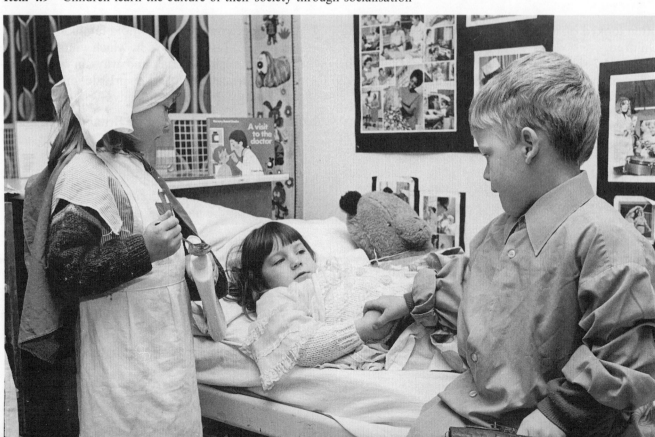

It's got a tea pot and cups and plates and you can make real drinks with it. And there's a washing brush.

Mrs Smith   Oh, that's the 'Little Miss' series of toys, isn't it, Arthur? I pointed them out to you the other day.

Mr Smith   'Little Miss'? Doesn't sound very suitable, does it? Er, well Seb . . . it's something for girls really, that teaset and dishes and things. Not really for boys.

Sebastian   Why?

Mr Smith   Well, it just is. Making the tea and washing up. Little girls practise for when they're mummies.

Sebastian   You're washing up, Daddy.

Mr Smith   Er.

Mrs Smith   Quite. Anyway he likes pouring water from one cup to another, don't you, love? You do it at school.

Mr Smith   Well, he can do that with a chemistry set, then. That's for boys.

Mrs Smith   Oh, they're not for girls, then? I see. I got my chemistry 'O' level – you failed yours.

Mr Smith   Don't confuse the issue, darling. Other boys of Sebastian's age play with Cosmic Hero dolls or 007 secret agent kits.

Mrs Smith   Aha! A doll!

Mr Smith   For boys, though. You know, you get extra models – his space ship, invaders from Mars, enemy robots. I never had a teaset when I was young.

Mrs Smith   Pity! Call this saucepan washed? Shame on you, 007!

Mr Smith   Very funny! Is the Queen coming then? OK, give it here.

Mrs Smith   Well at least a teaset's useful. He'll learn a social skill – unlike his father – and the chances of him having to repel an invasion from Martians, or even enemy robots, is rather remote.

Mr Smith   It develops the imagination. Stimulates their mind to create fantasy.

Mrs Smith   I bet that's on the box.

Sebastian   Mum, can I have a teaset?

Mrs Smith   You'll have to ask your Dad, Seb. He's the man with the money. That teaset's about three pounds fifty. Lot of money. Mind you, the Cosmic Hero is nine pounds admittedly. And 007's about twelve.

Sebastian   Dad, can I have a teaset?

Mr Smith   Yes, all right Sebby. If it's what you want.

1 What is Mr Smith's attitude toward Sebastian's request for a teaset for Christmas?

2 From the passage, and your own experience, comment on the differences between boys' dolls and girls' dolls.

3 How does the incidence portrayed here illustrate the different socialisation received by boys and girls? Give other examples from your own experience.

ACTIVITIES 5

The difference in the ways girls and boys are treated is even more pronounced in other cultures. Read the passage in Item 4.10, which outlines the case in a typical South Asian family, and answer the questions that follow.

1 Why are girls in South Asian families under much stricter surveillance than boys?

2 Outline your understanding of the 'dual standard of morality' referred to in the passage.

Girls are under stricter surveillance than boys, for it is felt that too much freedom might spoil a girl's reputation and thus damage her chances of making a good marriage. In addition the status and prestige of the family as a whole depends upon keeping its reputation, much of which rests with the chaste behaviour of its women, irreproachable. Many girls complain about the dual standard of morality which allows their brothers a good deal more freedom than they have themselves:

In Asian society the woman is a white piece of cloth, the man a black piece. If there are any dirty marks on the black cloth it will be difficult to see, but this won't be the case with the white cloth. The dirty marks will be seen. (*Girl typist*)

However, if he goes too far, a boy's behaviour may also make it difficult for a good match to be made for himself or for his sisters. Every story about an Asian girl running away from home, and such stories are often featured in the Asian newspapers which are published in Britian, increases the anxiety of all parents about the corrupting influence of British norms on their own daughters. They may withdraw their daughters from school and speed up the arrangement of their marriages.

from Verity Saifullah Khan (ed.), *Minority Families in Britain* (Macmillan, 1979)

Item 4.10   Girls in a South Asian family

3 What might some Asian parents mean if they refer to 'the corrupting influence of British norms'?

4 In what ways are boys and girls treated differently in your own community? Give examples from your own experience or observation.

Checklist

We can summarise the social functions of the family as:

1 biological and supportive functions
  a It provides a socially acceptable situation in which sexual needs can be satisfied.
  b It supports human reproduction in the social setting.
  c It provides a place for bringing up children.
  d It provides for the satisfaction of individual emotional needs.

2 social and economic functions
  a It transmits culture, and socialises the young into society.
  b It acts as an agent of social control, regulating the behaviour of its members.
  c It provides economic support for its members.
  d It provides a position for the individual in society, giving him or her a place from which to relate to the wider society.

11.4 Alternatives to traditional family life

The family performs numerous functions in society, but this does not necessarily mean that there is no possibility of anything else taking its place. There have been many planned experiments which have tried to find other ways by which, for instance, children can be brought up in society. Examples of experiments in communal living, where children are the concern of the society as a whole, are groups such as the Israeli kibbutzim and the communes of the People's Republic of China. However, it would be misleading to think of these experiments as providing complete alternatives to the family in society. For instance, making other groups responsible for social functions such as child rearing does not mean that the family has no significance in society. It means, rather, that the family is freed from that particular

activity because of the different demands of a communal society.

Many sociologists have researched the kibbutz, because it provides a way of testing the idea that whatever social arrangement are designed, the family will never altogether disappear. In the early kibbutzim, infants were taken to children's houses after only a short time with their parents. This physical separation from their family continued into adult life. The children grew up together and were looked after by specially trained nurses (called *metaplets*) and teachers, only being at their parents' home or seeing their parents for a few hours each day. Women with children were therefore free to take on any work, and women worked on the same terms as men. Today, these patterns are changing and the separation between parents and children is less complete. In many kibbutzim, children return to spend the night at their parents' flat, and more women are involved in the traditionally feminine types of work such as working in the communal kitchen or laundry.

In the communes of the People's Republic of China, communal services such as free creches, nurseries and canteens support the family in its social role. These services release members of the family for participation in the work of the commune.

ACTIVITIES 6

Item 4.12 is a description of a kibbutz to which one might apply to live and work as a volunteer. Read it and answer the questions that follow.

1 Imagine you are a volunteer on Kibbutz Misgav Am and write a short account of a day spent there.

2 The socialisation of children in a kibbutz is very different from that in a traditional family. Discuss how the kibbutz and the nuclear family are alike and how they are different from each other in the way they organise the socialisation of children.

Key terms

- Israeli kibbutzim
- metaplets
- kibbutznik
- volunteer

The kibbutz is a communal, socialistic society in which all the means of production are owned by the community as a whole. It is a society in which everything owned, everything produced and everything earned is shared by all members. It is not a perfect way of life but is an honest, committed attempt to live a life based on friendship, equality and democracy.

Founded in 1909 the kibbutz movement provided groups of people with common beliefs and aspirations with an opportunity to build their own way of life and support themselves with an economy based on agriculture. Many kibbutzim have now diversified energetically and profitably into manufacturing industry, and now operate factories producing a range of products ranging from footwear to sophisticated electrical instruments for both the home market and export.

In the early days the kibbutz was common property. The showers were for everyone; in the clothes store, the clothes belonged to everyone, even the underwear. The 'kibbutznik' did not even own a watch and had no time that was his own. There was no room in the kibbutz for the expression of personal style or taste. Everything belonged to the collective and the collective belonged to everyone, in every way and at all times. Today financial success and basic socialism have produced a way of life that is having a real effect on the cultural, economic and ideological life of Israel. How then does a kibbutznik live today?

Work

The kibbutz member can be assigned to any job on the kibbutz; his status is not affected by the work he performs, as all jobs are considered to be of equal importance. Members wishing to work outside the kibbutz may do so and turn their income over to the kibbutz.

Personal project

The division of wealth in the kibbutz is decided according to the principle 'to each according to his needs'. These needs are filled almost entirely in the form of sevices, housing, clothing, food, education, health, care, etc. The kibbutz may also allow each member an allowance to spend on consumer goods and luxuries.

Housing and children

Members live in single or double accomodation with living rooms, small kitchen, bathroom and toilet. In most, but not all kibbutzim, children live in special children's homes and not with parents. Community living is taught from a very early age with children living, eating and studying together. Mothers visit their children frequently during the day and after work each day parents and children spend several hours together.

Clothing

All clothing on the kibbutz is handled by the laundry and repair department. Deposited laundry is returned at the end of the week, washed, ironed and mended. Many kibbutzim keep a record of clothing owned by each member and certain items are replaced automatically when they are seen to be worn out.

Although kibbutzim are highly organised and often mechanised they generally face a labour shortage. Over the years a system has evolved that enables the many young people that travel to Israel from all over the world to live and work on a kibbutz, generally sharing the same conditions as the members. These young people are known as 'volunteers'.

adapted from John Bedford, *The Kibbutz Volunteer* (1986)

Item 4.11   The Israeli kibbutz: an alternative to the family

(1) KIBBUTZ MISGAV AM
Galil Elyon M.P. Tel: (067) 40632.
Founded: 1945.
Members: 95. Volunteers: 30–35.
Responsible for volunteers: Dahlia Halev.
Work available: Apples, fish ponds, cowsheds, laundry, kitchen, dining room, textile factory. 6 hour 6 day week. 2 extra days off monthly.
Free: Cheap cigarettes, aerogrammes, coffee, tea, washing powder, light bulbs, matches.
Accommodation: Wooden shacks with communal toilets and showers. 1–3 to a room. No kosher food.

Sports/Entertainments: Basketball, weekly films, fortnightly dances.
Other Facilities: Swimming pool, clubhouse with TV, refreshments and table games, shop.
Main Languages: Hebrew, English.
Excursions: 3 one day trips in 6 months.
Other Information: Minimum stay 1 month. Ages 18–30. Groups and individuals. Most northerly kibbutz, with army section permanently stationed. Small fairly poor kibbutz. Bus stop on kibbutz. 10 km from main road.
Kibbutz Movement: Hameuchad.

from John Bedford, *The Kibbutz Volunteer* (1986)

Item 4.12   Kibbutz life

UNIT 12   The family in the UK today

12.1 Social class, work and family life

It has long been recognised by sociologists and others that social class has an influence over the way family life is organised. Chapter 3 introduced the idea of social class, and it would be hard to imagine social class *not* influencing family life.

In some traditional working-class areas the extended family still plays a vigorous part in the experience of growing up in a family. These areas usually have a history of employment in difficult and strenuous manual occupations such as coal-mining, working on the docks, shipbuilding and deep-sea fishing. Families have lived and worked in these areas for generations, with members of the extended family living close to one another – often next door or on the same street. This makes it possible for relatives to see a lot of one another, and to be at hand whenever help is needed. This pattern of relationships is characteristic of traditional working-class communities.

In such a traditional working-class community, a woman usually expects to keep up a close relationship with her mother after marriage. This is not difficult as her mother usually lives close by. Family life often centres on the close relationship which exists between 'Mum' and her married daughters. Young and Willmott, two sociologists who studied the traditional working-class area of Bethnal Green in London, found that there was a considerable degree of contact between married daughters and their mothers.

ACTIVITIES 7

Conduct a short survey of your class. See how many people have 'family' living close by. Count the number of people who see a grandparent at least once a week. Comment on the kinds of family (nuclear or extended) that are to be found within your class or school. Try to explain your results.

In looking at the relationship between husband and wife in traditional working-class families we must remember that this relationship usually takes in the relationship between the wife and her mother. The lives of husband and wife are closely bound up with what is going on round at 'Mum's place'.

The wife's role is usually thought of as looking after the children and the home. The husband is the breadwinner and domestic chores or helping with the children are not seen as being appropriate to the masculine role. Husbands and wives also carry on leisure time activities separately, husbands spending time with their workmates and women with female relatives and friends. The separation between husband and wife often extends to the point where the wife does not know, or think it any of her business to know, how much money her husband earns. This type of *conjugal role relationship* (relationship between husband an wife) is termed *segregated conjugal role*.

ACTIVITIES 8

In what ways are 'conjugal roles' changing now? Think about changes which may have happened in a typical husband's attitude towards:

a his wife.   c domestic chores.
b his children. d leisure time.

Item 4.13 shows the relationships in a traditional working-class family. Draw a similar diagram for your own family. Draw the stronger relationships in thicker lines.

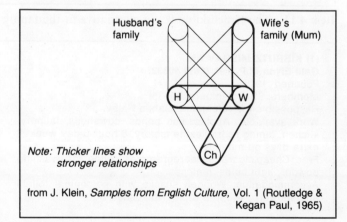

Note: Thicker lines show stronger relationships

from J. Klein, *Samples from English Culture*, Vol. 1 (Routledge & Kegan Paul, 1965)

Item 4.13   Relationships in the traditional working-class family

Item 4.14   'My husband is at home all the time and that makes for sharing'

Conjugal role relationships have changed. Husbands and wives increasingly act as partners, sharing activities to do with the home and the children. In other words, segregated conjugal roles are changing to become *joint conjugal roles*. For example, in her study of housebound mothers, Hannah Gavron notes a young working-class wife who recalls: 'My father was never at home, not so's you'd notice, while my husband, well he's at home all the time and that makes for sharing.' Indeed, in a later study, in the 1970s, Young and Wilmott identified the *symmetrical family*, in which the roles of husband and wife are increasingly similar and in which joint conjugal roles are more typical.

In her study, Gavron describes how many of the working-class mothers, at home with young children and living away from the friends and family that they had known when they were growing up in a traditional working-class area, were very miserable and looked to their husbands as the only relief they had from isolation and loneliness. Gavron suggests that, in these circumstances, joint conjugal roles are an expression of a desire for emotional closeness on the part of working-class couples.

Ann Oakley contributed to this debate about the changing pattern of conjugal roles in the family with her study of housewives. In the 1970s she studied a small sample of housewives, all with at least one child under five, and investigated the women's attitudes to housework. She tried to discover how much help male partners actually gave in the home, and what were thought to be the ideal or proper roles of the sexes. Oakley was unable to support the idea of close joint conjugal roles. She found that the most usual pattern was for male partners to share more in childcare than housework, with 'childcare' tending to involve playing with children rather than doing jobs like bathing them or changing nappies. Housework was always perceived by the women as primarily their duty rather than that of their male partners.

The nature of conjugal roles in the family, therefore, is not something upon which sociologists readily agree.

Key terms

- segregated conjugal roles
- joint conjugal roles

Many recent changes in the wider structure of society have affected the old, traditional working-class communities. For example, rehousing schemes have drawn families away from *close-knit communities* and this has affected relationships between members of the extended family. Willmott and Young noted the effects of this change on the organisation of the family in their study of the traditional working-class Bethnal Green families living on a new housing estate on the outskirts of London. The separation of the nuclear family from the extended family group encourages the nuclear family to spend more time with each other and to spend money on their home, their children and *home-centred activities*.

The life of the nuclear family is more private and self-contained. It is carried on free of close contact with everyone else in the neighbourhood. This *privatisation* is described by Willmott and Young as a change from face-to-face relationships to 'window-to-window' relationships. John Goldthorpe and David Lockwood also noted the presence of the privatised family pattern amongst the working class in their study, *The Affluent Worker*. In this they studied the family, working life and political view of the relatively well-paid car workers in Luton.

The social structure of the middle-class family today is typically the nuclear family pattern. The middle-class family is generally interested in 'getting on'. This desire for upward social mobility is reflected in a willingness to move to new areas if this means a better job or promotion. This results in the nuclear family often living many kilometres from members of the extended family group. Middle-class residential districts are areas where there is a shifting population, and few people either are related to one another or know one another closely. This type of community is called a *loose-knit* community.

In the loose-knit community, the husband-and-wife are likely to have mutual friends of both sexes, and leisure time is frequently spent by husband and wife together. In *The Captive Wife*, Gavron suggests that middle-class conjugal roles, in contrast to privatised working-class conjugal roles, are a way in which husband and wife show that they expect the individual to be able to carry on and enjoy a high level of independence within marriage.

Key terms

- home-centred activities
- privatisation
- loose-knit community
- close-knit community

12.2 The family life of the UK's ethnic minority groups

It is just as impossible, of course, to do justice to the tremendous diversity of the family life of the UK's ethnic minority groups as it is to do justice to the similar diversity found amongst the population at large. In this section, therefore, only an indication of typical differences can be provided and attention is paid particularly to the family life of South Asians. Item 4.15 describes an Asian household in the UK.

ACTIVITIES 9

Read Item 4.15 and answer the questions that follow.

1 What does the writer mean by 'chain migration'?

2 What are the consequences for the family of such chain migration?

3 Describe in your own words some of the most important features of family life for South Asians, as described by the writer.

4 Outline some of the differences between, and similarities to, family life as described by the writer and your own family life.

Asian households in Britain may often be smaller than those in the villages of the sub-continent, because very often only a section of the family has settled in Britain. As time passes however, and as sons grow up, marry and have children of their own, the household begins to increase in size. Many families make great efforts to remain together, but the small size of most British houses often makes it necessary to establish several residential and domestic units, although the ties between them may remain very close. It is still common for young couples to spend the first few years of their married life living with the boy's parents, and invariably one son and his wife and children will continue to live with them, even if others move out. It is extremely rare to find elderly people living on their own. Households where two brothers and their families live together are also by no means unusual. Chain migration, where early settlers called relatives to join them, has ensured that almost every family has an extensive network of kinsmen living in Britain. Frequently many of them will live in the same area, but the exigencies of the employment and housing markets usually mean that they will be geographically scattered. None the less the concept of being part of a large kinship group, with its concomitant loyalties and obligations, remains very strong. Residential units may be small and kinship groups fragmented and scattered but there is constant visiting and contact between them. The kinship group with its common identification with the village or areas of origin is still the most important focus of social interaction.

from Verity Saifullah Khan (ed.), *Minority Families in Britain* (Macmillan, 1979)

Item 4.15   An Asian household in the UK

An Asian child in Britain learns very early in its life that it is part of a wide and stable family group. The bonds of affection within this group, the security which it provides for its members and the group's sense of its own identity are very strong. From its earliest infancy a child will receive attention and care from a number of adults and older siblings. Even if the household is small, its members will spend much time exchanging visits with relatives and friends who, in the absence of the full kinship group, take on the role of quasi-kin. Small children are constantly carried, cuddled and kept amused and there is little separation of adult and child activities. The smallest children are taken on all family outings, they are present at all ceremonies and they are not sent away when adult functions and discussions are taking place. Allowances are made for children, but their needs are not seen as being very different from the rest of the family. They are participants in all family events and because of this they learn to behave responsibly at an early age. They learn by example and through play, which often imitates adult activity, the behaviour which will be expected of them as they grow up. Imitative play gradually develops into real help, so that by the time a child is seven or eight years old it will be taking an important part in the work of the household, looking after smaller children, performing minor domestic tasks and helping to entertain guests. As a member of the family group the child is expected to share everything with others. The emphasis is always on 'we' and 'ours' rather than on 'I' and 'mine' and the demanding of exclusive attention from parents is not greatly encouraged.

We have to start reminding them that they're not alone in the family from the time when they're very small. For instance, if my littlest one wants some sweets then I say that if he has them he'll have to share them with his brothers and sisters. That's how we do it, showing them that they have to think of others before themselves. Otherwise there's no hope for our kind of family. (*Sikh father*)

An Asian child's experience of the mutual co-operation which binds the family together is very intense, and constant exposure to the social life of the community is very effective conditioning. By the time children enter school they have been socialised into a very different set of values from those of their British peers.

from Verity Saifullah Khan (ed.), *Minority Families in Britain* (Macmillan, 1979)

Item 4.16   An Asian child in the UK

ACTIVITIES 10

Item 4.16 describes the way children are brought up in a South Asian family.

'By the time Asian children enter school, they have been socialised into a very different set of values from those of British children.' Using the passage provided, and your own experiences, say whether you agree or disagree with this statement and try to explain why you hold the opinion you do.

12.3 Changing family life in the UK

The family is part of society and therefore it influences, and is itself influenced by, changes in the wider social structure. Among the most significant of such changes have been the processes of *industrialisation* and *urbanisation* which began in this country in the eighteenth century.

Industrialisation brought the factory system. This meant a decline in the hand-production of goods, which was centred on production by the extended family carried on in the home, and the growth of machine-production of goods, carried on in factories in towns. Workers worked for wages, and their labour and the goods that they produced were effectively owned by the factory owner. Some of the traditions of the family-centred method of production carried over into the factory system. For example, the factory system inherited the custom of child labour and the belief that this was socially acceptable. Child labour only began to be limited after the passing of various Factory Acts in the 1830s and 1840s.

The growth of factories brought with it the growth of towns. This urbanisation resulted from the influx of workers from the countryside, leaving behind the older generation of the extended family, and seeking better wages in the factories. Home-centred production had meant all family members working long, irregular hours in order to complete production on time and ensure their livelihood. When work was

transferred to the factory, family members worked long hours, but they were more likely to be regular hours. Also, they were likely to receive regular wages. Despite this, the disadvantages were severe. Urban conditions were very bad indeed, and malnutrition was rampant in the working classes and the urban poor.

Today the family in Britain is part of a fully industrialised and urbanised society. In contrast to the nineteenth century, mass-produced goods, such as foodstuffs, cars, televisions, electric irons and vacuum cleaners, are commonplace, everyday things. Most paid work is carried on at a place of work outside the home, and it is usually members of the nuclear family rather than the extended family who live together under one roof.

Industrialisation and urbanisation have been powerful forces in changing the structure and function of the family in Britain over the last two centuries. This has occurred through the changes which have followed from work being taken outside the home, and also through legislative and other changes which have arisen to make modern, industrialised society a better place to live in. For example, the work of trade unions and the services of the Welfare State have helped to guarantee the family some income even in times of unemployment or ill health. Children are able to receive free education at state schools until they are sixteen. Many married women go out to work and legislation exists to safeguard equality between the sexes in many areas.

Key terms

- industrialisation
- urbanisation

▶ UNIT 13 Divorce

The nineteenth century saw the family and marriage as inseparable. Their image of marriage was as an enduring, stable relationship, sanctified by God. Christian marriage implied a lifelong, faithful cohabitation of husband and wife, dutifully concerned with the procreation and rearing of children. This was part of the middle-class idealisation of family life.

13.1 Divorce statistics

Did you know that . . .

– the older a couple are at marriage the less likely they are to divorce?

– spouses who marry in their teens are almost twice as likely to divorce as those who marry between the ages of 20 and 24?

– if present trends continue, one in three marriages could end in divorce?

– if present trends continue one child in five will see their parents divorce before the child reaches the age of sixteen?

– the divorce rate in England and Wales is one of the highest in Europe? In 1986, 168 000 divorce decrees were made absolute in England and Wales – out of every 1000 married couples in the population, about 13 divorced.

ACTIVITIES 11

Look at Item 4.18, which shows divorces granted to husbands or wives, and the grounds of the divorce.

1 Look first at the grounds for divorce used by husbands. What percentage of husbands petitioned for divorce on the grounds of adultery? What percentage petitioned on the grounds of cruelty?

2 Look now at the grounds for divorce used by wives. What percentage of wives petitioned for divorce on the grounds of adultery? What percentage petitioned on the grounds of cruelty? What grounds for divorce was most commonly used by wives?

3 The Divorce Reform Act 1969 came into effect in 1971. The graph shows the effects of this clearly.

   In 1971 what were the commonest grounds for divorces granted to:
   a husbands?
   b wives?

   What explanations can you give for the high proportion of divorces granted on these grounds in 1971 and their rapid decline in subsequent years?

Item 4.18   Divorce – party granted decree: in thousands

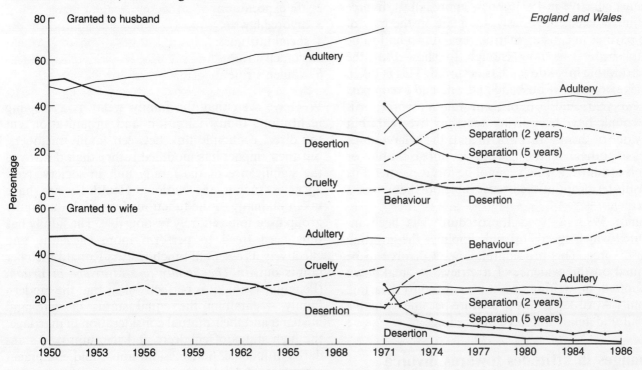

Source: Secular changes in divorce in England and Wales by class of decree – a socio-legal analysis, John Haskey, *Biology and Society*, Vol. 3, 1986

from *Social Trends 16* (HMSO, 1986) and *Social Trends 18*

13.2 Understanding divorce statistics

In attempting to make sense of divorce statistics several factors have to be taken into account.

Population structure and characteristics

The population has more than doubled since the nineteenth century. Also, a higher proportion of the population is married. The increase in the expectation of life that has occurred since the nineteenth century exposes marriage to a greater period of risk in which divorce can occur.

Legal changes

With the Matrimonial Causes Act of 1857, divorces began to be less costly and therefore accessible to more people. However, it has taken over a hundred years more for divorce laws and other legal provisions to reach their present state which makes it possible for almost anyone to obtain a divorce. Under the Divorce Reform Act (1969), which became effective in 1971, a new approach to divorce was introduced. Previously, the guilt on the part of one partner in causing marital breakdown had to be established. It is now enough to show that the 'irretrievable breakdown' has occurred. This is taken to have occurred if husband and wife had lived apart for two years and both of them want a divorce, or if the couple have been living apart for five years but only one of them wants a divorce. If the behaviour of one or other of the parties is unreasonable or involves adultery which cannot be forgiven, then this constitutes proof of the irretrievable breakdown of a marriage.

Since 1973, a 'special procedure' has been instituted which speeds up and simplifies the granting of a divorce. This procedure allows a divorce to be granted on the evidence of irretrievable breakdown submitted in writing, without any court hearing. From 1 April 1977, this procedure became available for all undefended divorce proceedings.

Changes in attitudes towards divorce

It has been suggested that there is greater tolerance of divorce and this has encouraged more people to petition for divorce. Changes in the law tell us something about changes in publicly held social attitudes towards divorce, as do changes which have occurred in the Church of England's position on divorce. In 1966, the Church of England had made clear its opinions on divorce in the publication *Putting Asunder*. In this, the Church of England supported the view which is now part of our law; that is, that irretrievable breakdown of marriage is the appropriate basis on which to grant divorce.

Changes in women's role

It has also been suggested that because women are now freer to make their own way in the world, own their own property and earn their own wages, divorce is not the daunting prospect it was in the nineteenth century. Then, the social stigma attached to divorce and the lack of women's rights made divorce largely impossible. At the present time many more wives than husbands petition for divorce.

Checklist

Factors affecting divorce statistics include:

1 number of marriages.
2 life expectation.
3 divorce laws.
4 social attitudes.
5 women's rights.
6 women's role.

We have seen that the family today is a thriving institution. Industrialisation and urbanisation cut the direct economic link between family members, but their impact has modified rather than destroyed the significance of the family unit in society. New agencies, such as the National Health Service, have taken on many of the functions for which the family group used to be entirely responsible. The family has thus been freed to perform more efficiently and effectively its essential functions. As Ronald Fletcher points out, in *The Family and Marriage in Britain* (Penguin, 1966), 'it is perfectly clear that the modern family – entailing the equal status of wife and husband and their mutual consideration in marriage; the high status of children; and the improved standards of income, housing and household equipment – aims at, and achieves, a far more satisfactory and refined provision for [the performance of essential functions] than did either the pre-industrial family or the family of early industrial Britain.'

REVIEW

If you have studied and understood this chapter you should be able to . . .

- describe the main features of
  a nuclear families, and
  b extended families.
- define or explain the terms
  a monogamy,
  b polygyny, and
  c polyandry.
- give an account of the way families contribute to society, including in your answer an account of the family's social functions.
- explain how the family can reinforce sex roles through the process of socialisation.
- outline the attempts different societies have made to find alternatives to traditional life in families, including in your account some of the advantages of any alternative you might discuss.
- define or explain with examples the terms
  a joint conjugal roles, and
  b segregated conjugal roles.
- give an account of the way social class affects conjugal roles in the family.
- give examples of the way children are brought up in South Asian families.
- define or explain the terms
  a industrialisation, and
  b urbanisation,
  and briefly indicate how these changes have affected the family.
- explain why any study using official divorce statistics must treat those statistics with care.

COURSEWORK SUGGESTION

Study the different kinds of family units and family life found in your school. Interview pupils who live in nuclear families and those who live close to, or with, their grandparents in a extended family structure. Also interview pupils who are members of Britain's ethnic groups. Try to interview pupils who come from communities different from your own. Write a report, providing clear ideas about the way family life is conducted and the impact this has on the socialisation of the children, the conjugal roles within the family and the way the family spend their leisure time. Consider similarities as well as differences in the families you study.

ASSESSMENT QUESTIONS

1 Read the source material and answer the questions that follow. Answer all the questions; they may be attempted in any order. The marks shown should be taken as guides to the lengths of answers expected.

SOURCE A

'Love is now considered important to marriage in most parts of the world. But only in societies like ours is the ideal of romantic love all powerful. From early childhood we are socialised into falling in love – not just by parents and friends but by popular songs, films, TV programmes, magazines and the other mass media. This influence is so strong that young people may be led to expect too much from marriage, and be bitterly disappointed when the passion of courtship is cooled by the daily routines of married life.'

R. J. Cootes, *The Family* (Longman, 1974)

SOURCE B

Margaret Mead spent a lot of time with Manus people in New Guinea in the 1920s before the impact of modernized societies like America and Australia had much influence on their way of life. In Manus societies marriages were arranged and the relatives lived together in extended family groups.

'The relationship between husband and wife is usually strained and cold. The blood-ties with their parents are stronger than their relationship to each other, and there are more factors to pull them apart than to draw them together.

The bridegroom has no attitude of tenderness or affection for the girl whom he has never seen before the wedding. She fears her first sex experience as all the women of her people have feared and hated it. No foundation is laid for happiness on the wedding night, only one for shame and hostility. The next day the bride goes about the village with her mother-in-law to fetch wood, and water. She has not yet said one word to her husband.

This sense that husband and wife belong to different groups persists throughout the marriage, weakening after the marriage has endured for many years, never vanishing entirely.'

J. L. Thompson, *Examining Sociology* (Hutchinson, 1980)

SOURCE C

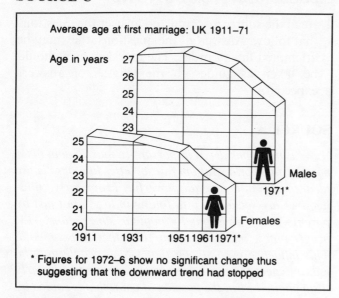

Average age at first marriage: UK 1911–71

Age in years

Males 1971*

Females 1971*

1911   1931   1951 1961 1971*

* Figures for 1972–6 show no significant change thus
suggesting that the downward trend had stopped

R. J. Cootes, *The Family* (Longman, 1974)

SOURCE D

*Percentage of women who had lived with their husbands
before their marriage*

Great Britain

	Percentage	
	Year of Marriage	
	1971–73	1977–79
First marriage for both partners: age of woman at marriage		
Under 20	4	16
20–24	8	17
25 and over	10	34
All ages (percentages)	7	19
Second or subsequent marriage for one or both partners:		
All women (percentages)	43	59

Adapted from *Social Trends 12* (HMSO, 1982)

SOURCE E

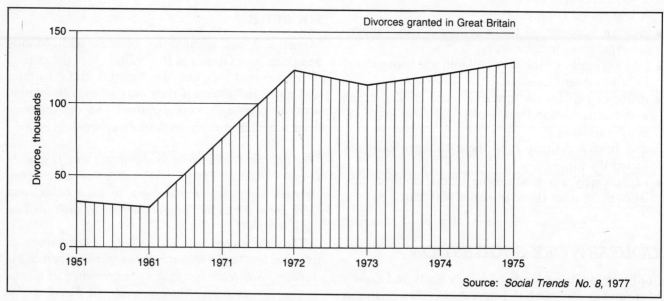

Divorces granted in Great Britain

Divorce, thousands

150

100

50

0

1951   1961   1971   1972   1973   1974   1975

Source: *Social Trends No. 8*, 1977

Reproduced from R Whitburn, *Investigating Society: Talking to People* (Macmillan, 1979)

SOURCE F

'Though the 1980s couple go into marriage on technically equal footing, true equality within marriage is still something of an ideal. The idea of the "househusband" is still fairly rare, as Ann Oakley found when she looked at the domestic division of labour in The Sociology of Housework *(1974). She asked 20 working class and 20 middle class housewives how far their husbands helped out with the housework and looking after the children. Fewer than a quarter of the husbands gave the kind of help that could be described as doing an equal share of the work – and these tended to be middle class.'*

'Society Today', 13/11/80, from *New Society*

a State four ways in which 'we are socialised into falling in love.' (2)

b i What was the average age of marriage in 1911 for females? (Source C) (1)

  ii What has been the trend, for each sex, of the "Average age at first marriage" during this century? (Source C) (1)

c What does Source E show about divorce? (3)

d Does the concept of 'romantic love' apply to marriages in all societies? Explain your answer, with reference to Sources A and B. (4)

e Some sociologists argue that there is now greater equality in marriage. To what extent does Source F support or oppose this view? (4)

f What can be learned from the Sources about the ways in which marriage in Britain has changed during this century? (6)

g Source B deals with an example of a society very different from our own. Why are sociologists concerned to look at such examples? (9)

London & East Anglian Group for GCSE Examinations

2

Marriage & Divorce in the United Kingdom

	1960	1971	1979
Marriages (thousands)	393.6	459.4	416.9
Divorces (thousands)	25.8	79.6	148.2
Re-marriages (one or both parties) (thousands)	57.2	90.8	137.9

(Source: *Social Trends* 1981 HMSO)

a i In which of the three years mentioned in the table did the greatest number of divorces take place? (1)

  ii How many more re-marriages were there in 1979 than in 1960? (1)

b State two possible reasons why the number of marriages fell between 1971 and 1979. (3)

c Divorce is the legal ending of a marriage. What are the alternatives to divorce when marital relationships break down? (4)

d Account for the increase in the number of divorces since 1960. (6)

London & East Anglian Group for GCSE Examinations

---

3 The question carries 15 marks. The mark allocations to sections of the question are shown in the right hand margin.

Study the data below and then answer the questions which follow.

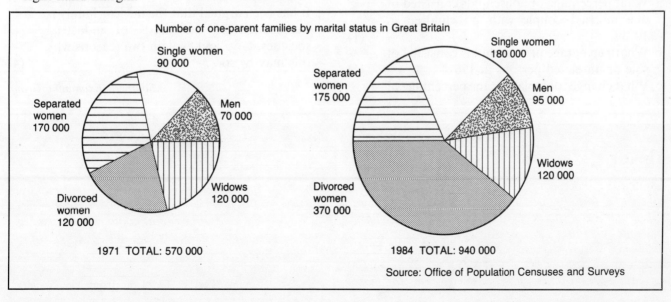

Number of one-parent families by marital status in Great Britain

Single women 90 000
Separated women 170 000
Men 70 000
Divorced women 120 000
Widows 120 000
1971 TOTAL: 570 000

Single women 180 000
Separated women 175 000
Men 95 000
Widows 120 000
Divorced women 370 000
1984 TOTAL: 940 000

Source: Office of Population Censuses and Surveys

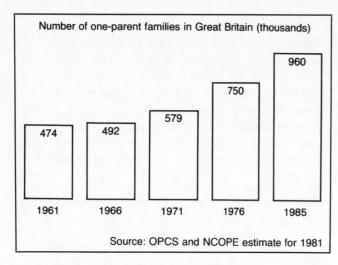

Number of one-parent families in Great Britain (thousands)

				960
474	492	579	750	
1961	1966	1971	1976	1985

Source: OPCS and NCOPE estimate for 1981

(Source: National Council for One-Parent Families: *Information Sheet No. 5* and *Key Facts* October 1987)

a How many one-parent families were there in 1984? (1)

b What type of person was most commonly found as head of a single parent family (i) in 1971, and (ii) in 1984? (2)

c How might a sociologist explain the change in the type of person most commonly found as head of a single parent family in 1971 and 1984? (2)

d Give **three** reasons which might explain why the number of single parent families has increased. (3)

e Some people believe that the increase in single parent families causes problems for British society. What reasons might they give, and what arguments and evidence could be produced to oppose their view? (7)

adapted from *Northern Examining Association*

4

Household composition, England and Wales, 1961 & 1971

	1961 Households %	1971 Households %
Households containing		
Sole or unrelated persons only	17	22
Married couple only, no children	26	27
Married couple, children	48	43
Lone parent, children	6	7
Two or more families	3	1

a What percentage of households consisted of one married couple with no children in 1971? (1)

b What percentage of households consisted of sole or unrelated persons in 1961? (1)

c What change took place in the percentage of households comprising married couples with children between 1961 and 1971? What is the sociological term used to describe such a household? (2)

d Give **four** reasons for the increase in the divorce rate in Britain this century. (4)

e Identify and explain **two** ways in which the role of the family has changed since the Industrial Revolution. (4)

f Identify and explain **two** changes that have occurred in role relationships in the family in this century. (4)

g It has been argued that the nuclear family is well suited to the needs of industrial societies. Give and explain **two** reasons why this may be so. (4)

Southern Examining Group

5 *Education*

AIMS

At the end of this chapter you should be able to:

- recognise and describe the important social functions education performs for individuals and societies.
- describe the way the education system has developed to its current organisation along comprehensive lines.
- outlines the impact social differences such as social class, gender and race have on educational achievement.
- show a critical awareness of the importance of the curriculum and the 'hidden curriculum' to students' educational chances and to society.
- explain the kinds of alternative to formal schooling which have been adopted by some parents and their children in the UK.

UNIT 14 The education system

14.1 The social functions of education

ACTIVITIES 1

In looking at the function of education ask yourself why you come to school. (Try to go beyond the simple fact that you *have* to come!) Try to think of what you hope to get out of school. You should also ask other members of your class and your friends the same question. You will get a lot of different answers but if you look carefully you may be able to group similar answers together. Try to put a label to each group of answers which sums up what the people were trying to say. By doing this you will have discovered some of the functions or purposes of education. Compare the ideas you have discovered for yourself in this way with the functions discussed in this unit.

To prepare young people for earning a living is an obvious economic function of education, but education has other functions as well, which are perhaps no less important. The broad transmission of *culture* is more possible in the school than in the family. The school has a stabilising function in that it usually tries to preserve the existing order of things from our cultural heritage. Culture, in this context, means a way of life characterised by generally accepted standards of behaviour, beliefs, conduct and morals. Each country has its own special culture, but within the culture of a nation there are class differences which make for working-class and middle-class cultures. British education has largely been dominated by middle-class culture, mainly because most teachers and educationalists are themselves the products of a middle-class upbringing.

As society has changed, schools have changed their values. For example, many schools no longer insist on school uniform for all their pupils; the curriculum is far wider and choices are much greater. To a lesser degree schools may themselves have been instrumental in bringing about changes. There is now less conformity about the ideas that should be transmitted on topics such as law and order, marriage, sex and religion.

The political functions of education have changed radically. Until modern times British political leaders came from a exclusive social background, and it can be argued that too high a proportion of ministers and senior civil servants still come from certain famous public schools. But it is now recognised that everyone must be educated so that they may share and then take the responsibility for the political leadership of society by using a vote. Ideally the education system should be organised so that the best leaders in society emerge because their abilities are encouraged through opportunities in all kinds of school.

Until comparatively recently it was generally agreed that education had a selective function, meaning that, because of disparities of talent and ability among us all, some form of grading was necessary – for example, some children being selected for grammar schools at the age of 11. There is now some debate as to whether this is either desirable or workable. The tests proposed by the Conservative government for pupils aged seven, 11 and 14 are, it is said, meant to assess progress, not as a basis for selection. Today all political parties subscribe to the belief of equality of opportunity and later units of the chapter look specifically at equality of opportunity in relation to pupils' social class, sex, ethnic origin and the region of the country in which a pupil lives.

Item 5.1   A high proportion of ministers and senior civil servants still come from certain famous public schools

Checklist

The functions of education are:

1 economic
2 stabilising
3 political
4 selective.

14.2 The growth of education

The state education system in Britain dates from the nineteenth century. It became clear then that an industrial society needed an efficient labour force. The governing classes realised that it was in their own interests to have a better educated working class. A working class that could read, write, and understand simple arithmetic could operate machinery more efficiently.

In the early 1830s only about one tenth of the population of this country had any schooling. In 1833 the government initiated an annual £20 000 educational grant which went mainly to the National Society for the Education of Anglicans, and to the British and Foreign Society for the education of nonconformists. These two voluntary societies were providing most of the schools. The foundations for a national educational system were laid in Forster's Education Act of 1870. This Act was supposed to provide adequately for elementary education, but it would be a mistake to believe that Britain had a universal compulsory system from 1870. The new locally elected school boards set up by the Act had great difficulty in getting the children to the schools and it took two more Acts to make education compulsory:

1 Sandon's Act of 1876 stated that it was the duty of parents of children aged between five and 13 years to see that they received elementary instruction.

2 Mundella's Act of 1880 made it the duty of every school board to get to school all its children of school age.

The next vital piece of educational legislation was Balfour's Act of 1902 which set up local education authorities in place of the school boards. The LEAs now provided public secondary education: new maintained secondary schools were built and the old endowed grammar schools were also aided from the rates. A proportion of scholarship places were offered to the bright children from elementary schools.

The Fisher Act of 1918 abolished fees in elementary schools; it also gave LEAs the power to provide nursery schools and to raise the school-leaving age to fifteen. During the Second World War the Norwood Report (1943) considered a re-structuring of secondary education as being necessary. In 1944, R.A. Butler introduced the now famous Education Act which was to revise all aspects of the education system completely. Most educational developments for the next twenty years were based on this Act.

The 1944 Act laid down important principles:

1 There should be free education for all.

2 Regard should be given, as far as possible, to the wishes of the parents.

3 Full-time and part-time education should be provided for those over compulsory school-leaving age.

4 Educational planning should be based upon local experience, interest and knowledge.

5 There should be set up a three-tier educational system consisting of three stages:
  a Primary (2–11)
    nursery (2–5)
    infant (5–7)
    junior (7–11): now often called 'middle' (8–12)
  b Secondary (11–15+) tripartite system
    modern
    grammar (now mainly comprehensive)
    technical
  c Further/Higher
    technical colleges
    art schools
    agriculture institutes
    teachers' training colleges (now colleges of education)
    universities

6 The school-leaving age should be raised to 16 (implemented 1972–3).

7 There should be equal opportunity for all.

The secondary tripartite organisation of education divided schools into grammar, secondary modern and technical.

Item 5.2   R. A. Butler

Item 5.3 Today 90 per cent of pupils attend comprehensive schools

Today 90 per cent of pupils attend comprehensive schools admitting all pupils without reference to their ability or aptitude. As we shall see in the next topic, the tripartite system relied on selecting pupils at 11 for a particular kind of school.

14.3 The tripartite system

The basic assumption was made that it was possible to categorise children by their abilities as either academic or manual in their skills. A particular type of schooling should then be provided accordingly; the more academic children should go to grammar schools, the less academic to secondary modern and technical schools.

The 11+ examination almost always decided the separation of secondary schooling. This examination usually involved tests in English, arithmetic and 'intelligence'. The pattern of examination varied slightly from one local education authority to another, and some, for example, gave an emphasis to the primary teachers' confidential reports. But mostly the kind of school that children would attend after the age of 11 depended upon their either passing or failing this examination in their last year in the primary school.

Item 5.4 shows the percentage of children attending the different kinds of school in 1958. As can be seen, just under one fifth of children attended grammar schools, while almost two thirds went to secondary modern schools.

	%
Grammar and direct grant schools	19.1
Secondary modern	63.0
Independent	5.1
Technical	2.8
Special	1.3
Unallocated	8.7
	100.0

from J.W.B. Douglas, *The Home and the School*
(MacGibbon and Kee, 1964)

Item 5.4 Distribution of 12-year-old children in secondary schools in June 1958

14.4 The comprehensive system

The term *comprehensive* is a general one as there are many kinds of comprehensive school. Some are all-through comprehensives, which means that pupils may complete their entire secondary education in the same school from 11 to 18; others have pupils transferred from middle schools at the age of 12–14; and in other authorities pupils attend comprehensive high schools and may choose to go to sixth-form colleges at the age of 16. Some comprehensive schools stream, band or set their pupils by general ability or subject ability, while others have little academic division in their classes. The common feature of all comprehensive systems is that children of wide-ranging abilities attend the same secondary school.

The Labour Government elected in 1964 decided to allow the development of comprehensive education by local authorities, which considered the needs of their own area and then put forward a plan to the Department of Education and Science. Circular 10, issued by the Department of Education in June 1965, requested LEAs to submit a plan for a comprehensive system of secondary education in their area.

Comprehensive schools served to answer some of the criticisms of the tripartite system which had been building up over the years. Some of these are listed below:

1 The 11+ examination was too rigid. Intelligence is not 'fixed' at 11 and many children are late developers. A poor performance on the day of the examination might determine a child's whole future career in an adverse way. Some bright people invariably perform badly under examination conditions.

2 There were wide regional disparities in the availability of grammar school places.

3 The system heightened and perpetuated class differences as a much larger proportion of middle-class children obtained grammar school places and gained more qualifications there.

4 Local education authorities often provided better facilities for their grammar schools than for their secondary modern schools.

5 The assumption that children were either academic or manual in their skills was not correct. There were not the facilities in many secondary modern schools for a number of children who would benefit from more academically-biased courses. Similarly some bright academic children would benefit from being taught manual skills.

6 Very few children who showed promise at secondary modern schools were transferred to grammar schools.

7 A growing number of pupils attending secondary modern schools wanted to continue their education past the school-leaving age, but provision for them was not widely enough available.

Similarly, the main advantages of the comprehensive system can be listed as follows:

1 The abolition of the 11+ examination took a great strain away from pupils who were being carefully prepared for this examination, often to the exclusion of more socialising influences. It also allowed schools to enlarge their educational horizons, and not to concentrate so many of their resources on securing 11+ passes.

2 Comprehensive schools can often provide greater resources: a small secondary school might not be able to afford or have space for large, well-equipped laboratories. The distribution of pupils to teachers (pupil-teacher ratio) decreases as a school gets larger.

3 As the comprehensive system has expanded, the *Open Sixth* has grown up. Here young people can remain at school in voluntary attendance after the age of 16 to increase their number of 16+ passes, or to prepare for further educational advancement such as GCE 'A' Level.

4 There is not likely to be such a wastage of talent, particularly among working-class children and late developers.

ACTIVITIES 2

1 Read the following account of the education system of the UK carefully.

The education system of the United Kingdom has three main stages: **primary** (including **nursery**), **secondary** and **further** (including **higher** education). The first two stages are compulsory for all children between five and 16 years old. Most pupils move from primary to secondary education in their eleventh year but some education authorities have **middle** schools, allowing the start of secondary education to be delayed. Primary education consists of three age ranges: nursery for the under-fives, **infant** for those children between five and seven or eight, and **junior** which takes pupils until they begin secondary school. While, as we have said in earlier units, 90 per cent of all pupils now attend **comprehensive** schools, these schools may coexist in some areas with **secondary modern, grammar** and **technical** schools. **Special schools** exist for children who are physically and mentally handicapped. Further education covers all **college** education after legally compulsory education, excluding those staying on at secondary school after 16 and those studying at **university**. Higher education covers all those advanced courses in universities, **polytechnics** and colleges which lead to qualifications above GCE 'A' Level, Scottish 'H' grade and Ordinary National Diploma and equivalent.

Draw a chart or diagram of the education system of the UK, incorporating in your work the information given in the above passage. Use the words in bold above when labelling your diagram. Remember that the way education is organised is a matter of political debate. Changes can take place, and you should find out about any recent changes from newspapers or your teacher.

2 Item 5.5 shows you the percentage of the population having different levels of qualification. Look at Item 5.5 carefully and see if you can find out what percentage of the population managed to get at least one GCE 'O' Level or CSE Grade 1.

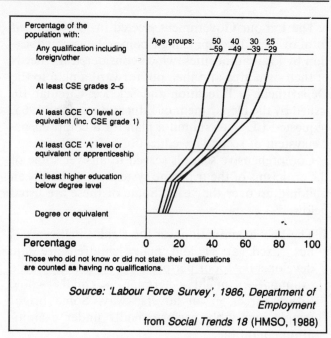

Those who did not know or did not state their qualifications are counted as having no qualifications.

Source: 'Labour Force Survey', 1986, Department of Employment

from *Social Trends 18* (HMSO, 1988)

Item 5.5   Qualification levels of the population: by age, 1988

Education and social differences

This unit goes on to look at the influences on educational chances of social class, gender, ethnic origin and where pupils live.

15.1 Education and social class

Many studies have shown that children from working-class backgrounds are less successful in school than those from middle-class homes. One important study by sociologists Brian Jackson and Dennis Marsden reveals that working-class children start school with a disadvantage which is rarely overcome. This disadvantage has nothing to do with inherited intelligence but has much to do with the home background, because the values of the education system are largely middle-class values. Success in middle-class terms is often measured in terms of achievement at school and the kind of job that one has.

ACTIVITIES 3

Look again at Chapter 3 and particularly at the unit on social class. See if you can list those things about a working-class background and upbringing which may hinder a pupil's academic achievement at school. You will find it particularly helpful to refer again to Items 3.13 and 3.14, which outline the middle-class perspective and the traditional working-class perspective as seen by sociologists Goldthorpe and Lockwood.

Jackson and Marsden in their study of 88 working-class grammar school boys in Huddersfield found a conflict between the different values of the home and school. The boys' achievement at school was seriously affected by such things as lack of homework facilities, and their parents' failure to understand the importance of homework. Parental support was found to be important: only those boys who had some connection with a middle-class situation (such as having a middle-class mother) completed the course. The working-class grammar school boys who did not have this connection rejected the grammar school values and sought support from and identification with their working-class peers.

Social factors which tend to improve the chances of greater educational achievement of middle-class children are:

1 greater parental concern with education.

2 books and speech at home designed to help a child's vocabulary.

3 middle-class speech patterns and norms of behaviour in school.

4 more opportunity for travel and stimulation through educational visits.

5 higher levels of parental expectation.

6 acceptance of the deferred gratification of 'study now and get a better job later'.

7 economic provision to stay on at school after the age of 16.

8 homework facilities (and even private tutors).

An important explanation is given by a sociologist called Bernstein, working in the 1970s. He points out how important language is in schools – many intelligence tests, for example, are based on skill with words – and suggests that working-class and middle-class people speak different kinds of language. Working-class people, according to Bernstein, use the *restricted code*, which has a limited vocabulary and simple sentence structures, and is mainly used to describe things rather than analyse or explain them. Middle-class people use the *elaborated code*, which has a larger vocabulary and more complicated sentence structures, and can be used to explain emotional and abstract ideas. Because most teachers are middle class and use the elaborated code, they tend to interpret more limited vocabulary and simpler sentences as showing less ability. Middle-class children therefore perform better in schools, even though intelligence tests involving arithmetic do not show such a difference between children of middle- and working-class backgrounds.

For the most part, teachers are themselves middle class, or have adopted middle-class life styles, speech patterns and vocabulary. This means that unless they take great care with their speech they may not be readily understood by working-class children. Middle-class children are more likely to have the benefits of early-reading books and to hear a wider vocabulary. Often they are taught the advantages of deferred gratification: to put off immediate pleasure or satisfaction and to enjoy themselves after something has been accomplished – for example, not to watch television until the toys have been cleared up, or, when older, not to go out until homework is finished. Middle-class children are more concerned with achievement, as the virtues of education and a good career are emphasised by their parents.

The following example is often given to sum up the difference in the relationship between a typical working-class mother and child and a typical middle-class mother and child:

Working-class mother:'Don't jump in the puddles!' (*Child continues jumping.*) 'Don't jump in the puddles or I will give you such a clout.'

Middle-class mother: 'Please keep out of the puddles, or your new shoes will be ruined.' (*Child continues jumping.*) 'If you don't stop, Mummy will get very cross.'

The working-class child is given a simple direct order; when the order is disobeyed the consequences are immediate and possibly painful. The middle-class child is, by way of contrast, informed why he or she should not jump in puddles. Reasons and consequences are given to the middle-class child, while the working-class child is given an order and a threat. While this is clearly an over-simplified example, it does illustrate the way middle-class children are more prepared for learning and reasoning at school.

ACTIVITIES 4

Whatever the explanation, it is clear that middle-class children achieve more educational success than do working-class children. Look at the information in Items 5.6 and 5.7 and see what conclusions you can draw about the extent of equality of educational opportunity between the classes. Item 5.6 is derived from figures appearing in the General Household Survey and Item 5.7 is derived from the Universities Central Council on Admissions (UCCA).

1 What two variables are related together in Item 5.6?

2 Mention two occupations which you might find in each of the socio-economic groups. You might refer again to Chapter 3 to help you do this.

Highest qualification level attained by socio-economic group of father

Persons aged 25-49 not in full-time education   Great Britain 1984-1985 combined

Highest qualification level	Socio-economic group of father							
	Professional	Employers and managers	Intermediate non-manual	Junior non-manual	Skilled manual	Semi-skilled manual	Unskilled manual	Total
Higher education (above GCE A level)	57%	32%	37%	28%	14%	10%	8%	20%
Other qualifications (at or below GCE A level)	35%	48%	49%	49%	41%	37%	31%	42%
No qualifications	8%	20%	14%	23%	45%	53%	61%	38%
Base=100%	1144	5950	1596	1546	13130	4446	1812	29624

from *General Household Survey Report*, 1985, HMSO

Item 5.6   Effect of father's social class on educational achievement

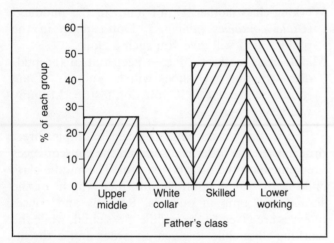

Item 5.7   Percentages receiving no educational qualifications: by father's social class

Social class	Acceptances (%)		
	1985	1986	1987
Professional	21.0	20.4	20.3
Intermediate	48.1	48.2	48.0
Skilled non-manual	10.4	10.7	11.1
Skilled manual	12.7	12.5	12.9
Partly skilled	6.6	6.9	6.6
Unskilled	1.2	1.2	1.1

from UCCA, *Statistical Supplement to the Twenty-fifth Report 1986-7*, 1988

Item 5.8   Universities: acceptances by social class, 1985-7 – UK

3 Item 5.6 shows that 61% of persons with unskilled manual fathers attained no educational qualifications. What percentage of persons with professional fathers get no educational qualifications?

4 Look at Item 5.7, which shows the percentages of each group receiving no educational qualifications. Draw a similar bar chart for each group, but this time show the percentages getting high educational qualifications.

5 Item 5.8 shows the percentages of students accepted for a place at a university in 1985–7. Work out from the figures the average percentages for middle-class students accepted at a university. Put these figures into a table. Remember to give your table a heading and clearly show what your figures refer to.

6 What explanations can you give for the differences shown in the table you have just compiled?

15.2 Education and gender

The increase in girls' education since the nineteenth century has been important in extending their opportunities. In the early nineteenth century, there were few schools for girls and these were intended for the daughters of middle-class families. Much of the earliest efforts for girls' education had to do with providing suitable training for governessess.

By the end of the century, the Girls' Public Day School Company had opened 33 secondary schools, educating in all more than 7100 girls. Meanwhile, the passing of the 1870 Education Act made elementary education free and compulsory for boys and girls from all classes. However, it was not until the passing of the 1944 Education Act that secondary education became free and compulsory for all boys and girls.

Higher education for girls began largely in the last half of the nineteenth century. Girton College, Cambridge, began in 1869 at Hitchin and then moved to Girton in 1873. In 1880 Newnham College for Women in Cambridge was established. In 1879 two more women's colleges, Somerville Hall and Lady Margaret Hall, opened in Oxford, but none of these colleges awarded degrees. In 1880 women were admitted as degree students to London and Manchester Universities. Cambridge University began awarding women degrees in 1921. Women were admitted to full membership of Oxford University only in 1920 and Cambridge in 1948.

These developments do not mean that today there are no differences in the educational chances of boys and girls. We have already seen, in Unit 15.1, that the educational performance of the working class was worse than that of the middle class. When we look at boys and girls, however, the gap is not one of performance but of subject choice and attitude.

Item 5.9   Higher education for girls began in the second half of the nineteenth century

If you can beat them, you should join them

LAST YEAR, for the first time, more girls than boys left school with an A level pass: 18.5 per cent of girls leaving at 18 did so with at least one A level, compared to only 17.9 per cent of boys, notching up another peg the superior performance of girls right through the school examination system.

At 16, 11 per cent of girls left school last year with five or more O levels, compared to 9.1 per cent of boys, and 29.3 per cent gained up to four O levels compared to 24.6 per cent of boys. At the lower end of the ability range, 14 per cent of boys left with no exam passes at all, but only 10.3 per cent of girls.

It is often assumed when people talk about the problems of girls' education that the difficulty is one of low performance. As the 1984 statistics show, it isn't. Nor has it even been. Right through primary and secondary school, girls tend to turn in better academic results than boys. In the days of the eleven plus

they used to have to fiddle the books to make sure that equal numbers of girls and boys were allowed into grammar schools. Without a little 'adjustment' of the figures far more girls than boys would have won places.

Girls now maintain their academic advantage right through to the end of the sixth form. But not, as the Equal Opportunites Commission pointed out last week, into higher education. The tendency of girls to go into less skilled, lower paid work than boys, and to steer themselves away from further and higher education qualifications, persists, largely because the impressive performance of girls at school is still predominantly in the 'wrong' subjects.

At A level 70 per cent of the passes in maths go to boys, in technical drawing no less than 97 per cent and in physics, 79 per cent. Only in biology, amongst the sciences, do girls getting A levels

outnumber boys, while in chemistry they achieve 41 per cent of the passes. The proportions of girls opting for science and maths has been increasing – in chemistry dramatically – but it is still, according to a recent EOC survey, disappointingly low. Girls shy away from economics and, to a lesser extent, from geography too, while boys turn away from sociology (25 per cent of A levels) and commercial and domestic subjects at 16.

Most worrying of all, according to the EOC, has been a drop in the last five years in the proportion of girls taking computer studies at A level, another subject where they are outnumbered four to one by boys. Parents should realise that girls need home computers too, comments the EOC, and software manufacturers should design more non-aggressive games to attract girls.

from the *Guardian*, 28 January 1986

Item 5.10   Girls' choice of examination subjects

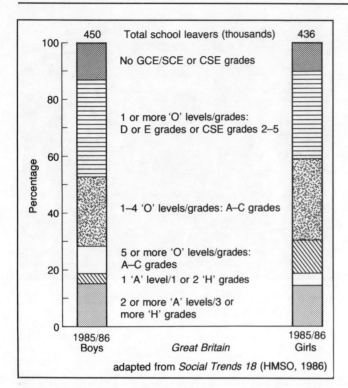

Total school leavers (thousands)

450 — 1985/86 Boys
436 — 1985/86 Girls

No GCE/SCE or CSE grades

1 or more 'O' levels/grades: D or E grades or CSE grades 2–5

1–4 'O' levels/grades: A–C grades

5 or more 'O' levels/grades: A–C grades

1 'A' level/1 or 2 'H' grades

2 or more 'A' levels/3 or more 'H' grades

Great Britain

adapted from *Social Trends 18* (HMSO, 1986)

Item 5.11   School leavers – highest qualification: by sex

Girl friendly schooling

Although girls do better on average at the primary level and achieve better school-leaving examination results their choice of career does not reflect their academic success. Only 40 per cent of women are graduates and 90 per cent of all entries to technical subjects are from boys, thus effectively debarring girls from many FE and HE courses and ensuring that they will eventually be forced into the lower paid jobs.

That girls still make such traditional subject choices is not surprising when we read that teachers of maths, physical sciences, and craft, design, and technology have the most stereotyped attitudes towards women, often actively discouraging girls from choosing their subjects.... 42.3 per cent of the teachers questioned thought that a woman's career was not as important as a man's. Nearly 18 per cent considered that a woman's most important job was to look after the comforts of her man and children. More than 70 per cent thought she should give up work when she had children.

from the *Guardian*, 28 January 1986

Item 5.12   How teachers see girls

ACTIVITIES 5

Look at Items 5.10 and 5.11.

1 In Item 5.10, what does the Equal Opportunities Commission (EOC) mean when they say girls at school often choose the 'wrong' subjects?

2 Why is the Equal Opportunities Commission 'disappointed' that girls do not opt for science and maths in larger numbers?

3 You might choose to conduct a survey of your sociology class. List all the subject options people do, and draw up a bar chart to show how many boys and girls are in your sociology group. List as many things as you can that might explain your findings. You will find more help on how to do this given in the coursework suggestion at the end of Chapter 3.

As we saw in Chapter 3, there are a whole network of factors affecting the way girls see themselves and their role in society. Item 5.12 is another extract from *The Guardian* indicating how these factors can spill into school and affect the way girls choose their options.

The need to provide equality of educational opportunity for both boys and girls has recently been referred to as the need for 'girl friendly schooling', as the extract in Item 5.12 shows. This is derived, of course, from the computer jargon of 'user friendly' programs, but it does seem to express the right idea very well. The Equal Pay Act of 1970 and the Sex Discrimination Act of 1975 both provide the basis in law for moves to establish better chances for girls at school. The Sex Discrimination Act makes it illegal not to provide equal treatment and equal access to all educational facilities to all pupils in a school. It would be illegal, therefore, for your school to prevent girls from choosing technical drawing and boys from choosing typewriting and keyboard skills. The Sex Discrimination Act of 1975 also marked the setting up of the Equal Opportunities Commission, whose job it is to promote equal opportunities between the sexes. Their objective is to encourage schools to ensure that all pupils can study both arts and sciences up to the school leaving age and to create a learning environment where no subject is regarded as more appropriate for study by one sex than the other. The EOC will accept complaints from anyone who believes boys and girls are not given equal chances.

Craft is still the most obvious area of sex-differentiation in the school curriculum, particularly at secondary level, and the traditional allocation of girls into Home Economics and boys into Craft, Design and Teachnology (CDT) is proving difficult to change. A typical complaint was received from a parent regarding a school under the Hereford and Worcester Local Education Authority (LEA) where girls and boys were being allocated to different craft subjects. A visit to the school and discussions with senior staff and LEA representatives revealed inadequate staffing and accommodation facilities for CDT in the junior section of split-school, and the Commission was able to make representations to the County Education Officer concerning the school's difficulty in meeting a statutory requirement. Financial constraints had caused the shcool building programme to be frozen and until the programme is implemented, the school has agreed to make additional provision in the form of extra-curricular CDT activities in order to increase the CDT experience of all pupils. The separation of girls and boys for craft subjects was an administrative exercise to halve the accommodation problem, the educational implications of which had not been wholly considered. The Commission is of the opinion that to teach all children for half of the time is a better basis for a balanced curriculum at examination level than to give half the children no experience of the subject at all....

Information Technology (IT) is a relatively new addition to the school curriculum, but already there are indications that girls are becoming distanced from it. Certainly the number of girls taking 'O' and 'A' level Computer Studies is very small in comparison with the number of boys taking the subject. In November the Commission produced two publications, *Information Technology in Schools* and *Working with Computers* which present guidelines for teachers and role models for girls, respectively. Both publications will be included in an advertising campaign scheduled for 1984 which will encourage girls to consider the opportunities which are offered by Information Technology at school and at work. The Commission has also embarked upon a joint initiative with Croydon Local Education Authority to evaluate the effectiveness of IT courses which have been planned to increase girls' participation.

from the *Annual Report of the Equal Opportunities Commission* (EOC, 1983)

Item 5.13   Sex differentiation in the school curriculum

ACTIVITIES 6

Read Item 5.13 and answer the questions that follow.

1 Why did the EOC investigate the teaching of Craft, Design and Technology in a school in Hereford and Worcester?

2 Try to explain simply, and in your own words, what the problem at the school was and why it happened.

3 What did the EOC do, and what did the EOC recommend?

4 The extract mentions at least two ways in which the EOC operate to encourage the provision of equal opportunities for both girls and boys. What arc these two ways?

Item 5.14   Sex stereotyping is damaging because it assumes that a person's sex limits his or her sphere of activity

15.3 The school curriculum

We saw in the topics on education and social class, and on education and gender, that we can identify a number of social factors which influence in individual's chances of doing well in the education system. We saw that working-class children seem to fail more often in the education system than do middle-class children. Sociologists, however, have recently begun to look at the education the working-class child failed in, as well as looking at the working-class child and that child's home and family background. This means that sociologists have studied the curriculum, or course of study, which students have to follow in school.

ACTIVITIES 7

1 List the subjects you are studying at school. Add up the hours and minutes you spend on each subject in a week. Add a certain amount of time for homework as well.

2 List the subjects again but this time putting first the subjects you spend most time on with the others following in order. Why do you think you only study these subjects? Why do you think you spend more time on some than others?

Sociologists have asked the question 'what *counts* as knowledge in the curriculum?'. Clearly there are all sorts of things you *know* which do not count as knowledge to be included in the school curriculum – details about pop stars, facts about football teams, and information relating to hobbies, for example. A sociologist called M.F.D. Young said there was a relationship between the fact that some kinds of knowledge 'count' and other kinds of knowledge do not, and the way teachers treat pupils: 'If . . . there is a clear distinction between what is taken to count as knowledge, and what is not, . . . it would follow that [there will be] a rigid hierarchy between teacher and taught, [otherwise] control by the pupils would be implied and the process of . . . selection would become open for modification and change.' Young is saying that teachers decide what 'counts' and do not allow pupils a say. He goes on to suggest that some knowledge is given 'high status' and some knowledge is given 'low status'.

ACTIVITIES 8

Look again at the list of your subjects you made in Activities 7.

1 Which subjects have 'high status' (that is, are more important) and which subjects have only 'low status'?

2 In your school which kinds of pupils do a lot of high status subjects and which pupils do a lot of low status subjects?

3 Is sociology high status knowledge?

Young said that there is restricted access to high status knowledge – that is, not everyone has a chance to master it. As a result some pupils will be labelled 'failures' only because they have not had a chance to acquire high status knowledge. Young went on to say that if we re-evaluated what counts as high status and low status knowledge then there would be a massive redistribution of the labels 'educational success' and 'educational failure' and a consequent redistribution of the rewards of money and power. In this way Young illustrated for the first time the importance for sociologists of looking at the curriculum children have to follow as well as looking at the social class, sex and family background of the child.

ACTIVITIES 9

1 If high status knowledge consisted of the names and details of pop stars or football players, how many of your teachers would be educational successes and how many would be dunces?

2 Why do you think some knowledge has high status and some has low status? List three reasons for each and compare them with the rest of the class.

15.4 The hidden curriculum

If the official school curriculum, then, consists of all those things it is intended students should learn from school, the hidden curriculum consists of all those unintended lessons students learn from school. It may sound odd but the things you will remember longest about school are probably not the things you were *taught*, but all those other things you 'picked up' along the way.

Before we get down to the time-table I think we should plan the hidden curriculum

from *The Social Science Teacher*, October 1978, vol. 8, no. 1

Item 5.15   The hidden curriculum

ACTIVITIES 10

You have been asked to write a guide to your school for new students. The guide is to be 'by students and for students' and has been given the provisional title *How to Survive (your) School.*

1 List three bits of advice you would give to new students to help them get by and cope.

2 Compare these ideas with your classmates and make up a full list from all your ideas.

Looking at the ways students do homework is one of the simplest ways of understanding what the hidden curriculum is. If the 'official' or intended homework is reading, students often do not actually bother to do it. This is because it is, of course, difficult for a teacher to tell whether it has been done or not. Students, in other words, translate the official curriculum into tasks which have to be done because

they can be assessed. In the same way students try to get clues as to what may 'come up' in an examination. If it is not expected to come up students will not revise it even though it may be in their official curriculum. A sociologist called Snyder said that the hidden curriculum was made up of those tasks students had to complete in order to get the highest possible grades with the least possible effort.

ACTIVITIES 11: Play-reading

(Two students, Andrea and Julie, introduce Jenny, a new girl, to the school.)

Andrea   Oh, it's not that bad when you've learnt the ropes.

Julie   No, it might look bad but the English homeworks are just reading a lot of the time and Austen's a softie. He never tests you on them.

Andrea   Yeah, so it's sort of optional really.

Julie   And the biology's usually copying out diagrams from the textbook.

Andrea   Just make sure your pencil's sharp and you underline the headings in red, and you'll get an A!

Julie   Mind you, she makes you work hard in the lesson, Darwin does. Keeps you quiet anyway.

Jenny   Who's Mr Marks?

Julie   He's history.

Jenny   I used to like that. What's he like?

Andrea   He's strict. Doesn't let you muck about, but he's a good teacher. He gives you lots of worksheets in lessons. I've got a pretty good memory for dates, so I'm not too bad. He got my older brother through the exam last year.

Julie   That's pretty amazing if you knew her brother.

Jenny   What's the English like? That's supposed to be my best subject.

Julie   It used to be mine until last year. I used to get an A every other essay for being 'imaginative' and 'vivid', and my spelling didn't matter too much. With Austen I'm lucky to manage a C because of my spelling mistakes.

From L. Fursland and R. Fielding 'The Hidden Curriculum', *Social Science Teacher*, vol. 14, no. 1 (Autumn 1984)

1 What does Andrea mean when she says 'it's not that bad when you've learnt the ropes'? What does she mean when she says 'it's sort of optional really'?

2 What has happened to Julie's performance in her English lessons? Explain your answer.

3 The pupils are describing the lessons quite differently from the way their teachers would describe them. Can you think of any other examples, from your own experience perhaps, which illustrate that what *actually* goes on is not always what teachers *think* is going on?

4 Look again at the ideas you drew up for your survival guide to your school in Activities 10. Do any of your ideas have anything to do with the hidden curriculum?

5 Have you ever given the same kind of advice as Julie and Andrea are giving Jenny?

Students learn a lot from schools which it is not *intended* that they should. Students have to learn how to do as they are told, how to lose time waiting for things to happen, and how to put up with being bored! Sociologists have listed the following things as being among the unintended lessons of schooling.

Schooling and education are the same thing.
Education ends when schooling ends.
Learning is the result of teaching.
Passive acceptance is better than active criticism.
Discovering knowledge is beyond school students.

In addition to these items students will learn the following:

to tolerate boredom.
to accept being assessed by others.
to compete against friends to please the teacher.

A sociologist called Jackson said that while the three 'r's of the official curriculum were reading, writing and arithmetic, the three 'r's of the hidden curriculum were the rules, routines and regulations students must learn to survive schools. Sociologists think the hidden curriculum is important because of the effect it can have on students' attitudes and, in turn, on society. Two American sociologists, Bowles and Gintis, think the hidden curriculum channels and prepares some students to take menial, repetitive and boring jobs in the world of work when they leave school.

ACTIVITIES 12

What do you learn at school besides your subjects? Think about the lessons of the hidden curriculum sociologists have listed and see if you can come up with some others. What 'lessons' do you learn from:

the way your classroom seating is arranged?
the way you are taught?
the responsibilities you are given?
the notice which is taken of your opinions and feelings?

The hidden curriculum can also teach pupils a good deal about politics, economics and sex roles too – for example, the history on the school curriculum tends to show the world from a male perspective and to highlight the achievements of men rather than women.

16.1 School's out

We have seen how the education system is organised in the UK, and how the organisation of schools has changed from the tripartite system to the comprehensive system. We have also seen how different sociologists have different ideas about the consequences of our schools on society and on individual pupils. There are some parents, too, who are unhappy with the consequences of formal education.

ACTIVITIES 13

Read Item 5.16 and answer the questions that follow it.

1 Why did Daisy's parents decide to take her away from school?

2 Why do you think the education authorities were discouraging? What worries do you think they had?

3 Describe the kind of education Daisy now gets at home.

4 What difference in Daisy's attitude and approach do her parents report seeing now Daisy no longer goes to school?

5 What special qualifications did Daisy's mother and father have?

Some parents feel that school is not right for a particular child or children. Jane Chaudhuri, a history graduate married to an engineer husband, has two children and three foster children. They all go to school except Daisy, who is now 11½.

Jane said: 'I took her out when she was ten, because she was the one who wasn't happy at school. She didn't like it, she wasn't doing particularly well, and she kept having tummy aches in the morning. It seemed silly to send her when she and I were going through such misery over it.'

Jane is one of the parents who has managed to win the approval of the education authorities, in her case the Inner London one. When Daisy stopped school, she wrote and told them, and they asked her to submit a programme. They altered the programme, and were rather fierce and discouraging at first. 'Once they realised we were serious, they were better,' Jane said. 'An inspector visits from time to time.

I started off teaching her at 9 o'clock each morning, but it has got more fluid. We just do it as it crops up during the day. Sometimes she reads and writes on the kitchen table. We follow some of the education broadcasts, and she spends one afternoon a week in the local library working on one of her 'projects'.

At school she complained that as soon as she got interested in something she had to go on to something else, but now she can follow things through. We have quite a few outings to galleries and museums. My husband does some science and maths with her.

There is no strain about it. She is so much happier. She used to be shy but now chats quite confidently to both adults and children.'

from Caroline Western, 'School's Out', *She*, 1980

Item 5.16 Daisy stopped school

Item 5.17 Families have the right to give their children home-based education instead of school

It may have surprised you to read about Daisy. In the early 1960s Mrs Joy Baker went to the High Court in order to win the legal right to educate her children at home, against opposition from Norfolk Education Authority. Mrs Baker was one of the first people to fight publicly for the right to give her children homebased education instead of sending them to school. Other families wanting to do the same thing set up an organisation called Education Otherwise in 1977. Education Otherwise takes its name from the 1944 Education Act, England and Wales, which states: 'It shall be the duty of the parent of every child of compulsory school age to cause him to receive effecient full-time education suitable to his age, ability and attitude, either by regular attendance at school or otherwise.'

In the UK, then, education is legally compulsory but *school* is not. Education Otherwise support parents wishing to provide a positive homebased alternative to formal schooling. A growing number of parents are taking this option. In Item 5.18 Dick Kitto, a member of Education Otherwise, describes the kind of families involved.

'Roughly speaking, we seem to cater for three categories of families. The first is the dissatisfied parent, perhaps intellectual and middle class, with academic aspirations for his child, who really wants a good education of the sort provided by the public school system. They want what school offers, but better. They pressurise their kids, and want them to get into university.

The second category are the potential drop-outs from current society. They don't approve of where society is going, or of the part that education plays in this. Even if they can't drop out, they want to stop their kids being institutionalised from the age of five to the age of 90. This is the anarchic element who reject school and society.

As you can imagine, an organisation that contains these two groups has to display a good deal of diplomacy and tact.

The third group are the ordinary people who have not thought that much about education, but are forced to do so when they find that their children are not benefiting. Perhaps their children are being bashed around, becoming school-phobics, the school is disorganised, there is gang warfare, they want to learn and they can't. These families are not basically committed to taking their children out of school, but they are driven by desperation.

The majority of our enquiries come from this uncommitted centre.'

from Caroline Western, 'School's Out' *She*, 1980

Item 5.18   Education otherwise

ACTIVITIES 14

1 List the kinds of reasons parents might give for wanting to take their children out of the formal education system.

2 Imagine you are a parent. Write a letter to the Director of Education explaining why you wish to educate your child at home.

REVIEW

If you have studied and understood this chapter you should be able to . . .

■ outline briefly each of the main functions of the education system.
■ explain the main changes which took place in the change from the tripartite system to the comprehensive system, including in your account an outline of the advantages and disadvantages of both systems.
■ outline the advantages that might help middle-class children at school.
■ account for the poorer performance of working-class children in the education system as compared to middle-class children.
■ explain what the sociologist Bernstein meant by the terms:
  a 'restricted code', and
  b 'elaborated code'.
■ outline in a paragraph the way the education system can affect the socialisation of girls.
■ suggest ways that schools could be changed to help improve girls' educational chances.
■ explain the term 'the hidden curriculum'.
■ list some of the things which students might learn from the hidden curriculum.
■ outline the arguments for and against formal schooling.

COURSEWORK SUGGESTIONS

1 Education and gender

Try to find out whether there are any differences between boys and girls in their subject options at the end of the third year. You might decide to concentrate on one or two subjects specifically (such as craft, design and technology, typewriting, home economics or computing) and interview boys and girls in these options about the reasons for their choices. Alternatively you might decide to look at the patterns in as many subjects as you can and think about a range of factors which might explain the patterns you find such as school organisation and discipline, teacher attitudes, careers guidance, the media and advertising, parental and peer group pressures, etc. Remember, if you do not find very great differences between boys and girls at your school you can still produce an interesting project explaining why your school is the way it is.

You might need to interview your headteacher and other teachers for this project. Prepare your questions and test them on other students in your group first.

2 The hidden curriculum

Try to find out what students learn from the hidden curriculum. Concentrate on the idea that students selectively neglect work which cannot be assessed. You might decide you will find out what students *really* learn at your school through the hidden curriculum. Refer again to Unit 3 on tools of sociological enquiry.

You might conduct some interviews with students to get some ideas and then design a questionnaire to give to other students, or you might decide to have a go at listing a few questions and test them on others in your sociology class. When you are ready collect your data and then write an account of the hidden curriculum at your school. You should include in your account anything your respondents said that illustrates particularly well something you want to show.

ASSESSMENT QUESTION

The mark allocations to sections of the question are shown in the right hand margin.

'There is a poor match between education and the world of work. We are less 'efficient' than our competitors overseas. Only 5.5% of the labour force in the U.K. are graduates compared with 7.1% in West Germany. Only 30% of British people have intermediate vocational qualifications (including apprenticeships), compared with about 60% in West Germany.'

(Adapted from: *New Society*, February 1982)

a According to the above information, what percentage of the work force in Britain are graduates? (1)

b According to the above information, what percentage of West Germans have intermediate vocational qualifications? (1)

c Identify and explain **two** ways in which a British government might attempt to improve the 'efficiency' of education as a preparation for work? (4)

d Identify and explain **two** other functions of education apart from the preparation of young people for the world of work. (6)

e Many studies have shown that children from working class homes are less successful at school than those from middle class homes. Suggest reasons why this may be so. (8)

Southern Examining Group

6 *Population*

AIMS

At the end of this chapter you should be able to:

- explain why the study of population is so important.
- understand and use population statistics such as birth rate, death rate and migration statistics.
- show an awareness of the composition of the population of the UK in terms of age, sex and ethnic origin.
- discuss world population statistics and trends.

UNIT 17 The study of population

17.1 The census

Every ten years since 1801 the government has appointed investigators to count and gather information about every inhabitant of the UK. The last UK census was conducted on 5 April 1981. It was one of the most detailed surveys ever carried out by the government.

The survey showed that the population of England and Wales had grown from just under 9 million in 1801 to just over 49 million. This survey was conducted by the Registrar General's department (the Office of Population Censuses and Surveys – OPCS) which appointed several thousand temporary civil servants, mainly local government workers and teachers, known as *enumerators*. Each enumerator was assigned a certain number of households in his or her locality. Computers have been used to process census information since 1961, but, although the most modern techniques are employed, it still takes several years for all the information from a census to be processed and analysed by the Registrar General.

Today the changes that are taking place in the population and in society as a whole are so consider-able and rapid, compared with those of a century ago, that it has been found necessary to conduct a small census of ten per cent of the population every five years: this is known as a *midpoint sample survey*. The OPCS also carry out five continuous social surveys – the General Household Survey, the Family Expenditure Survey, the Labour Force Survey, the International Passengers Survey and the National Food Survey – to maintain accurate records on population and social change.

On 5 April 1981, all householders were bound by law to give details of everyone staying in their household on the night of the census. Included in the census were people in hospitals, hotels, prisons and ships in UK ports. The police sought out vagrants to prevent people being omitted. If all the enumerators had missed just one household from their lists the numbers unrecorded from the census would, it is estimated, have equalled the number of inhabitants of a town the size of Nottingham.

Census data is one of the most precise forms of demographic material, but other sources of information on population are available to the government.

United Kingdom								Indices 1986=100
	Population index[1]							Social and economic needs of different age groups of the population
	1971	1981	1986	1991	2001	2011	2025	
People aged:								
Under 1	120	97	100	109	101	95	101	Maternity services, health visiting, preventive medicine
1–4	127	94	100	108	110	98	105	Day care, nursery education
5–15	121	113	100	97	110	104	101	compulsory education
16–19	85	105	100	84	80	92	78	Further and higher education, training, employment
15–44 (Females)	86	95	100	100	95	91	89	Maternity services
20–49	90	94	100	105	101	99	94	Employment, housing, transport
50–59/64[2]	109	104	100	98	115	123	130	Pre-retirement training, early retirement
60/65[3]–74	98	102	100	99	94	107	122	Retirement pensions
75–84	73	90	100	105	109	106	132	Retirement pension, health care, home helps, sheltered housing,
85 or over	68	84	100	124	164	186	191	retirement homes

[1]Includes 1985-based projections.
[2]59 for females, 64 for males.
[3]60 for females, 65 for males.

Source: Office of Population Censuses and Surveys; Government Actuary's Department

from Social Trends 18 (HMSO, 1988)

Item 6.1   Selected social and economic needs of population groups: by age

Since 1837 the registration of births, deaths and marriages has been compulsory, and in 1984, some 637 000 births, 349 000 marriages and 567 000 deaths were registered in England and Wales. There are now ten miles of shelving at the Registrar General's Office with thousands of volumes containing over 250 million entries!

These figures do provide some guide to population trends, but all sources need to be supplemented by the census material. In some countries registration goes much further than in the UK. In most countries in Europe, citizens are required by law to register their address with the police, and in some countries all adults must carry an identification card which contains some demographic data.

ACTIVITIES 1

1 Why do you think governments need to know in such detail about the population of their country?

2 Consider how different population changes (like changes in different age groups) might affect the social and economic services needed by a population. Item 6.1 will help you to answer this question.

Remember: the 'population index' provides a simple way of comparing population size for any particular year. 1986 is given the value 100 and other years are given an index number which is greater or lesser than 100 depending upon population size.

▶ UNIT 18 The size of the population in the UK

The UK's population in 1986 numbered 56.8 million, putting the UK fifteenth in the world in terms of population size. The figures in Item 6.2 show the populations for England, Wales, Scotland and Northern Ireland separately.

The UK's total population is expected to be 57.7 million in 2001, 58 million in 2011 and 60 million in 2025.

The *optimum population* is said to be the level which, with existing technology and know-how, can maximise output per head. In populations above the optimum size standards of living will decline, but populations below it will not be able to produce as much as they could.

Thomas Malthus advanced one of the first important theories of population in 1798. He believed that the population increased at a faster rate than a nation's ability to produce food, so the population increase was threatened and limited by periodic famine. A high birth-rate increase meant that in theory a population would double itself every twenty-five years – it would increase at a geometric rate – but food production could not match this increase, as it only rose gradually – at an arithmetic rate. According to Malthus, no normal increase in food production could sustain a population at a constant rate of growth.

Malthusian theory has not applied in this country, but has some validity in countries such as Bangladesh or Puerto Rico where food supplies have barely kept pace with the population increase.

18.1 The birth rate

Demographers usually express the birth rate in numbers of *live births per thousand of the population*. This is termed the *crude birth rate* because it is only an approximate measurement of fertility. Counting only the numbers of women of child-bearing age (generally taken to be between 15 and 44) would produce a more accurate figure. The crude birth rate will tell demographers and sociologists something about family sizes in a country: a decline in birth rate will mean that the size of families is decreasing, although the overall population may be increasing due to people living longer, or more people entering the country than leaving it.

In 1986 there were 755 000 live births in Britain, 4000 more than in 1985. The crude birth rate stayed the same at 13.3 during the same period. In 1986 there were 13.3 births per 1000 of the total population (including all ages). As Item 6.4 shows this was 61.1 *births per 1000 women of child-bearing age (15–44)*. This statistic is termed the *general fertility rate*.

	Population (000's, mid-1986 estimate)
England	47 254
Wales	2 821
Scotland	5 121
Northern Ireland	1 567
United Kingdom	56 763

from *Britain 1988: An Official Handbook* (HMSO, 1988)

Item 6.2   Population statistics for the UK

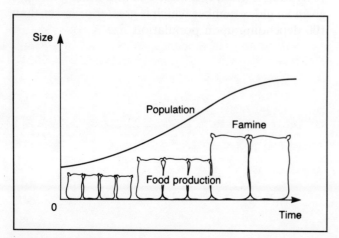

Item 6.3   Malthus's projection of food production and population growth in theoretical terms

ACTIVITIES 2

Study Item 6.4 and answer the questions that follow.

1 During which year was the total number of live births the greatest?

2 In 1984, 28 out of every 1000 women aged between 15–19 had a child.
   Which age group had the highest birth rate?
   Which age group had the lowest birth rate?

Great Britain								
	Total live births (thousands)	Crude birth rate[1]	General fertility rate[2]	Age-specific live birth rates[3] per 1 000 women aged					
				15–19	20–4	25–9	30–4	35–9	40–4
1981	704	12.8	61.5	28	106	129	68	22	5
1982	692	12.6	59.9	28	106	126	69	23	5
1983	694	12.7	59.6	27	99	126	71	23	5
1984	702	12.8	59.6	28	96	125	73	23	5

from *Social Trends 16* (HMSO, 1986)

United Kingdom					
	Total live births (thousands)	Crude birth rate[1]	General fertility rate[2]	Mean age of mothers at birth (years)	Total period fertility rate[4]
1985	751	13.3	61.4	27.7	1.80
1986	755	13.3	61.1	27.7	1.78

Source: Office of Population Censuses and Surveys
from *Social Trends 18*, (HMSO, 1988)

[1] Total births per 1,000 population of all ages.
[2] Total births per 1,000 women aged 15–44, includes also births to mothers aged under 15, and 45 or over.
[3] Births to mothers aged under 15, and 45 or over, are included in the age groups 15–19 and 40–44 respectively.
[4] The average number of children which would be born per woman if women experienced the age-specific fertility rates of the period in question throughout their child-bearing life span.

Item 6.4   Live births: totals and rates

3 Which age group has had the greatest fall in its birth rate between 1981 and 1984?

4 Which age group has had the greatest increase in its birth rate between 1981 and 1984?

5 Can you give any reasons which may help to explain your answers? Use Item 6.5 to help you.

Checklist

1 The crude birth rate is births per 1000 of the population.

2 The general fertility rate is births per 1000 women of child-bearing age (15–44).

During this century the birth rate in Britain has declined steadily except during the periods which followed war time in 1920 and 1947. The crude birth rate remained fairly constant at 16 live births per 1000 between the wars; after the last war it rose slightly but the 1984 figures show an uneven decline to a rate of 12.8 per 1000 of the population. By 1986 this had risen to 13.3 per 1000 of the population. Reasons for the stability of the birth rate this century may include the following:

1 The general rise in standards of living has been attributed to, and recognised as being made more possible with, smaller families.

2 As women have improved their status and gone out to work in greater numbers they have not

It looks very much as though there is a link between women's jobs and the falling birth rate. Very few industrial countries now have a birth rate high enough to stop the natural size of the population from shrinking. The West has already arrived at the zero population growth preached so despairingly by ecologists at the start of the 1970s. It has happened right across the social spectrum: fastest, in the past decade, among working-class families who have tended in the past to have the most children. Interestingly, with the onset of a recession in which women's jobs have been unusually vulnerable, the birth rate showed a small upturn at the end of the 1970s – and that showed up first in the UK, the country where unemployment struck first.

Some of the evidence linking the fall in the birth rate and women's jobs emerged at a conference this month at the Aspen Institute, Berlin. One of the conference participants had been doing an international survey of families with one child which decide not to have a second. In Germany, the usual explanation was: 'With a second child, the wife would have to give up her job.'

from the *Guardian*, 27 May 1982

Item 6.5   The falling birth rate

wished for large families and constant child-bearing.

3 Improved contraceptive techniques and the greater availability of contraception have allowed better family planning.

4 The provisions of the Welfare State have meant that parents need not rely upon their children to support them in old age, and so large families are no longer needed as an 'insurance'.

The slight rise in the birth rate during the 1960s may have been due to improved economic conditions. Better material circumstances and upward social mobility for some could have caused them to follow the upper professional classes' tendency to have larger families. Perhaps another reason was the younger age at which people were getting married. As people marry earlier they also have their family at an earlier age, thereby making it appear that the birth rate is increasing. The birth rate fell low enough to give zero growth rate in 1976. If the 1970s trend had continued, with the lowest birth rate since the war, we would have had a decreasing population. In 1978 however, the trend reversed again, with a rise in part due to couples having children that were put off earlier.

ACTIVITIES 3: Play-reading

Read the play-reading and answer the questions which follow.

(Two women, Eva and Janice, are chatting in a consultant's waiting room.)

Eva   I thought, you know, six kids was enough – so I decided to have the operation.

Janice   I'm not surprised! I've only half your number but I've decided to call it a day. Must cost you a fortune in child minder fees.

Eva   Oh no, I'm at home with them. Well, two are at school now, but I look after the other four.

Janice   You deserve a medal, love! The same four old walls all day would drive me mad. Still, you take them out, I suppose – you've got all week. Ours are quite keen on museums – we go on a Saturday.

Eva   Don't you miss them?

Janice   Well, when the time's so precious you value it more – but yes, I do, and I wonder what it'd be like to go out during the week, give them more attention and so on. But my job's important to me as well. I want to be regarded as something more than a mum.

Eva   Well, as for museums, with my lot it's like a Viking raiding party. And libraries – if they spot a 'Quiet please' sign it's like a red rag to a bull.

Janice   I can imagine.

Eva   You have yours minded, then?

Janice   The youngest is – the two oldest are at school. They're pretty independent – they let themselves in, get their own tea. It's good for them to realise the world doesn't revolve around them and Mum and Dad have their lives too.

Eva   Yes *(sigh)* – I thought it was so vital, you see, to give them all lots of attention when they were little – but when you've got six . . . Still, no more if medical science has its way. I might go back to work someday too.

Janice   You know, some overpopulated poor countries give things like transistor radios away to people who've been sterilised.

Eva   Give me some soundproof ear-plugs any day!

1 Why does Janice, who has three children, go out to work?

2 Why did Eva, who has six children, decide to stay at home to look after them?

3 Is it easier these days for mothers to go back to work when they have children? How might this affect the birth rate?

4 Why don't many fathers give up work to look after their children?

18.2   The death rate

The *crude death rate* is the number of *deaths per 1000 of the total population* in a given year. Items 6.6 and

Year	Life expectancy (years)
1841	41
1871	43
1901	50
1931	61
1971	71
1977	74
1979	Males: 70 / Females: 76
1981	Males: 71 / Females: 77
1984	Males: 72 / Females: 77

Item 6.6   Life expectancy in the UK

Year	Crude death rate (per 1000)
1930–2	17.2
1950–2	14.1
1960–2	13.1
1966	12.9
1972	12.6
1975	11.8
1978	12.0
1981	Males: 12.0 / Females: 11.4
1985	Males: 12.0 / Females: 11.7
1986	Males: 11.8 / Females: 11.5

Item 6.7   Crude death rate in the UK

United Kingdom											Rates per thousand population and thousands	
	Age										All ages	Total deaths (000's)
	Under 1*	1–4	5–14	15–34	35–44	45–54	55–64	65–74	75–84	85+		
1961												
Males	24.8	1.1	0.4	1.1	2.5	7.5	22.3	55.1	125.0	258.6	12.6	322.0
Females	19.3	0.8	0.3	0.6	1.8	4.5	11.1	31.5	89.1	215.9	11.4	309.8
1971												
Males	20.2	0.8	0.4	1.0	2.4	7.2	20.5	51.4	114.7	235.6	12.2	328.5
Females	15.5	0.6	0.3	0.5	1.6	4.4	10.3	26.8	75.2	189.5	11.1	316.5
1976												
Males	16.4	0.7	0.3	1.0	2.2	7.2	20.1	51.4	118.5	250.8	12.6	341.9
Females	12.4	0.5	0.2	0.5	1.5	4.4	10.5	26.6	75.9	203.0	11.8	338.9
1981												
Males	12.7	0.6	0.3	0.9	1.9	6.3	18.1	46.3	106.3	226.6	12.0	329.1
Females	9.5	0.5	0.2	0.4	1.3	3.9	9.8	24.7	66.9	178.4	11.4	328.8
1985												
Males	10.3	0.5	0.3	0.8	1.8	5.6	17.5	45.0	104.8	223.6	12.0	331.6
Females	8.3	0.4	0.2	0.4	1.2	3.4	9.9	24.7	64.7	178.6	11.7	339.1
1986												
Males	10.9	0.4	0.2	0.8	1.7	5.5	17.0	43.6	102.0	217.1	11.8	327.2
Females	8.1	0.4	0.2	0.4	1.1	3.3	9.5	24.0	63.2	172.4	11.5	333.6

* Rate per 1,000 live births.

Source: Office of Population Censuses and Surveys
from Social Trends 18, (HMSO, 1988)

Item 6.8   Death rates: by age and sex

6.7 show how the death rate in the UK has decreased, and how life expectancy has thereby increased, since 1841.

Since 1960 the crude death rate has remained more or less stable at around 12 deaths per thousand of the population. Item 6.8 shows crude death rates by both age and sex.

The decline in the death rate over recent years is due to a number of factors:

– better nutrition.
– improved standards of living.
– medical advances.
– better health care and personal hygiene.
– better working conditions.

Official statistics show that deaths from infectious diseases (notably tuberculosis) have virtually disappeared. Deaths caused by circulatory diseases (including heart attacks and strokes) now account for nearly half of all deaths. The next largest cause of death is cancer (responsible for nearly a quarter of deaths).

18.3 Infant mortality

ACTIVITIES 4

Using Item 6.8, find the crude death rate of:

1 male children under one year of age.

2 female children under one year of age.

The death rate of children who are born alive but die before the age of one year is referred to as *infant mortality*. Item 6.9 shows the decline in the infant mortality rate from 1851.

This considerable decline in infant mortality is an important factor in increased life expectancy. The infant mortality rate is used frequently as an index of social and economic progress. Although social and economic advances were made in late Victorian times, the infant mortality rate remained around the figure of 150 per 1000. There was a failure to apply knowledge of medical science and the living conditions of a great number of the working class

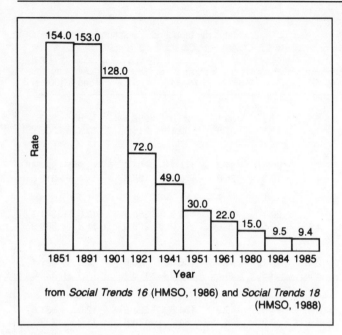

Item 6.9   Infant mortality in the UK per 1000 live births

from *Social Trends 16* (HMSO, 1986) and *Social Trends 18* (HMSO, 1988)

remained poor. Only in the first decade of the twentieth century, when poverty decreased, standards of hygiene improved, and the midwifery services were extended, was there a noticeable decline in infant mortality.

The introduction of pencillin, and the development of more effective vaccines during the war further lowered the infant mortality rate. Since 1945 the figure has continued to fall. Boys have a higher infant mortality rate than girls. In 1984, 10.7 boys per 1000 died under the age of one year. The rate for girls in the same year was 8.4 per 1000.

Other industrial countries have experienced similar trends in their infant mortality rates. Britain lags behind certain European countries but is better than others. The poorer nations have the highest infant mortality and the lowest life expectancy. In most countries of Africa, Asia and South America it is estimated that half the children die before reaching 15 years, while in Europe the average figure for child deaths before 15 is about five per cent. The infant mortality in India today can be compared to Britain a hundred years ago. In South Africa there are marked differences in the approximate rates for different races:

Whites	20
Blacks and Coloureds	100
Asians	60

These figures reveal the importance of social and economic conditions to survival in infancy. The social and economic deprivation of Blacks, Coloureds and Asians under South Africa's apartheid is well documented – look at Items 6.10 and 6.11.

Checklist

1 The crude death rate is deaths per 1000 of the total population.

2 The infant mortality rate is deaths within the first year of life per 1000 live births.

Item 6.10   White home in South Africa

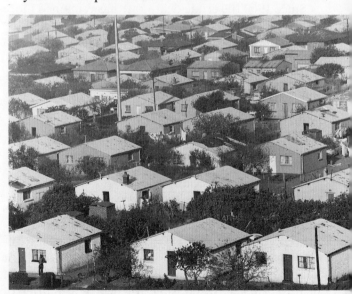

Item 6.11   Black homes in Soweto, South Africa

UNIT 19 Emigration and immigration

To many people the term 'immigrant' is synonymous with black immigrants from Commonwealth countries in the Caribbean, India and Pakistan. In fact, in 1983 only 24 per cent of immigrants to the UK came from Pakistan and the Commonwealth. As Item 6.13 shows, 30 800 of the immigrants settling in the UK in 1983 were from the European Community, compared with 25 300 from the Indian subcontinent and 18 200 from the African Commonwealth. Black people in the UK make up less than 4 per cent of the total population, and increasingly this percentage is made up of the children of New Commonwealth parents who were born in the UK. Not as immediately recognisable as Commonwealth immigrants or their descendants are several thousand immigrants of European origin and those from Australia, Canada, New Zealand and South Africa who have entered Britain in the past 35 years. About 25 000 US citizens are resident in the UK (excluding those on the diplomatic staff and in the armed forces), and so are a further 75 000 citizens of other European countries.

Thousands of people have left the UK since World War II. About a third have emigrated to Australia, a third to Western European countries, a sixth to Canada and a tenth to the USA. In this period the total number of people emigrating from the UK has exceeded those immigrating by about a quarter of a million. Between June 1978 and June 1979, for the first time, more people (6000) entered the UK than left the country. This was repeated in 1983 when 202 000 new residents settled in the UK and 185 000 emigrated, resulting in a net addition to our total population, by immigration, of 17 000. Item 6.12 shows this, and Item 6.13 shows the destination of those leaving the UK in 1984.

Most migrants to and from the UK since 1951 have been looking for better material conditions in the new country. Until an Act of Parliament in 1962 which severely restricted the kinds of people who could immigrate into the UK, most immigrants were unskilled or semi-skilled workers. At first Commonwealth immigrants undertook industrial work which was often poorly paid and offered few chances of promotion. The National Health Service, for example, employs a large number of Commonwealth doctors and nurses. Since 1982 there have been further Acts of Parliament designed to control immigration, making it harder for immigrants to gain entry and residency. The Commission for Racial Equality suggest that immigration is now largely confined to those people with job skills still in short supply in this country, and to those being reunited with their families (more than halved from about 50 000 in 1972 to 21 000 in 1983).

The data exclude movement between the United Kingdom and the Irish Republic

from *OPCS Spotlight 4* (HMSO, 1985)

Item 6.12 Net loss due to migration: in thousands

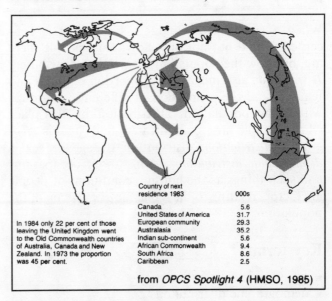

Country of next residence 1983	000s
Canada	5.6
United States of America	31.7
European community	29.3
Australasia	35.2
Indian sub-continent	5.6
African Commonwealth	9.4
South Africa	8.6
Caribbean	2.5

In 1984 only 22 per cent of those leaving the United Kingdom went to the Old Commonwealth countries of Australia, Canada and New Zealand. In 1973 the proportion was 45 per cent.

from *OPCS Spotlight 4* (HMSO, 1985)

Item 6.13 Where people go

Item 6.14   Population changes in
the UK

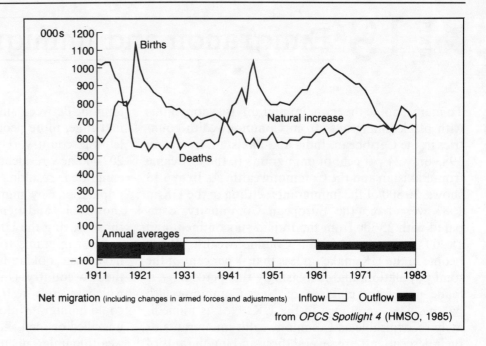

Net migration (including changes in armed forces and adjustments)   Inflow ☐   Outflow ■

from *OPCS Spotlight 4* (HMSO, 1985)

Migrants from the UK now tend to be skilled workers and many are professionally qualified. For example, several hundred doctors leave the UK annually for the USA. In terms of the qualifications of those entering and leaving the UK, the balance is roughly even.

ACTIVITIES 5

Produce a histogram (bar chart) to show:
a where immigrants to the UK come from.
b where emigrants from the UK go to.

► UNIT 20   Population distribution

When a government conducts a census it is concerned to find out not only how many people there are, but how the population is spread or distributed. *Distribution* also means the proportion of males and females, and the proportion of different age groups within the population. Distribution by the place where people are concentrated and live is *geographic distribution*; distribution by age or sex is *demographic distribution*; details about occupations and such things as the housing conditions of people are factors relating to the *economic distribution* of the population.

Key terms

- geographic distribution
- demographic distribution
- economic distribution

20.1 Age and sex distribution

Although, as we have seen in the previous section, the *numbers* of the total population have remained relatively stable over the last decade, the *nature* of the population has changed, noticeably in its age and sex structure. As Item 6.15 shows, in mid-1986 there were an estimated 29.1 million females and 27.6 million males in the UK. This represents an overall ratio of over 105 females to every 100 males, although in the younger age groups there are more males to females. It is the higher mortality of men at all ages which leads to the imbalance in favour of women. This imbalance increases with age so that there are more women than men among the elderly population.

United Kingdom										Millions
	0–4	5–14	15–29	30–44	45–59	60–64	65–74	75–84	85+	All ages
Mid-year estimates										
1951	4.3	7.0	10.3	11.1	9.6	2.4	3.7	1.6	0.2	50.3
1961	4.3	8.1	10.3	10.5	10.6	2.8	4.0	1.9	0.3	52.8
1971	4.5	8.9	11.8	9.8	10.2	3.2	4.8	2.2	0.5	55.9
1981	3.5	8.1	12.8	11.0	9.5	2.9	5.2	2.7	0.6	56.4
1984	3.6	7.4	13.3	11.2	9.3	3.3	4.8	2.9	0.7	56.5
1985	3.6	7.3	13.4	11.3	9.3	3.1	4.9	2.9	0.7	56.6
1986										
Males	1.9	3.7	6.9	5.8	4.6	1.5	2.2	1.1	0.2	27.6
Females	1.8	3.5	6.6	5.7	4.6	1.6	2.8	1.9	0.5	29.1
Total	3.6	7.2	13.5	11.5	9.2	3.1	5.0	3.0	0.7	56.8

Source: Office of Population Censuses and Surveys Government Actuary's Department

from Social Trends 18 (HMSO, 1988)

Item 6.15   Age and sex structure of the population

ACTIVITIES 6

Study Item 6.15 and answer the questions that follow.

1 How many millions in each sex does Item 6.15 show in the following age groups?
  a 0–4
  b 5–14
  c 0–14
  d 15–64
  e 65+

2 What *percentage* of the total population is shown in the following age groups?
  a 5–14
  b 15–64
  c 65+

3 Draw a bar chart to show these percentages.

Those under 16 are either infants or at school, and people over the working age of 65 are usually retired, so most of the *working population* is between the ages of 16 and 65. In fact there are nearly 28 million people of *working age*, that is, between 16 and 65 for males and between 16 and 60 for females. It does not include people of working age who are full-time students, or people who are sick, disabled or otherwise permanently unable to work, or people who are 'keeping home' or have retired early. It is the economically active members of the working population who provide the elderly with economic goods and services and who provide for the needs of

	000s
Employees in employment	21 594
Self-employed	2 627
Unemployed	3 180
Armed forces	322
Total working population	27 772

from Britain 1988: An Official Handbook (HMSO, 1988)

Item 6.16   The working population in Britain, 1986: in thousands

dependent young people and others. Society always has the job of looking after those at the top and lower ends of the age scale – the *dependent population*. Item 6.16 shows the make-up of Britain's working population in 1986.

Checklist

1 The working population is those people of working age who are working or actively seeking work, – the 'working population' includes the unemployed.

2 The economically active are those actually engaged in employment.

3 The dependent population is those in the population not economically active.

Since 1871 older people have formed a growing proportion of the population as a result of increased life expectancy. In 1900 the number of people over the age of 65 made up about five per cent of the population; today the figure is over 13 per cent, and this percentage is expected to be the same at the end of the century.

Until recently the fastest growing proportion of the population was the under-16 age group. But this trend has been reversed and we shall have a more balanced population in terms of age distribution by the end of the century, as about two-thirds of the population will be of working age and the rest will be infants or of school age, or those of retirement age.

When estimates of the working and non-working sectors of the population are made, factors such as the school-leaving age, developments in higher education, improved technology and automation must be taken into account. They affect the size of the working population and may also mean that people work fewer hours and choose to retire earlier.

20.2 Ethnic origin

ACTIVITIES 7

As Item 6.17 shows, 96 per cent of the population in the UK in 1984–6 was white. Study Item 6.17 and answer the questions that follow.

1 What is the total number of the following ethnic groups in the UK?
   a West Indian/Guyanese
   b Indian
   c Pakistani

2 Given that the total population, including people of all origins, is 54 230 000, work out the percentage of the total population which the above groups represent.

3 Comment on the age structure of the following ethnic groups:
   a white
   b West Indian/Guyanese
   c Indian
   d Bangladeshi.

4 What explanations can you give for any differences you have observed?

20.3 Geographic distribution

One of the most important features of the UK's population is that most of us live in towns, cities or other urban areas. The reason is simple: most of the jobs are in the towns and most of us like to live near our place of work. More than a third of the population live in just seven areas: Greater London, Manchester, Birmingham, Leeds, Liverpool, Newcastle and Glasgow. Because some urban areas are not separate local government units, but a mixture of different authorities which border one another, we refer to them as *conurbations*. A third of the people in Britain live in these conurbations, even though they account for less than three per cent of the total land area. If a line were drawn from Chester to Hull the *land area* of Britain would be divided in half, but two thirds of the population would live south of that line.

The concentration of population within a defined geographical area is termed *population density* and it is usually expressed in terms of the number of people living within a square kilometre. England, with an area of 130 439 square kilometres, has 46 546 million people. This is a density of 359 people for each square kilometre. Item 6.18 shows the figures for

Great Britain						Percentages and thousands		
	Percentage in each age group					Total all ages (= 100%) (000's)	% UK-born	% resident in English metropolitan areas
Ethnic group	0–15	16–29	30–44	45–59	60 or over			
White	20	22	20	17	21	51 107	96	31
All ethnic minorities of which	34	28	20	13	4	2 432	43	69
West Indian or Guyanese	26	33	16	19	6	534	53	81
Indian	32	27	23	13	5	760	36	66
Pakistani	44	24	17	12	2	397	42	66
Bangladeshi	50	20	14	15	1	103	31	79
Chinese	28	28	28	11	5	115	24	52
African	26	31	27	12	4	103	35	75
Arab	17	40	28	10	5	66	11	62
Mixed	53	27	11	7	3	235	74	58
Other	28	25	30	12	4	119	28	63
Not stated	29	24	18	13	17	691	68	37
All ethnic groups	21	22	20	17	20	54 230	93	33

Source: Labour Force Survey, combined data for 1984 to 1986 inclusive, Office of Population Censuses and Surveys

from Social Trends 18 (HMSO, 1988)

Item 6.17   Total population by ethnic origin and age, 1984–6

	England	Wales	Scotland	Northern Ireland	United Kingdom
Population (000's)	46 846	2 808	5 150	1 573	56 377
Area (sq km)	130 439	20 768	78 783	14 120	244 110
Population density (persons per sq km)	359	135	65	111	231

from *Britain 1986: An Official Handbook* (HMSO, 1986)

Item 6.18   Population density in the UK

Wales, Scotland, Northern Ireland and England separately, and for the UK as a whole.

ACTIVITIES 8

Look at Item 6.19, which gives the size (area) of the main urban areas in the UK along with their populations in thousands. Work out the densities for each urban area and draw up a table with the areas in order of population density. (In Item 6.19 the urban areas are given in order of the size of their total population in thousands rather than their population density.)

	Area		Population (000s)
	sq.km	sq.miles	
Greater London	1,580	609.7	6,775
Birmingham	264	102.0	1,004
Glasgow	198	76.3	725
Leeds	562	217.0	711
Sheffield	368	141.9	534
Liverpool	113	43.6	483
Bradford	370	142.9	463
Manchester	116	44.9	451
Edinburgh	261	100.6	438
Bristol	110	42.3	392
Coventry	97	37.3	310
Belfast	140	54.0	304
Cardiff	120	46.3	280

from *Britain 1986: An Official Handbook* (HMSO, 1986)

Item 6.19   Size and population of the main urban areas, mid-1986

ACTIVITIES 9

The government publish a book of statistical data on each region of the UK, called *Regional Trends*. You will find a copy in a main library near your school. The extract from *Regional Trends* in Item 6.20 refers to the West Midlands.

See whether you can get hold of a copy of *Regional Trends* at a library and find out about your own region.

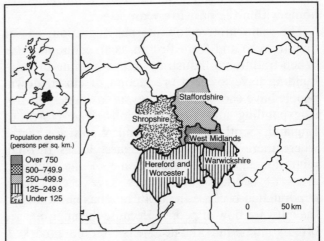

from *Regional Trends 1987* (HMSO, 1987)

Main demographic characteristics
The population of the West Midlands rose by nearly 9% from 1961 to 1985, compared to 7% for the UK as a whole, though the region's population was almost unchanged between 1980 and 1985 while the UK total continued to rise by around ½%. In common with the countrywide tendency for people to move away from more urban areas, the population of the metropolitan area around Birmingham fell 6% from 1971 to 1985 while the population of the rest of the region (Hereford and Worcestershire, Shropshire Staffordshire and Warwickshire) rose by 9%.

The West Midlands metropolitan area had the largest single concentration of all the major urban areas, nearly a quarter of the GB population in households, of people of Pakistani ethnic origin in the period 1983 to 1985. Nearly a fifth of those of Indian origin also lived in this area.

The birth rate in the West Midlands, at 13.6 live births per 1,000 population in 1985, was higher than everywhere except Northern Ireland and the North West, and rose to 14.4 in the West Midlands metropolitan area (and within that to 15.8 in Birmingham). The regional perinatal mortality rate, at 12.1 still births and deaths of infants under one week old per 1,000 live and still births during the period 1983 to 1985, was the highest in the country at regional level and rose to 14.7 in Shropshire, the highest sub-regional rate.

Item 6.20   Population density in the West Midlands

20.4 Internal migration

Demographers are often concerned with the movements of population within a country. The numbers involved and the rate at which this *internal migration* takes place have important consequences. In some places there may be a considerable depopulation, while elsewhere the population may rise considerably within a short space of time. Because the data on internal migration had been inadequate previously, the 1971 census asked a question on the movement of home within the past five years.

The main motive for internal migration, as for migration to and from Britain, is an economic one. When traditional industries such as mining or shipbuilding have lowered production or closed down, people have chosen to move away to where industry is expanding and there are jobs. The North of England, Scotland, Ireland and Wales are places where there have been the highest losses through migration since the 1930s. Some of the highland areas of Scotland and Wales have been greatly depopulated because the birth rate has not matched the outward flow of people. Because the migrants are often young adults the decline is even more marked, as they might otherwise have brought up children in the area. The Midlands and the South of England have gained in population through migration from other parts of the country and also from the natural increase in population. This trend was most marked during the economic depression of the interwar years when unemployment caused many to move to the newer light industries of the Midlands and the South. After the war the drift to the south continued. The rate of retirement migration has increased in recent years, mainly to the south coast of England and East Anglia.

Movement of population to towns and cities began in Britain in medieval times, and London's population more than trebled during the reign of Elizabeth I. This movement to the towns accelerated considerably in the industrial revolution of the nineteenth century. In the 1920s residential suburbs grew up around many of the larger towns, where housing estates were built within easy travelling distances. This process is called *suburbanisation*. Since 1945 some 32 new towns have been built. Twenty-one are in England, two in Wales, five in Scotland and four in Northern Ireland. Most took an existing town or village as a beginning point, and they were built to carry the overspill of population from already overcrowded cities and encourage the gradual spread of industry to new areas. The new towns have a total population of over two million.

The movement to suburbs and new towns is known as *urban dispersal*. Before the war suburbanisation was often haphazard as builders spread the houses along routeways into towns and cities. This was called *ribbon development*. After the war central and local government authorities planned urban dispersal to protect the countryside and at the same time provide accommodation. The demand for housing is now growing considerably, particularly around London, so that some local authorities are faced with the problem of either protecting the green belt around cities or providing more houses.

Some commuters to London travel more than a hundred miles to get to work each day. The number

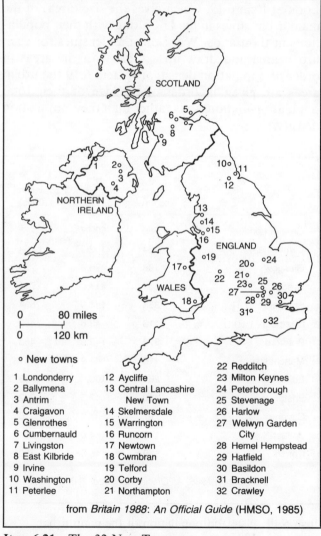

0   80 miles
0   120 km

○ New towns

1 Londonderry
2 Ballymena
3 Antrim
4 Craigavon
5 Glenrothes
6 Cumbernauld
7 Livingston
8 East Kilbride
9 Irvine
10 Washington
11 Peterlee

12 Aycliffe
13 Central Lancashire
        New Town
14 Skelmersdale
15 Warrington
16 Runcorn
17 Newtown
18 Cwmbran
19 Telford
20 Corby
21 Northampton

22 Redditch
23 Milton Keynes
24 Peterborough
25 Stevenage
26 Harlow
27 Welwyn Garden
        City
28 Hemel Hempstead
29 Hatfield
30 Basildon
31 Bracknell
32 Crawley

from *Britain 1988: An Official Guide* (HMSO, 1985)

Item 6.21   The 32 New Towns

of inhabitants of Greater London is declining and people have left the city centre, mainly for the home counties of Essex, Hertfordshire, Surrey and Kent. The old centres of many of the large cities have been left almost to decay. The poorer housing conditions of these places are often inhabited by the less well off, including elderly people and some New Commonwealth immigrants.

Key terms

- depopulation
- retirement migration
- suburbanisation
- new towns
- urban dispersal
- ribbon development

 # 21 Population trends

21.1 World population trends

Astonishingly, there are more people alive today than have ever died. This massive increase has been fairly recent in terms of world history, and it creates problems (primarily for the poorer nations of the world). Although the populations of advanced technological countries in Europe and the USA stabilised between the wars, the populations of the third world nations continued to increase. In the richer developed nations there is fairly even age distribution, with about a quarter of the population aged under 15 years, but in third world countries the percentage of children is much greater – 40 or 50 per cent. This is one of the reasons why there will be a high population growth rate over the next generation.

The reasons for the growth in world population are similar to those which caused Britain's population to rise a century ago. The death rate is falling due to better knowledge of hygiene and medicine, particularly as epidemic diseases today can be controlled, through immunisation and vaccination, at relatively low cost. Because of the lower infant mortality and higher birth rate, many more children survive to adulthood, but contraception is not nearly as widely practised as in developed countries. Possible reasons for this include the following:

1 Ordinary people are often unaware that limiting the size of their families may have advantages. In many countries extra children are seen as extra workers for the family, and in some the desire to have sons outweighs all considerations of family size.

2 Contraceptive techniques may be expensive or unknown.

3 There may be religious objections to contraceptive devices, as in Roman Catholic countries.

4 Improved farming methods have helped to feed some of the growing numbers – for example, a 'miracle rice' which yields twice as many grains has been successfully introduced to some countries.

Whether the world's resources of minerals and foodstuffs will be able to support such a large increase in population is still in doubt. Some economists and scientists maintain that there are not enough resources to give even half the world's population a standard of living equivalent to that of the average European at present. Feeding and controlling the world's population growth are among today's greatest and most urgent problems. Malthus's dreadful predictions of a century and a half ago are a reality in some parts of the world today, and many more may suffer in the future.

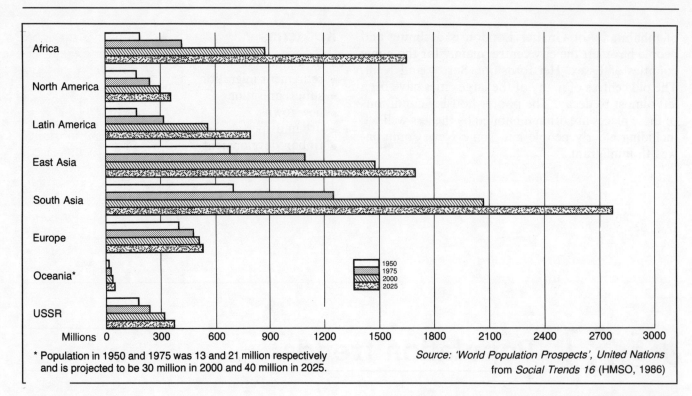

* Population in 1950 and 1975 was 13 and 21 million respectively
and is projected to be 30 million in 2000 and 40 million in 2025.

Source: 'World Population Prospects', United Nations
from *Social Trends 16* (HMSO, 1986)

Item 6.22   World population growth, 1950–2025

ACTIVITIES 11

Study Items 6.22 and 6.23 and answer the questions
that follow.

1 In your own words explain the meaning of 'expectation of life at birth'.

2 What is the expectation of life at birth in the UK
for:
a males?
b females?

3 In which country is expectation of life at birth for
males:
a highest?
b lowest?

4 How might you begin to explain these differences?

5 Which countries seem to have the highest proportion of:
a under 15-year-olds?
b over 60-year-olds

	1984	Percentage aged		Expectation of life at birth (years)	
		Under 15	60 or over	Males	Females
United Kingdom	56.5	*21*	*20*	69.8	76.2
Belgium	9.9	*20*	*18*	68.6	75.1
Denmark	5.1	*20*	*20*	71.1	77.2
France	54.9	*22*	*18*	70.1	78.2
Germany (Fed. Rep.)	61.2	*18*	*20*	69.9	76.6
Greece	9.9	*22*	*17*	70.1	73.6
Irish Republic	3.5	*31*	*15*	68.8	73.5
Italy	57.0	*22*	*17*	69.7	75.9
Luxembourg	0.4	*19*	*18*	66.8	72.8
Netherlands	14.4	*22*	*16*	72.4	79.2
European Community	272.8	..	..	..	..
Portugal	10.2	*26*	*15*	65.1	72.9
Spain	38.7	*27*	*15*	69.7	75.0
Sweden	8.3	*19*	*22*	73.0	79.1
Australia	15.5	*25*	*14*	71.4	78.4
USSR	275.0	*36*	*13*	64	74
Egypt		*40*	*6*	51.6	53.8
Tanzania	21.1	*46*	*4*	48.8	52.2
Zimbabwe	8.0	*51*	*3*	51.8	55.3
China	1,051.6	..	..	66.0	68.6
India	746.7	*39*	*6*	46.4	44.7
Japan	120.0	*23*	*13*	73.8	79.1
Canada	25.1	*23*	*13*	70.2	77.5
USA	236.7	*22*	*16*	69.9	77.8
Brazil	132.6	*37*	*6*	57.6	61.1
Peru	19.2	*43*	*5*	52.6	55.5

from *Social Trends 16* (HMSO, 1986)

Item 6.23   Population and population structure:
selected countries

21.2 Population growth

Four stages in Britain's population growth

Stage 1   until 1750   Until about 1750 the rate of growth was slow – about one million each century from the year AD 1000. This period had a high birth rate and a high death rate. Poor agriculture and diet, lack of knowledge of medicine and hygiene, and occasional plagues were the principal reasons for this slow population growth.

Stage 2   1750–1870   During this time Britain's population trebled owing to a high birth rate and a falling death rate. Agriculture improved, with higher yields and better stock through breeding. From 1840 onwards public health measures controlled sanitation and water supplies, and people began to live in cleaner conditions with less risk of disease.

Stage 3   1870–1920   A falling birth rate and a falling death rate slowed down the rate of population growth. Plentiful food from imports as well as home production ensured adequate feeding for most people. Bye-laws and government control of hygiene

and sanitation became more stringent, medicine made significant advances and life expectancy increased. Family sizes fell as birth control became widely practised. Living standards rose.

Stage 4   1920 till today   The modern period has a low birth rate and a low death rate. Infant mortality is very low, and life expectancy has greatly increased. There has been gradual, slow increase in population, due primarily to increased life expectancy. The Welfare State and higher living standards have meant a minimum provision of welfare for all and better general material well-being. Epidemic diseases have been almost eradicated, while concern about the environment has grown. During the last decade the total population has remained relatively stable, as Item 6.24 shows.

21.3 A population policy for Britain?

From the beginning of this century until the mid-1960s demographers, economists and politcans were mainly concerned that Britain's population was ageing. This was due to increasing life expectancy and a declining birth rate. In the 1950s and 1960s life expectancy continued to increase, but the birth rate began to increase as well. It was then suggested that Britain's population would become too large by the end of the century. In 1961 a population of 70 million was projected as likely by the year 2001. For an already densely populated country, a further increase in population would perhaps cause many problems:

1 environmental problems such as pollution and loss of natural amenities.

2 economic and social problems such as diminishing natural resources.

3 lack of housing.

4 strain on education and welfare services.

The 1971 census showed a decline in the birth rate and the population projection for 2001 was lowered to 63 million. After 1971 the birth rate continued to decline but it began to rise again in the late 1970s. Demographers are now projecting a very slight increase in overall population by the end of this century to 58 million, and there is again concern about an ageing population.

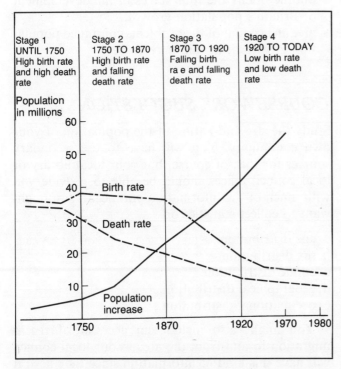

Item 6.24   Four stages in Britain's population growth

A number of reasons may account for the decline in the birth rate recorded in the 1971 census. One answer must be the greater knowledge and availability of family planning. Local authorities and the National Health Service run family planning centres where advice on contraceptive methods and devices is freely available. Since the Abortion Act of 1967 many unwanted pregnancies have been terminated legally, which may have increased the number of abortions. Economic factors such as high unemployment can also affect the birth rate. The Family Planning Association estimate that as many as one pregnancy in three is unplanned; this would suggest that, with ever increasing knowledge of contraception and the introduction of simpler and more reliable methods, the birth rate and overall population will continue to decline.

The size and structure of a population have far-reaching social and economic consequences. Governments and local authorities may often have to base long-term planning decisions costing millions of pounds on projected population statistics. The number of places in teacher training was reduced by one third in 1976 on the evidence of the declining birth rate of the previous five years. So there would be advantages to the government if it had a population policy. How might it try to encourage population decline?

The experience of other countries, such as France after the war, has shown that it is fairly easy to encourage population growth through generous state benefits and allowances for people who have larger families. Encouraging population decline poses many more problems. If benefits and child allowances were not given to large families, then the poor, who tend to have large families, would suffer more and it would be harder for them to escape poverty than at present.

REVIEW

If you have studied and understood this chapter you should be able to . . .

- explain what the census is, and how it is conducted.
- define or explain the terms:
  a optimum population,
  b crude birth rate, and
  c general fertility rate.
- account for the stability of the birth rate in Britain this century.
- account for the decline in the death rate in Britain in recent years.
- define or explain the terms:
  a crude death rate,
  b infant mortality,
  c emigration, and
  d immigration.
- outline the make-up of Britain's population in terms of age groups, sex and ethnic groups.
- explain the patterns of internal migration seen in Britain. Include the idea of urban dispersal in your answer.
- suggest reasons for the reluctance in third world countries to use contraception to control population growth.
- outline briefly the four stages in the development of Britain's population growth.
- give an account of the problems continued population growth in Britain may cause.

COURSEWORK SUGGESTION

Study the size and nature of the population of your own community. You will have to use secondary sources for this, of course, but your local library or local council offices should be able to provide you with much of the information you need. You might want to collect statistics on:

a age distribution.
b sex distribution.
c ethnic distribution.
d geographical distribution.
e occupational distribution.

You might also include an account of recent migration to and from the area. Your local council will have this kind of information since they need it to plan their future provision of services.

ASSESSMENT QUESTIONS

The mark allocations to sections of the questions are shown in the right hand margin.

1

a Explain the difference in meaning between the terms 'birth rate' and 'fertility rate'. (4)

b What changes have occurred in the birth rate in Britain since 1900? (5)

c Account for the changes in the birth rate in Britain since 1900. (6)

London & East Anglian Group for GCSE Examinations

2 The following diagrams show the birth rates and death rates in three societies over a period of time.

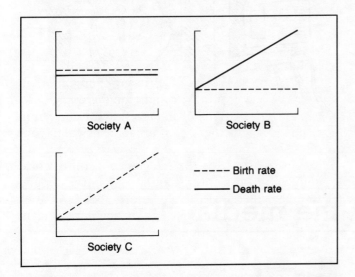

a From the diagrams:
  i what is happening to the population size in society B; (1)
  ii what is happening to the population size in society C; (1)
  iii what is happening to the population size in society A? (1)

b Name **two** factors other than birth rate and death rate which affect population size. (2)

c Define the term birth rate. (2)

d Define the term infant mortality rate. (2)

e Suggest **three** measures which might reduce the high death rate in society B. (3)

f Identify and explain **two** reasons why the infant mortality rate is higher in social class 5 (unskilled manual workers) than in social class 1 (e.g. top managers). (4)

g Draw a diagram which shows the relationship between birth rate and death rate in a society with an ageing population. Give **three** social consequences of an ageing population. (4)

Southern Examining Group

7 The mass media

AIMS

At the end of this chapter you should be able to:

- identify and describe the main forms of the mass media.
- recognise the influence of social class on newspaper reading and television viewing habits.
- explain the role of the mass media in the socialisation process.
- show a critical awareness of the role of the media in the creation of stereotypes.
- outline the problems posed by the existing pattern of ownership and control of the media.

► UNIT 22 The forms of the media

Clearly if we are to participate in the society in which we live we must communicate with other people. A great deal of communicating is performed on a person-to-person basis by the simple means of speech. If we travel in buses, stand in football match queues, or eat in restaurants, we are likely to have conversations in which we impart information or ideas, receive news or comment, and very likely have our opinions challenged by other members of society. Face-to-face contact is by no means the only form of communication and during the last two hundred years the art of mass communication has had a profound impact on contemporary society. Communication is no longer merely concerned with the imparting of information. The modern communications industry influences the way people live in society by allowing access to:

information,
education,
entertainment.

Item 7.1   Newstands sell local and national papers, and a variety of magazines and journals

The printing, broadcasting and advertising industries are all involved with informing, educating and entertaining.

Denis McQuail, a sociologist particularly interested in the mass media, argues that the history of the media begins with the *printed book*, a form which played a part in the transformation of the medieval world. It was as much as two hundred years after the invention of printing before we could recognise a *newspaper* marked by a regular appearance openly on public sale and providing information, advertising and gossip. Most of the population, however, did not read a daily newspaper until after World War I. Film began at the end of the nineteenth century. *Radio* and *television*, in their relatively recent history, have taken positions of power among other media, because of their ability to observe directly and give accounts of events as they happen.

While the mass media may take the form of the press, television, radio, books or films, it is the power of the press and broadcasting which most interests sociologists. The mass media of primary importance to sociologists therefore, can take any of the forms shown in Item 7.2.

A   The Press
1 The national press
2 The regional and local press
3 'Ethnic' publications
4 Free distribution newspapers
5 Periodicals
  a 'general'
  b 'specialised'
  c 'trade'
  d 'technical'
  e 'professional'
  f 'house' magazines
  g the 'alternative' press

B   Television and radio
1 British Broadcasting Corporation (BBC)
  a BBC 1
  b BBC 2
  c Radio 1, 2, 3 and 4
  d BBC Local Radio (30 stations)
  e BBC External Services
  f BBC World Service

2 Independent Broadcasting Authority (IBA)
  a ITV (15 ITV companies)
  b Channel 4
  c Independent Local Radio (43 stations)
3 The Welsh Fourth Channel Authority (WFCA)
4 Hospital radio (200 stations)
5 Campus radio (20 stations)

Item 7.2   Forms of the mass media

▶ UNIT 23 The press

23.1 The national press

As we have seen, 'the press' covers a wide range of printed material from the common newspaper or magazine to specialist trade and technical periodicals most people will never have a need to read. Item 7.3 shows the national press, that is newspapers that are available all over the country (although as you can see some of the newspapers have higher *circulation figures* than others).

ACTIVITIES 1

Study Item 7.3 and answer these questions.

1 Which of these national newspapers has the highest circulation figure?

2 Which four of these national newspapers have the lowest circulation figures?

3 Perhaps you have seen some of these newspapers. If so, can you think of any explanations for these circulation figures from your knowledge of what these papers are like?

4 What effect do you think the circulation figures have on:
a the 'power' of the newspaper to influence opinion?
b the use of the newspaper for advertising?

5 Describe the kind of person you think typically reads:
a *News of the World.*
b *Financial Times.*
c *Daily Mail.*
d *The Times.*
e *Sun.*
f *The Guardian.*
g *The Independent.*

Item 7.3   National newspapers

Title and foundation date	Controlled by	Circulation* average Jan.–June 1987
National dailies		
'Populars'		
Daily Express (1900)	United Newspapers	1,697,229
Daily Mail (1896)	Associated Newspapers Group	1,759,455
Daily Mirror (1903)	Mirror Group Newspapers (1986)	3,122,773
Morning Star (1966)	Morning Star Co-operative Society	25,000
The Star (1978)	United Newspapers	1,288,583
The Sun (1964)	News International	3,993,031
Today (1986)	News International	307,256
'Qualities'		
Daily Telegraph (1855)	The Daily Telegraph	1,146,917
Financial Times (1888)	Pearson	279,762
The Guardian (1821)	The Guardian and Manchester Evening News	493,582
The Independent (1986)	Newspaper Publishing	292,703
The Times (1785)	News International	442,375
National Sundays		
'Populars'		
News of the World (1843)	News International	4,941,966
Sunday Express (1918)	United Newspapers	2,214,612
Sunday Mirror (1963)	Mirror Group Newspapers (1986)	3,013,285
Sunday People (1881)	Mirror Group Newspapers (1986)	2,932,472
The Mail on Sunday (1982)	Associated Newspapers Group	1,688,015
News on Sunday (1987)	News on Sunday Ltd	n.a.
'Qualities'		
Sunday Telegraph (1961)	The Daily Telegraph	720,902
Sunday Times (1882)	News International	1,220,021
The Observer (1791)	George Outram & Co/The Observer	773,514

*Circulation figures are those of the Audit Bureau of Circulations (founded in 1931 and consisting of publishers, advertisers and advertising agencies) and are certified average daily or weekly net sales for the period. The circulation figure of the *Morning Star* is otherwise audited.
n.a. = not available; the newspaper was first published in April 1987.

from *Britain 1988: An Official Handbook* (HMSO, 1988)

Try to explain your answer as fully as you can. Now look again at your answer to question 4 and see if you want to change or add to it.

6 The table divides the national newspapers into either 'populars' or 'qualities'. What do you think these terms mean? Look again at your answer to question 5 and see what differences there are between the kind of person you think reads the 'populars' and the kind you think reads the 'qualities'.

7 How do 'populars' differ from 'qualities' in terms of their:
a style?
b content?
c format?

It has been said that the popular papers are frequently of the tabloid type and are likely to concentrate upon sensationalism, human interest stories, sport, prominent headlines and many photographs, while the quality press is of the large broadsheet format and concerns itself with informative journalism and commentaries upon politics, economic problems, literature and the arts. Do you agree with these ideas? Collect examples which illustrate your answer.

Item 7.4 Social class readership of newspapers (1)

1987							
Newspaper	A (%)	B (%)	C1 (%)	C2 (%)	D (%)	E (%)	Total approx. %
Daily Express	3	18	31	28	12	9	100
Daily Mail	4	20	32	26	11	8	100
Daily Mirror	1	6	18	37	26	13	100
The Sun	1	6	18	35	26	15	100
Daily Telegraph	12	39	30	12	4	4	100
Financial Times	12	40	33	8	5	1	100
The Guardian	7	43	27	12	7	3	100
The Times	16	41	26	9	5	3	100
Any national morning paper	3	15	22	29	19	12	100

from *National Readership Survey 1987* (JICNARS, 1987)

Item 7.5 Social class readership of newspapers (2)

Newspaper	A	B	C1	C2	D	E	% of total population
Daily Express	18	18	20	16	13	11	16
Daily Mail	17	17	17	11	8	7	13
The Mirror	6	11	22	35	37	20	16
The Sun	6	11	22	37	40	19	28
The Daily Telegraph	38	24	11	3	2	2	8
Financial Times	9	5	2	1	0	0	2
The Guardian	9	8	4	1	1	0	3
The Times	14	6	3	1	1	0	2
Any daily paper	72	69	70	75	75	56	71

Note: The columns in Item 7.5 add up to more than 100% because many people (all social classes) read more than one newspaper.

from Ivan Reid *Social Class Differences* (Grant McIntyre, 1981)

23.2 The social class of newspaper readers

As you would expect, and as your answers to the previous questions might show, it has long been recognised that different newspapers are read by different types of people. More specifically, surveys have shown that the different social classes in our society tend to read different newspapers. Item 7.4 is based on information provided by the Joint Industry Committee for National Readership Surveys (JICNARS) and shows the *social class composition*, or *social class profile*, of all the readers of each publication.

It is possible to provide information about social class and newspaper readership in a different way. Item 7.5 shows the percentage *of each social class* which reads each publication.

The research which gives rise to these figures is continuous, and involves over 30 000 interviews each year.

ACTIVITIES 2

In your own words, explain what Item 7.4 and Item 7.5 are showing. Be careful to explain the difference between each table. Remember Item 7.4 shows the readership profile for *each newspaper*, and Item 7.5 shows newspaper reading habits for *each social class*.

23.3 Distributing the national press

Simon Jenkins, one-time feature editor of *The Sunday Times*, a past editor of the *London Evening Standard*, and currently the political editor of *The Economist*, argues that Fleet Street is no longer just another aspect of what academics now call the 'mass media' industry, playing its allotted role alongside television and radio, local newspapers and specialist magazines. It is, says Jenkins, a unique commercial phenonemon based on archaic structures of finance, production and distribution. Jenkins describes one aspect of distributing Fleet Street newspapers in Item 7.6 to illustrate his point.

Britain is able to enjoy a wide range of titles on its breakfast table as a result of yet another of its characteristics – a compact population supporting a heavily subsidized railway network. This network enables millions of awkward and grubby bales to be manhandled to their eventual destinations by an army of men working 'unsocial hours' through the night. It is likewise dependent on thousands of newsagents, whose sole incentive for getting up at five or six in the morning is the few pence they make on each copy (they keep about a quarter of the cover price). And they are in turn dependent on a ready supply of schoolboys who must get up equally early to deliver the papers and thereby earn a small addition to the pocket money. (The world's press is alarmingly reliant on the schoolboy work ethic.) This lengthy and tenuous chain is weakening each year. In the past three years, 3000 newsagents gave up their businesses, no longer prepared to work such hours for so little reward. Competing with bigger stores for their other goods, they are simply closing down and not being replaced. And as newspaper circulations fall, it becomes less and less economic to distribute the ones that remain. A change in rail freight pricing policy, an alteration in child labour regulations, even an increase in parental generosity towards pocket money, could savage newspaper sales.

from Simon Jenkins, *Newspapers: The Power and the Money* (Faber, 1979)

Item 7.6   Distributing the newspapers

23.4 The local press

ACTIVITIES 3

Read the account in Item 7.7 of the regional press in England, and answer the questions that follow it.

1 List the regional or local newspapers which appear in your area. Divide them into:
a morning and evening papers.
b daily and weekly papers.

2 From the account in Item 7.7 write down:
a the number of local newspapers produced outside London (including both morning and evening daily papers and Sunday local papers).

Regional Newspapers (England)

The regional newspapers of England (outside London, 98 morning or evening dailies and Sundays and some 950 newspapers appearing once or twice a week) provide mainly regional and local news. The daily newspapers also give coverage of national and international affairs. Generally, regional evening newspapers are non-political, while the morning newspapers adopt a more positive political stance and tend to be independent or conservative in outlook.

Of the morning papers the *Yorkshire Post* (Leeds) and the *Northern Echo* (Darlington) have circulations of over 87 400 and 89 900 respectively, and two provincial Sunday papers – the *Sunday Sun* (Newcastle upon Tyne) and the *Sunday Mercury* (Birmingham) – sell nearly 124 000 and 172 000 copies respectively. Circulation figures of evening papers start at about 11 000 and most are in the 20 000 to 90 000 range: those with much larger sales include the *Manchester Evening News* and the *Birmingham Evening Mail* (both over 275 000), the *Wolverhampton Express and Star* (over 243 700), and the *Liverpool Echo* (over 200 000). Weekly papers are of mainly local appeal and are also a valuable medium for local advertising. Most have circulations in the 5 000 to 30 000 range.

There is currently one London evening newspaper. *The London Standard*, with a circulation of some 503 900: plans have been announced for the launch of a new evening paper, to be called *The London Post*. A number of evening newspapers are published in the outer metropolitan area. The hundred or so local weeklies include papers for every district in Greater London, often in the form of local editions of an individual paper.

from *Britain 1986: An Official Handbook* (HMSO, 1986)

Item 7.7   Regional newspapers

b the two local evening papers with the highest circulation figures. How do the circulations of these newspapers compare with the circulation figures of the national newspapers shown in Item 7.3?

3 How does the account say local daily and local weekly newspapers differ?

4 What is the circulation of the one London evening newspaper and how does this compare with the circulation of *The Times* and the *Guardian*?

5 Try to find out what has happened to *The London Post* since this account was written.

23.5   Other publications

In addition to the traditional-style national and local press, free distribution newspapers are becoming more important. Ethnic minorities also increasingly have newspapers and magazines that deal with their special interests.

ACTIVITIES 4

Study Item 7.8 and answer the questions that follow.

1 What is the benefit to advertisers of free distribution newspapers?

2 Look at the following list of periodicals or magazines. Put them into one of the seven categories of 'periodicals' mentioned in Item 7.8.

Woman's Own	*Radio Times*
New Society	*Investor's Chronicle*
The Economist	*Marketing*
Punch	*Social Science Teacher*

ACTIVITIES 5

Study Item 7.9 and answer the questions that follow.

1 How many daily and Sunday newspapers were there in:
a 1976?
b 1986?

2 What has happened to the number of local free newspapers during the same period?

Ethnic minority publications

More than 70 newspapers and magazines are produced by members of the ethnic minorities, over 40 of which are printed in Asian languages and the rest in English. Most are published weekly or monthly. They include the Asian newspapers *New Life* and *Asian Times*, *The Weekly Gleaner* – a local edition of the *Jamaican Gleaner* – and *West Indian World*. *The Voice* and *Caribbean Times* are aimed at the black population in general as is the magazine *Root*. An Arabic daily, *Al-Arab*, is also produced in Britain.

Free distribution newspapers

Some 730 free distribution newspapers (mostly weekly and financed largely by advertising) are now published in Britain, just over half of them produced by established newspaper publishers. The have enjoyed rapid growth in recent years and now have an estimated total weekly circulation of some 30 million.

Europe's first daily free distribution paper, the *Daily News*, was launched in Birmingham in 1984.

The periodical press

The 6000 periodical publications are classifield as 'general', 'specialised', 'trade', 'technical' and 'professional'. There are also about 500 'house magazines' produced by industrial undertakings, business houses or public services for the benefit of their employees and/or clients. The 'alternative' press probably includes several hundred further titles, most of them devoted to radical politics, community matters, religion, the occult, science or ecology.

from *Britain 1986: An Official Handbook* (HMSO, 1986)

Item 7.8   Other publications

	1976	1985	1986
Daily & Sunday newspapers	134	125	128
Weekly newspapers	1091	907	867
Local free newspapers	–	732	842
Periodicals			
Trade, technical, professional (incl. scientific & academic)	*4956	5109	5507
Consumer & specialist consumer		2302	2341
Free consumer magazines	–	221	304
Directories, etc	1414	1755	1979

*Total of periodicals

from *Benn's Press Directory 1986–87* (published annually by Benn Publications Ltd.)

Item 7.9   Number of periodical titles

115

▶ UNIT 24   Television and radio

1922

18 Oct   The British Broadcasting Company was formed.
1 Nov   Broadcast receiving licence introduced (ten shillings).
14 Nov   Daily broadcasting began from the London station of the British Broadcasting Company (2LO).

1927

4 Jan   The British Broadcasting Corporation constituted under Royal Charter for ten years. John Reith Director-General.
23 Apr   The first broadcast running commentary on a F.A. Cup Final match. Cardiff City v Arsenal.

1928

30 Oct   Inauguration of experimental transmission of still pictures by the Fultograph process from Daventry.

1936

2 Nov   First regular high definition television service in the world began transmission from Alexandra Palace.
11 Dec   Abdication broadcast by King Edward VIII.

1948

11 Oct   First television broadcast from No. 10 Downing Street (interview with Commonwealth Prime Ministers).

1955

2 May   First vhf radio broadcasting station brought into service at Wrotham.
10 Oct   Colour television test transmissions began from Alexandra Palace.

1964

20 Apr   Opening of BBC 2 and introduction of 625-line transmission.

1966

2 Jun   First direct television pictures from the Moon.

1985

23 Jan   Start of 6 month experiment in televising House of Lords.
27 Mar   New licence fees of £58 for colour and £18 for black and white announced by Home Secretary. Setting up of Peacock Committee to review BBC financing.
23 Apr   Radio Shropshire, the 30th BBC Local Radio station opened.
24 Jun   Radio Bedfordshire opened.
13 Jul   BBC transmits *Live Aid* programme to record world audience estimated at 1,500 million.

from *BBC Annual Report 1986* (BBC Publications, 1986)

Item 7.10   BBC dates

In this section we will concentrate on television, as television is the more powerful of the two media and has received more attention from sociological research. Factual information about radio can be found in the annual guides of both the BBC and the IBA, available at most libraries.

The BBC (British Broadcasting Corporation) has been providing a regular high definition television service since 1936. The first regular independent television programmes began in London in 1955; independent television is controlled by the IBA (Independent Broadcasting Authority). BBC 2 opened in April 1964 and Channel 4 began broadcasting in November 1982.

Item 7.10 shows some key dates in the development of the BBC.

It is the Independent Broadcasting Authority's aim so far as possible not to broadcast material unsuitable for children at times when large numbers of children are viewing.

Constraints on this policy arise from two factors: first there is no time of the evening when there are not some children viewing, perhaps even in quite substantial numbers; and secondly, any attempt to provide a wide range of programmes appropriate for adults and including serious subject-matter will entail the broadcasting of some material that might be considered unsuitable for children.

The IBA does not accept that, because some children are always likely to be present in the audience, there should be no adult material included in the programme output of Independent Television. The necessary compromise between these constraints and the IBA's general aim is embodied in the IBA's Family Viewing Policy for evening viewing.

The policy assumes a progressive decline throughout the evening in the proportion of children present in the audience. It expects a similar progression in the successive programmes scheduled from early evening until closedown: the earlier in the evening the more suitable, the later in the evening the less suitable.

Within the progression, 9.00 p.m. is fixed as the point up to which the broadcasters will normally regard themselves as responsible for ensuring that nothing is shown that is unsuitable for children. After nine o'clock progressively less suitable (i.e., more adult) material may be shown, and it may be that a programme will be acceptable, for example, at 10.30 p.m. that would not be suitable at 9.00 p.m. But it is assumed that from 9.00 p.m. onwards parents may reasonably be expected to share responsibility for what their children are permitted to see.

Violence is not the only reason why a programme may be unsuitable for family viewing. Other factors include bad language, innuendo, blasphemy, explicit sexual behaviour, and scenes of extreme distress.

from *TV Times*, 19–25 April 1986

Item 7.11   Family viewing policy

24.1 Family viewing policy

Both the BBC and the IBA are required to work within certain guidelines imposed by Parliament. The Home Secretary is responsible for the regulations of broadcasting, but allows the BBC and IBA independence in the day-to-day conduct of their affairs. There are codes of practice adopted by both authorities. Item 7.11 shows the 'Family Viewing Policy' of the IBA as it appeared in the *TV Times* of April 1986.

ACTIVITIES 6

Read Item 7.11 and answer the questions that follow.

1 How do the IBA decide whether material is 'suitable' or not for family viewing?

2 Why is the policy sometimes difficult to implement?

3 What assumptions do the IBA make about the viewing habits of their audience?

24.2 Television licences

ACTIVITIES 7

Item 7.12 shows the number of broadcasting receiving licences issued between 1927 and 1985. Study it, and answer the questions that follow.

1 Plot these figures as a bar chart or histogram. First plot the total number of licences issued, then plot the issue of monochrome (black and white) licences and finally plot the issue of colour licences.

2 How many television licences were issued in 1985? How does this compare with the total circulation figures of all national newspapers?

Item 7.12 Broadcasting receiving licences, 1927–85

Licences at 31 March	Total	Issued free for blind persons	Issued for payment Radio and television combined		
			Radio only	Monochrome	Colour
1927	2 269 644	5 750	2 263 984		
1930	3 092 324	16 496	3 075 828		
1935	7 011 753	41 868	6 969 885		
1940	8 951 045	53 427	8 897 618		
1945	9 710 230	46 861	9 663 369		
1947	10 777 704	49 846	10 713 298	14 560	
1950	12 219 448	56 376	11 819 190	343 882	
1955	13 980 496	62 506	9 414 224	4 503 766	
1960	15 005 011	54 958	4 480 300	10 469 753	
1965	16 046 603	34 355	2 759 203	13 253 045	
1968	17 645 821	27 564	2 529 750	15 068 079	20 428
1970	18 183 719	22 174	2 279 017	15 609 131	273 397
1971*	15 943 190	–	–	15 333 221	609 969
1975	17 700 815	–	–	10 120 493	7 580 322
1976	17 787 984	–	–	9 148 732	8 639 252
1977	18 056 058	–	–	8 098 386	9 957 672
1978	18 148 918	–	–	7 099 726	11 049 192
1979*	18 381 161	–	–	6 249 716	12 131 445
1980	18 284 865	–	–	5 383 125	12 901 740
1981	18 667 211	–	–	4 887 663	13 779 548
1982	18 554 220	–	–	4 293 668	14 260 552
1983	18 494 235	–	–	3 795 587	14 698 648
1984	18 631 753	–	–	3 261 272	15 370 481
1985	18 715 937	–	–	2 896 263	15 819 674

*Because of industrial action within the Post Office the figures for licences in force at 31 March 1971 and 1979 do not reflect the true position on those dates.
1. The Combined Radio and Television Licence was introduced on 1 June 1946.
2. The Supplementary Colour Licence was introduced on 1 January 1968.

3. The Radio Licence was abolished on 1 February 1971, and from the same date the Combined Radio and Television Licence was discontinued. Licences issued from that date were for television (monochrome or colour).
4. Figures do not include dealers' demonstration fees and concessionary licences for old people and the disabled living in approved residential homes.

from the *BBC Annual Report, 1986* (BBC Publications, 1986)

24.3 Programme content

Viewers are offered a wide range of different types of programme, as Items 7.13 and 7.14 show.

ACTIVITIES 8

Use Items 7.13 and 7.14 to draw a bar chart for each channel, dividing their transmitted output into the three common categories of 'informative', 'narrative' and 'entertainment' (consisting of light entertainment and sport).

Item 7.13 BBC programme analysis, 1985/86: television networks

	BBC 1		BBC 2		Total	
	Hours	*%*	*Hours*	*%*	*Hours*	*%*
BBC PRODUCTIONS						
Current Affairs	1,125	19·8	291	5·9	1,416	13·4
Features and Documentaries	333	5·8	701	14·4	1,034	9·8
Sport	761	13·4	773	15·8	1,534	14·4
Children's Programmes	753	13·2	20	0·4	773	7·3
Light Entertainment	518	9·1	217	4·4	735	7·0
News	410	7·2	51	1·1	461	4·4
Schools	–	–	512	10·5	512	4·8
Drama	295	5·2	144	3·0	439	4·2
Continuing Education	172	3·0	196	4·0	368	3·5
Religion	156	2·8	10	0·2	166	1·6
Music	16	0·3	126	2·6	142	1·3
Continuity	184	3·2	198	4·1	382	3·6
	4,723	83·0	3,239	66·4	7,962	75·3
British & Foreign Feature Films & Series	849	14·9	854	17·5	1,703	16·1
	5,572	97·9	4,903	83·9	9,665	91·4
Open University	118	2·1	786	16·1	904	8·6
Total	5,690	100·0	4,879	100·0	10,569	100·0

from *BBC Annual Report and Handbook 1987* (BBC Publications, 1986)

Item 7.14 Programme transmissions on ITV and Channel 4

ITV* *(Weekly average, year ended 3 April 1988)*

	Duration Hrs:Mins	Percentage %
News and News Magazines	11:55	10.4
Current Affairs & General Factual	14:22	12.6
Arts	1:02	0.9
Religion	2:36	2.3
Adult Education	1:38†	1.4
Schools Programmes	1:55	1.7
Pre-School Programmes	3:07	2.7
Children's Informative Programmes	1:00	0.9
Informative	37:35	32.9
Plays, Series, TV Movies	26:17	23.0
Feature Films	12:13**	10.7
Narrative	38:30	33.7
Children's Drama & Entertainment	9:04	8.0
Entertainment & Light Music	20:04	17.6
Sport	8:46	7.7
Total All Programmes	114:06‡	100%

NOTES
*   *Excluding TV-am transmissions of 22 hours 42 minutes per week.*
†   *To this total should be added 14 minutes per week of general factual material shown during peaktime which was accepted by the IBA as educationally valuable and supported by educational material and activities.*
‡   *The opening routine of each day for a nominal one minute is not specified above but is included in the total.*
** *This figure includes EC and other films exempted from the overseas quota which were previously included under the Plays, Series and TV Movies category.*

Channel 4 *(Weekly average, year ended 3 April 1988)*

	Duration Hrs:Mins	Percentage %
News	4:24	4.4
Current Affairs & General Factual	22:18	22.2
Arts	2:15	2.2
Religion	1:15	1.2
Education	8:14	8.2
Open College	1:58	2.0
Informative	40:24	40.2
Plays, Series, TV Movies	14:12	14.1
Feature Films	18:35**	18.5
Narrative	32:47	32.6
Entertainment & Light Music	13:44	13.7
Sport	8:26	8.4
ITV Schools Programmes	5:08	5.1
Total All Programmes	100:36‡	100%

NOTES
†   *The opening routine of each day for a nominal one minute is not specified above but is included in the total.*
** *This figure includes EC and other films exempted from the overseas quota which were previously included under the Plays, Series and TV Movies category.*

24.4 Viewing audiences

The average amount of television viewing per person per week in 1985/86 was 26½ hours. Item 7.15 shows the proportions of the population selecting any of the channels at some time during a week. The table also shows in hours and minutes the average amount of each channel viewed and the share of total viewing attracted by each channel.

ACTIVITIES 9

Study Item 7.15 and answer the questions that follow.

1 Of each person's weekly 24 hours and 35 minutes viewing, on average, how much was devoted to:
  a BBC 1?
  b BBC 2?
  c ITV?
  d Channel 4 (or the Welsh channel S4C)?

2 The daily and weekly 'reach' of each channel (that is, the percentage of the population selecting each channel at same time during the day or week) is shown.
  a What is the daily 'reach' of:
    i BBC 1?   ii ITV?
  b What is the weekly 'reach' of:
    i BBC 2?   ii Channel 4?

Item 7.15 Viewing audiences, 1985/86

	Reach % of population (aged 4+)		Viewing per head/week	Share of viewing
	Daily	Weekly	Hrs:Mins	%
BBC 1	64.6	92.0	9:22	36
BBC 2	35.3	80.6	2:57	11
Any or all BBC	69.1	93.0	12:19	47
ITV	65.2	91.5	12:04	46
C4/S4C	28.5	72.8	1:58	7
Any or all commercial	69.2	92.6	14:02	53
Any or all television	79.3	94.3	26:21	100

Item 7.16 Time spent watching television: by social class

United Kingdom

	February				August			
	1968	1970	1973	1976	1968	1970	1973	1976
Average weekly hours viewed								
Age groups:								
5–14	19.4	21.9	29.5	22.0	14.8	17.0	22.7	19.0
15–19	15.6	16.7	16.8	18.4	12.0	13.4	13.0	13.9
20–29	15.6	16.6	18.1	19.1	11.2	13.9	13.7	14.0
30–49	17.4	18.4	18.4	19.0	11.4	13.2	13.4	13.2
50 and over	17.5	18.4	19.0	20.4	11.6	14.3	14.3	14.5
Social class of adults (15 and over)								
A (top 5%)	13.9	14.6	15.0	16.6	10.2	11.4	11.2	11.3
B (next 25%)*	15.9	16.5	16.8	17.7	10.7	12.5	12.8	12.5
C (bottom 70%)	17.9	19.0	19.3	20.3	11.8	14.4	14.4	14.6
Overall average weekly hours viewed by all persons aged 5 and over	17.6	18.7	19.3	19.9	12.0	14.2	15.3	14.7

*Inserted by the author.

from *Social Trends, 1976*, CSO

3 Try to devise a short and simple questionnaire to give to your friends, family and neighbours. Try to find out how many hours viewing each person does in a week, and what proportion of that time is spent on each channel.

24.5 Social class and television viewing habits

Ninety-six per cent of all households now own a television set and, as we have seen, the weekly average amount of viewing is around 24½ hours. However, time spent watching television does vary with social class, as does the choice of television channel. Item 7.16 indicates some of the findings from BBC audience research.

The table indicates that time spent watching television varies with social class, age and time of year. Those in social class A watch less television in both winter and summer than those in classes B and C.

▶ UNIT 25 Socialisation and attitude formation

25.1 Socialisation

The media do play an important role in the socialisation of children and, of course, in the continuing socialisation process of adult life. The media offer experiences and information not available otherwise. The images presented by the media of women, ethnic minorities, the aged, youth and other social groups have all been studied by sociologists.

ACTIVITIES 10

Read the letter in Item 7.17, written to *The Lancet* by two doctors at an East London hospital, and answer the questions that follow it.

1 Read the first two sentences again. Summarise in your own words exactly what it is the two doctors seem to be suggesting.

2 About how many drug overdoses might the doctors usually have expected to be admitted to their hospital during the week in question?

3 How many drug overdoses were admitted during that week?

4 Apart from the influence of the television programme *EastEnders* on the increased rate of drug overdosing in Hackney during that week, what other explanation do the doctors suggest might be a possible cause?

Soap may seriously damage your health

SIR – On Sunday, March 2, the omnibus edition of BBC Television's soap opera *EastEnders* showed the character Angie taking an overdose. In the following week we experienced a 300% increase in the number of patients attending the accident-and-emergency department at the Hackney Hospital in East London for deliberate overdose. This was the straw that nearly borke the camel's back. As in other hospitals in central London the number of our medical beds has lately been reduced and our bed state was critical. On Sunday night we were putting up beds to cope with the influx. The following week a 'yellow alert' was declared, resulting in the cancellation of routine admissions.

In the week after the *EastEnders* programme 22 patients attended the accident-and-emergency department having taken an overdose. During the previous ten weeks the average had been 6.9 ± 3.4 (SD) During the previous ten years the average for the week in question was 6.7 ± 1.6 (four years' figures unavailable). Perhaps the long spell of cold weather contributed to the increase in overdoses in Hackney, but the close temporal relation with the screening of an overdose on a programme which is widely viewed and purports to reflect real life in our part of London makes a causal relation seem likely.

In these days when cash limits are rationing care is it unreasonable to ask the BBC to contribute towards the extra cost they have caused the City and Hackney Health Authority? Do the BBC programmers consider the likely consequences of screening self-destructive behaviour that is likely to be copied? Next time, could they please arrange for Angie to take an overdose in the summer when our bed state is not so acute?

Department of Medicine,
Hackney Hospital,
London E9

SIMON J. ELLIS
SUSAN WELSH

from *The Lancet*, 22 March 1986

Item 7.17   A letter to *The Lancet*

Item 7.18   Angie from *EastEnders*

5 What do you think are the 'likely consequences of screening self-destructive behaviour'? Do you think it is likely to be copied as the doctors suggest? Do you think the BBC have any responsibilities to be careful about this sort of thing?

Sociologists are concerned with the impact of the media on individuals and their attitudes and behaviour, and on society, social control and social change more generally. The mass media, as we can see from examples such as the criticisms of the overdose scene on *EastEnders*, is often blamed for hooliganism, vandalism, drug-taking, violence, crime, mugging and so on. It has also been blamed for social prejudice and for promoting subordinate and inaccurate images of women. The mass media are also constantly accused of being politically biased in one way or another. These are not easy problems to study.

ACTIVITIES 11: Play-reading

Read the play-reading and answer the questions that follow.

(9 p.m. Front room of Kent household. Mrs Kent sits watching TV. Enter Bruce, 12-year-old son.)

Bruce   There's a programme on in ten minutes, Mum. Are you watching anything?

Mrs Kent   No, But what's wrong with the portable in your bedroom?

Bruce   Don't know. Can't get a decent picture. It's all fuzzy.

Mrs Kent   What's the programme?

Bruce   It's a film: *The Kung Fu Squad*.

Mrs Kent   No, Bruce. I don't think it's the sort of thing you want to watch.

Bruce   But I *do* want to watch it.

Mrs Kent   That's not what I meant. It's rubbish by the sound of it. It'll just give you a lot of violent fantasies.

Bruce   No it won't. I've seen *Superman* twice but I'm not daft enough to try and fly out of the window.

Mrs Kent   Don't be cheeky, now. It's not the same. You know it isn't. Those sorts of films are no better than comic strips, fantasies. We're trying to get you to appreciate more educational programmes.

Bruce   Oh, I like all those too – the nature ones and that, but these are just as interesting. You watch soap operas, don't you? They're not real life.

Mrs Kent   I'm older. Anyway they're not full of violence and sex – well, not very full. But they're fairly true to life.

Bruce   If they were really real they'd show everyone watching telly. Or else they'd be arguing about what to watch.

Mrs Kent   I'm sorry, Bruce, but I think violence on television affects people.

Bruce   If my portable was working I could've seen it on that. You wouldn't've known then.

Mrs Kent   But I know now. If that's the sort of thing you see at night I'm not sure we should've let you have it.

Bruce   Oh Mum, there's more violence and rape and so on on the news at six o'clock. They show riots and give details of crimes. If I was going to be disturbed I'd be disturbed by that.

Mrs Kent   That's real life, unfortunately, not a glamorous fantasy-style violence. When you have children, Bruce, you won't want them to grow up too fast – do you understand?

Bruce   But yesterday, Mum, after the news about that little girl who was found strangled, you had a long talk to me and Ann; and she's only eight. You said we had to know about these unpleasant things so we'd know what to be afraid of.

Mrs Kent   Yes, but I don't think your education will be damaged if you don't see this film.

121

Bruce   Oh Mum! *Please*, I won't become a vandal. I promise.
Mrs Kent   Look, I'll video it and then I'll talk to your Dad whether to let you see it, when he gets back from his karate class.
Bruce   OK, Mum, Goodnight.

1 Is Mrs Kent correct to worry about Bruce watching films like *The Kung Fu Squad*?

2 Is Bruce right to say that there is no difference between programmes like the news and violent films?

3 Explain your own feeling about the influence of the media on attitudes and behaviour.

25.2 Agenda setting

What do you think it means to say that the media has 'the power to set the agenda of the public debate'? Items 7.19 and 7.20 give two views on this.

Agenda-setting, then, is the name given to the idea that the media can determine what is discussed by people and what people think is important. This idea is only partially correct, according to sociologist Denis McQuail. He argues that while people do think *about* what they are told they do not think *what* they are told. In other words, evidence does seem to suggest that the order of importance attached to issues by the media is similar to the order of importance attached to issues by the public and politicians. For McQuail, it is equally believable that it is the concerns of the public which sharpen the concerns of the politicians and the media. The mass media probably help the 'agendas' of the public and politicians to meet but the mass media do not necessarily *set* the agenda.

25.3 The Falklands dispute

One fairly recent example of an attempt by the government to interfere with journalistic freedom happened during the Falklands dispute.

ACTIVITIES 12

Read Items 7.21 and 7.22. Then discuss in your class the role *you* think a reporter should play in the event of war, and whether you believe the public does have 'an unlimited right to know' in all circumstances.

Journalistic freedom

Today, more than ever, the duty of the broadcast reporter is to maintain his impartiality and his freedom from bias in seeking out and examining the truth about our world – but the truth as he thinks it is, not as he thinks it ought to be. His job – backed by the IBA – is to play fair and do his best to be impartial.

The power to set the agenda of public debate has always been regarded as the broadcaster's most important responsibility. He exercises it through his own professional news sense – an honest attempt to decide what to report in the public interest.

'If you ask me who decides what is the public interest I can only reply – the working journalist', writes Robert Hargreaves, a former news correspondent with ITN and now IBA Chief Assistant (Television). 'If he allows someone else to decide for him – the Government, a pressure group, the courts or an ideology – then he has forfeited his freedom. If you deny the journalist that choice, you deny one of the basic principles of democracy.'

from *IBA Guide 1986*

Item 7.19   From the IBA

'We have to balance different points of view in our programmes but not necessarily within each individual programme. Nothing is more stultifying than the current affairs programme in which all the opposing opinions cancel each other out. Sometimes one has to use that method but in general it makes for greater liveliness and impact if the balance can be achieved over a period, perhaps within a series of related programmes.'

Sir Hugh Greene, former Director-General of the BBC

from *BBC Annual Report and Handbook*, (BBC Enterprises Ltd, 1986)

Item 7.20   From the BBC

When I started on this assignment, the Ministry of Defence reached deep into its files and came up with a pile of greying forms printed in the fifties. They laid down the role of a war correspondent, told me that I was to be treated as an Army Captain, that I came under the orders of the Operational Commander, that I couldn't leave the battle zone without his permission, and was subject to military censorship. It also pointed out that the normal job of a correspondent was to publish information – the normal wish of the military was to keep it secret. It was a fair warning of the battles to come.

from Brian Hanrahan, 'On Being a War Correspondent.' *From Our Own Correspondent*, Saturday, 19 June 1982

Item 7.21   The role of a war correspondent

The man with the major responsibility for how the world should hear about the war, and how much it should be told, was Sir Frank Cooper, permanent under secretary at the ministry of defence. A powerfully-built former RAF pilot, whose long career in the civil service had included the rigours of the Northern Ireland office where control of information is a daily matter of life and death, Cooper was in no doubt where his first responsibility lay. 'Obviously the public has got a right to know,' he was to say later. 'But I do not think it has got an unlimited right to know. You have got to give a very high priority to the security of our forces and the success of our operations.'

Max Hastings, writing for the *Daily Express* and the London *Standard*, and filing a weekly column for the *Spectator* magazine, managed to send back eloquent and remarkably detailed stories. Somehow, wherever he was, he appeared to have access to communications in a way that others did not. Hastings' secret was partly to have established good relations early on with those officers he judged would be best placed to help ensure his stories got to the right place, and partly to file copy that was congenial to the army.

'Most of us decided before landing that our role was simply to report as sympathetically as possible what the British forces are doing here today,' he wrote in one story under a heading 'None of Us Can be Neutral in This War'. In justification he quoted his father, a noted war correspondent in the Second World War: 'When one's nation is at war, reporting becomes an extension of the war effort.'

from The Sunday Times Insight Team, *The Falklands War: The Full Story* (1982)

Item 7.22 Has the public an unlimited right to know?

Item 7.23 Page 3 girl

25.4 The creation of stereotypes

ACTIVITIES 13

Stereotypes are fixed pictures of what we expect certain people to be. They are a bit like police identikit pictures: a composite of characteristics making up an overall picture. We have stereotypes with which to view every type of behaviour in society from that of police officers to that of punk rockers. One of the main sources of our stereotypes is the media. Look at Items 7.23 and 7.24 and answer the questions that follow.

1 What worries do people have about the 'page 3' girls?

2 List all the arguments for and against the proposal that 'page 3' pictures 'incite people to commit crime'.

from *Daily News*, 18 February 1986

Item 7.24 Do Page 3 pin-ups influence people?

3 What kind of image of women do you think 'page 3' pictures convey to readers? Why might such pictures degrade women?

▶ UNIT **26** Control of the mass media

ACTIVITIES 14

Bring in a range of national newspapers for the same day and look at what news they cover, and what their editorials and political commentaries say. What political opinions does each newspaper express? What opinions do the majority express?

An analysis of the political viewpoint of our national newspapers shows that more than two thirds in numbers of publications, and three quarters in circulation terms, of the newspapers listed in Item 7.3 consistently express political opinions to the right of centre. The explanation may lie in the ownership of most newspapers by a handful of millionaires or wealthy shareholders. As in other industries, there has been a trend in the media towards larger business corporations. Glover, a sociologist who has written about the mass media, argues that a very high percentage of what we see, hear and read comes from a small number of extremely large companies. Look again at Item 7.3 and list each newspaper under the company which controls it. You should see, for example, that News International (owned by a media proprietor called Rupert Murdoch) owns the *Sun, The Times* and the *News of the World*. It is clear, therefore, that News International is an extremely powerful company owning newspapers with high circulation figures.

Sociologists have argued that this kind of development in the ownership and control of the press leads to its one-sidedness and its support for the capitalist, ruling or dominant social classes. Sociologists do not suggest that this is a simple conspiracy – that the ruling classes consciously manipulate the media – but the cost of starting a new newspaper is extremely high and more or less prohibits alternative or minority opinions having effective coverage. The fierce competition for readers reduces the number of titles to choose from and ensures a safe and conservative outlook and editorial stance.

The problems posed by these features of the ownership and control of the media are recognised by the government. The law provides safeguards against the concentration of ownership of mass media in too few hands. It is not permitted, for example, for a local newspaper with monopoly in a certain area to have a controlling interest in the local radio station. It is also unlawful for a newspaper proprietor to acquire assets in other newspapers, if the resultant circulation exceeds 500 000, without first getting the written consent of the Secretary of State for Trade and Industry, who may well refer the matter to the Monopolies and Mergers Commission.

REVIEW

If you have studied and understood this chapter you should be able to . . .

- explain clearly the difference between popular newspapers, and quality newspapers.
- give an account of the way newspaper readership is affected by social class.
- give a simple account of Britain's television viewing habits.
- explain, with examples of your own, the way newspapers and television contribute to the process of socialisation.
- give a short explanation of the idea of agenda setting by the media.
- define or explain the word 'stereotype'.
- give examples of the role the media plays in creating stereotypes.
- give an account of the arguments for and against the idea that the mass media are to blame for crimes of violence.
- explain why the media tend to be conservative in outlook.
- outline in a paragraph how the government attempts to safeguard against owners of mass media becoming too powerful.

COURSEWORK SUGGESTION

As part of its continuing programme of audience research the BBC asked viewers to say which of 16 elements of a programme they found most offensive. Virtually all the 2639 adults who kept diaries for this research found at least one of the things listed in Item 7.25 offensive, and as many as 60 per cent found up to six, or even more, of them offensive. The results are shown in Item 7.25.

	Offensive (%)	Very Offensive (%)	Total (%)
Programmes of such poor quality that they were an insult to the viewers' intelligence	46	15	61
'Invasions of privacy' by over-enthusiastic reporters	41	9	50
Rudeness by interviewers	40	6	46
Unneccesary violence or brutality	35	10	45
Bad language, swearing	33	9	42
Parents shouting at or hitting children	36	6	42
Rudeness to the Royal Family	36	6	42
Deliberate exploitation of the human weaknesses of people	33	6	39
Making fun of religion	32	7	39
Inept or incompetent performance by actors, singers, comedians, etc.	33	5	38
Plays or films in which sex seems to be the only concern of the characters	29	9	38
People talking about intimate matters like their sex lifes	24	7	31
Misuse of the English language by those who ought to know better	25	3	28
People in pain	24	3	27
'Smuttiness' in comedy programmes	22	4	26
Nudity or semi-nudity	18	5	23

from *Annual Review of BBC Audience Research Findings*, 4 (1976)

Item 7.25   Proportions finding elements in programmes offensive

	1st choice (%)	1st, 2nd or 3rd choice (%)
For me, the *best* thing about television is that		
– it provides reliable, up-to-date information about what is going on in the world	41	75
– it gives me the opportunity I wouldn't otherwise have of seeing good plays, sporting events, Royal occasions, and so on	24	65
– it is the ideal way to relax in your spare time	12	40
– it brings the fun, glamour and excitement of 'show business' into your own home	3	20
– it is great company	9	31
– it really shows you what life is like and how other people live	5	43
No choice made	6	
	100	

from *Annual Review of BBC Audience Research Findings*, 4 (1976)

Item 7.26   The 'best things' about television

	1st choice (%)	1st, 2nd or 3rd choice (%)
For me, the *worst* thing about television is that		
– it stops me doing things in my spare time, like reading, gardening, odd jobs, etc.	17	40
– it stops us talking to one another in the home	17	43
– many programmes seem to encourage people to do things that I think are wrong, like swearing, being rude, being violent, and so on	20	47
– it undermines our society by paying too much attention to extremists and protesters	11	41
– it makes 'little tin gods' of people who are good at expressing themselves on the screen	6	32
– it discourages people from finding ways of entertaining themselves	22	68
No choice made	7	
	100	

from *Annual Review of BBC Audience Research Findings*, 4 (1976)

Item 7.27   The 'worst things' about television

Viewers were also asked to select the 'best things' and the 'worst things' about the television from a short list of possibilities. The precise question was 'Most of us would probably agree with most of the following points of view, but if you had to choose only two or three as being *the best things of all* about television for you, which ones would they be?''. People were asked to indicate their first, second and third choice. The same format was also used to discover the three things people thought were the worst of all about television.

The results achieved by this BBC research are given in Items 7.26 and 7.27. You could use this approach to discovering people's reactions to television as a starting point for a research project of your own.

ASSESSMENT QUESTION

This question is worth 15 marks. The mark allocations to sections of the question are shown in the right hand margin.

a What do you understand by the term 'mass media'? Give three examples.   (4)

b Why are sociologists interested in the mass media?   (5)

c In what ways could the mass media be said to influence behaviour?   (6)

London & East Anglian Group for GCSE Examinations

8 Politics

AIMS

At the end of this chapter you should be able to:

- identify different forms and sources of 'power' in Britain.
- show an awareness of the British political system.
- understand the nature of democracy, in Britain and elsewhere.
- explain alternative ways of participating in the political process.
- recognise the process and agencies of political socialisation.
- identify and describe the main factors affecting voting behaviour.
- interpret critically the results of opinion polls.

 ## UNIT 27 Power

Politics is really about power. Every political party wants to be the party in power – to win enough seats in Parliament so that they can form the *government* (rather than the *opposition*) so that they can make the decisions and policies. Political parties have to win power in an election. If the election is seen to be 'fair' then most people will accept the result – even if they do not like it. However, winning power in an election is not the only way to achieve it.

ACTIVITIES 1

Look at the photographs in Item 8.1 overleaf and see if you can explain the source of each person's 'power'.

As you have discovered for yourselves power is sometimes won by physical dominance over others, or sometimes by holding the purse strings and therefore having economic dominance over others. It may be that a person's position in an organisation gives him or her administrative or bureaucratic power over others, which contrasts with the power certain personalities and characters have simply because of who and what they are – people who, like Hitler and Christ, attract power by their *charismatic* or inspirational enthusiasm.

You will also have found that 'power' is not just about political parties. Power and politics are part of everyday life. In your family, friendship groups and places of work, power, politics and decision-making all play an important role. Although our emphasis in this chapter will be on national political organisations like political parties and pressure groups, you should be able to relate a lot of the ideas to the politics of your own everyday life.

A sociologist called Clive Harber listed examples of different ways power can be expressed in families, among friends and at school. He distinguishes between power used to influence people against their

Item 8.1   People with power of different kinds

will, and power which might be based on 'authority' – that is, power which is seen to be fair and acceptable. Harber notes four ways of forcing people to do something against their will: by persuasion, by threat of non-co-operation, by economic punishments or rewards, and by physical threat. Max Weber (see topic 6.2) described the three ways in which a person can have authority. Traditional authority is handed down, and has always been accepted as proper and fair. Charismatic authority, as we mentioned above, stems from a person's personality and character – which might be 'magnetic', inspiring and exciting. Others are given authority simply because of the type of person they are.

ACTIVITIES 2

Study Item 8.2 and answer the questions that follow.

1 Apart from the teachers, who else has authority within your school? Make a list and include the kind of authority you think each person has: traditional, charismatic or legal.

2 Item 8.2 shows that different teachers at different times may have to rely on all three types of authority. Upon what basis for authority might a teacher prefer to rely? Explain your answer.

3 List other people who might have to rely on tradition, charisma or the law at different times in order to do their job with the authority they need.

4 Try to give an example of your own for each of the entries in Item 8.2.

When we talk about 'the government' we usually mean the people who control the affairs of the nation in Parliament. The kind of government that we have in power is important because it can directly change

		Family	Friends	School
Authority	Traditional	Father as traditional authority in family.	His brother was leader of the gang before him.	Teacher at the school for ages.
	Charismatic	Older child with strong personality takes over from a weak parent.	Leader of the gang because of a strong personality.	Teacher controls 'difficult' class because of his/her popularity.
	Legal	Child taken into care by the state.	Gang leader always elected by the members.	Headmaster recognised as having ultimate authority in school by the state.
Power	Persuasion	Father offers sound advice on son's career.	One member of group can out-talk/argue all the others.	'Bad' pupil persuaded to see the error of his/her ways.
	Non co-operation	Child refuses to behave unless given sweets.	Refuses to go to pictures with mates unless they go to the film he wants to see.	Refuses to work normally in class unless allowed to sit where he wants.
	Economic	No homework done, no pocket money given.	I bought the ball, I choose the sides.	School prizes.
	Physical	Smack and to bed.	Bully.	Cane.

from C. Brown, *A Handbook of Political Education* (Association of Teachers of Social Sciences, 1986)

Item 8.2   What is power?

our lives and the way in which society is organised. Our study of politics will be the study of people who have power or who seek to exercise power in society and the way in which they are able to influence events.

Many of the words used in government and politics are taken from the language of the Ancient Greeks, whose civilisation was one of the first to experience many different kinds of government and to produce writing about political ideas. The word *politics* comes from the Greek *polis*, meaning a city; the ways in which different city-states were governed introduce us to some of the concepts of politics. When Athens was at its highest point of civilisation and power, in the fifth century BC, it was governed by an assembly of male citizens who decided all matters of policy and leadership by vote. Because Athens was governed by citizens (even though women and slaves were excluded) it was known as a *democracy*, from the word *demos*, meaning people. In Ancient Athens it was possible for all citizens to gather in one place, for each to be heard, and for them to take decisions.

ACTIVITIES 3

Think of a small group you belong to. It may be a formal group such as a youth club, or it may be just a small group of your friends at school. Describe as best you can the process of making decisions in your group. You may be unaware decisions are being made, but whether you all decide to buy crisps, stay in class or wander round the school at break is the result of some kind of group decision. These things do not just happen!

1 How is the decision made?

2 Who has the power to make the decisions for the group?

3 Is that power shared?

4 Where does that power come from?

In modern states with populations numbering millions no such direct participation in democracy is possible. In democracies today representatives are chosen to conduct the affairs of government on behalf of the electors.

When political attitudes are discussed we use the words 'left' and 'right' to denote how radical or how conservative these attitudes are. These words originated with the French National Assembly in the late eighteenth century. After the French Revolution in 1789 the National Assembly sat in a semicircle with the more extreme revolutionaries on the left and the more moderate politicians ranged towards the right. At Westminster the MPs sit either side of an aisle; the government and their parliamentary colleagues sit on the right hand side while the opposition sits on the left.

Just as there are constant changes in party policies, so too do politicians move along the left-right axis. In general terms parliamentary politicians adopt attitudes which are more to the centre than those of the rank and file membership of the political parties. *Rank and file membership* means the ordinary party members in the constituencies who do not work at politics full time. Politics is sometimes said to be the art of compromise, and when the reality of power and responsibility is felt many politicians tone down their previously expressed views and become more moderate.

Democracy can only really survive when the media are free to comment upon and criticise the actions of all politicians. As governments are answerable to the people at each general election they cannot afford to ignore public opinion too often on too many issues. The principal difficulties in maintaining democracy in a country of over 50 million people with only 650 representatives are to ensure participation through the existing system and to enable the public to make its voices heard. Such participation may take place through the political parties, or through a variety of interest groups, as we shall see.

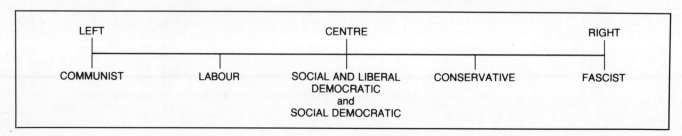

Item 8.3   Party positions in British politics

UNIT 28 Politics in the UK

Item 8.4   The Houses of Parliament

28.1 The institutional structure of the UK political system

Central government in the UK meets in the Houses of Parliament at Westminster. Parliament is divided into two *chambers*: the House of Commons and the House of Lords. Of these the House of Commons is the more important. It comprises 650 Members of Parliament who have been elected by the adult population. Each MP represents an area or *constituency* in the UK which contains an approximate average population of some 60 000 electors. Since 1872 voting for MPs has been by secret ballot.

Almost all the MPs belong to one of the major political parties: Labour, Conservative, Social and Liberal Democratic or Social Democratic. The party which has the largest number of MPs in the Commons usually forms the government because, being in the majority, it can best put its policies into action. After an election the leader of the party which has the most MPs is asked by the Queen to become Prime Minister, and to select members of his or her party to form the government.

Item 8.5   Voting

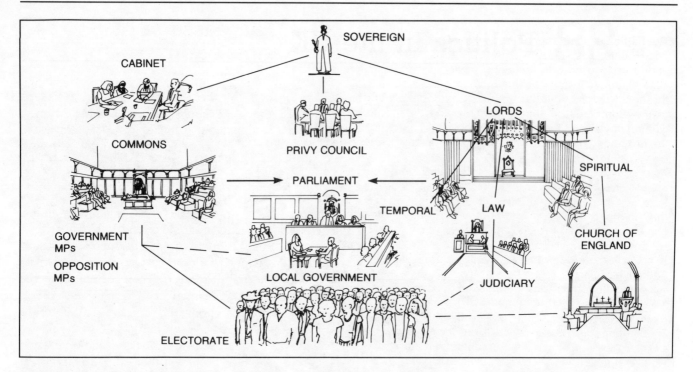

Item 8.6 Government in the UK

The government consists of MPs who have been chosen by the Prime Minister to run various ministries or departments of state. Ministers or secretaries of state are responsible for introducing any new laws in the form of *Acts of Parliament* (known as bills until they have passed through Parliament) concerning their departments, and for carrying out the wishes of Parliament with the help of civil servants. The second largest party in Parliament is known as the *opposition*, since its members seek to criticise and oppose many of the measures that the Government may introduce. Although they rarely succeed in defeating the government in a straight vote, they are constantly ready to take over and form a government should they win in an election. As an alternative government their leaders are sometimes referred to as the *Shadow Cabinet*.

Key terms

- government
- opposition
- central government
- Houses of Parliament
- House of Commons
- House of Lords
- constituency
- Act of Parliament

The House of Lords

The House of Lords contains three types of *peer* or lord: the *Lords Spiritual*, who are the two Archbishops of the Church of England and another 24 senior bishops; the *Lords Temporal* who hold hereditary titles (dukes, marquesses, earls, viscounts and barons), or who are people who have been given peerages for life only, under the Life Peerages Act of 1958, and who do not pass their title on to their heirs. The third group of peers are the *Law Lords* who are the most senior judges of appeal. Altogether about a thousand hereditary peers are entitled to sit in the Lords, but only a minority choose to attend. Most of the business in the Lords is conducted by the life peers who are usually elder statesmen and came to prominence in political life when they were MPs in the Commons. The principal function of the Lords is to have a second look at legislation from the Commons and to suggest constructive amendments to it. The Lords have the power to delay a bill for up to one year, but this is rarely used.

ACTIVITIES 4

Item 8.7 is an extract from Tony Benn's writings about the House of Lords.

The battle between the people and the Lords is an old one. Painfully, stage by stage, the Lords' Veto was ended in 1910 and the delaying power cut again in 1948. Changes in composition have also been carried through. Now the time has come to develop the work of the Commons so that it can replace the Lords without any loss of Parliamentary scrutiny. This is not an argument based on the political balance as it exists in the House of Peers. It is because it is inherently wrong that the Laws of this land should be submitted for approval to a body of men and women who lack any democratic mandate at all. It is not just that an inherited seat in Parliament is an anachronism – though it is. It is that the powers of patronage which are used by Prime Ministers to place people into Parliament by personal preferment are equally offensive.

Let me illustrate my argument with figures. The 635 MPs elected to the Commons in 1974 were put there by an electorate totalling just over 40 million people. By comparison 639 peers were put in the House of Lords by the last seven Prime Ministers. It cannot be right that seven men – however distinguished – can wield the same power to make legislators as do forty million voters. The simplest way to cut out this patronage is to end the Chamber which lives on it. I believe there would be strong public support for Parliamentary democracy to be strengthened in this way, and the day will come when it will be done.

Tony Benn, MP, in *Teaching Politics*

from L. Robins, T. Brennan and J. Sutton, *People and Politics in Britain* (Macmillan, 1985)

Item 8.7   Should the Lords be abolished?

1 What does the writer mean when he says:
   a the House of Lords lacks a 'political mandate'?
   b Prime Ministers have 'powers of patronage'?

2 How is the composition of the House of Lords decided?

3 What advantages does a 'second chamber' have for Britain?

Key terms

- House of Lords
- peer
- Lords Spiritual
- Lords Temporal
- Law Lords

28.2 The passage of legislation

Almost all new legislation starts from the *Cabinet*, which consists of the Prime Minister and his or her most senior colleagues. It is only some 20 or so of the most important ministers and secretaries of state who meet regularly at 10 Downing Street to discuss matters of policy. The Cabinet is chaired by the Prime Minister. It is possible for an individual MP to introduce new legislation through a *private member's bill* but it has little chances of success unless the government is prepared to lend its support.

Before a bill becomes an Act and therefore part of the law it is considered on three occasions, known as *readings*. The first reading is just a formality; at the second reading the general principles of the bill are debated in the Commons; then it passes to a committee of MPs for further examination before it passes back to the Commons for a third and final debate. If the measure has been approved in all its three readings in the Commons it goes to the Lords where the procedure is repeated. Finally it is sent to the Queen for formal signature (known as the *Royal Assent*), after which the bill becomes an Act of Parliament and hence part of the law of the land. See Item 8.8.

Royalty plays very little part in government. The Sovereign is the symbolic Head of State, whose most important governmental function today is confined to the right to advise and warn governments on various aspects of their policies.

ACTIVITIES 5

If you were a backbench MP who wanted to put forward a private member's bill and you had your name drawn out of the ballot, what new law would you try to get passed? Which other people or groups might you get to help you? How would you muster support for your cause?

28.3 The separation of powers

Ministers and their Civil Service departments are termed the *executive* because they execute, or carry out and see through, the wishes of Parliament. Parliament is known as the *legislature* because it makes changes in the law and may introduce new

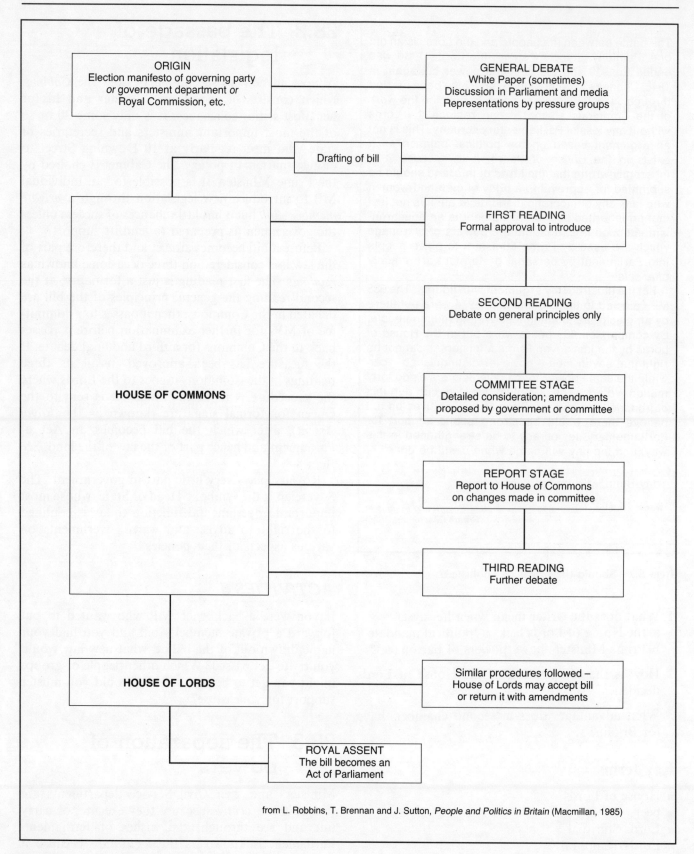

ORIGIN
Election manifesto of governing party
or government department *or*
Royal Commission, etc.

GENERAL DEBATE
White Paper (sometimes)
Discussion in Parliament and media
Representations by pressure groups

Drafting of bill

HOUSE OF COMMONS

FIRST READING
Formal approval to introduce

SECOND READING
Debate on general principles only

COMMITTEE STAGE
Detailed consideration; amendments
proposed by government or committee

REPORT STAGE
Report to House of Commons
on changes made in committee

THIRD READING
Further debate

HOUSE OF LORDS

Similar procedures followed –
House of Lords may accept bill
or return it with amendments

ROYAL ASSENT
The bill becomes an
Act of Parliament

from L. Robbins, T. Brennan and J. Sutton, *People and Politics in Britain* (Macmillan, 1985)

Item 8.8   From bill to statute

legislation. If there is any dispute about the interpretation of the law the *judiciary* or judges decide the dispute.

Checklist

1 The executive is the ministers and civil servants who carry out the wishes of Parliament.

2 The legislature is Parliament, which makes and changes the law of the land.

3 The judiciary is the system of law courts and judges who interpret the law and give judgements in cases and disputes.

The highest court in the land is found in the House of Lords (see Chapter 10). The three branches of government (legislative, executive, judicial) are complementary to each other, but are separate. Although Parliament (the legislature) is theoretically supreme, the government (executive) is able to function efficiently because it commands a majority of supporters in the Commons. The judiciary is independent of the legislature and executive. While the executive is given considerable power to govern it is, nevertheless, ultimately answerable to the legislature, the sovereign, and possibly to the judiciary. Should a government seek to extend its authority and become no longer answerable to the legislature (that is, to members of Parliament and hence to the electorate)

it would become undemocratic. A general election must be held at least every five years, though governments rarely remain in office for the full period. The electorate, therefore, is able to express its approval or disapproval of the government's policies at regular intervals.

28.4 Post-war Prime Ministers

As leaders of their political parties and leaders of the country, Prime Ministers are important and powerful people. Their power derives from their majority support in Parliament and their right to choose their own ministers and government. The chart in Item 8.9 shows the changes in government and Prime Ministers the UK has experienced since World War II.

28.5 Local government

The central government at Westminster directs and controls the affairs of the nation as a whole, but a large number of the functions of government are either shared with local authorities or directed entirely on a local level. This makes for more administrative efficiency, and regional and local needs are best met by local democracy because they vary greatly. The basic functions of local government may

Item 8.9 Changes in government since 1945

Elections	Period of Office	Prime Minister	Party	
		Churchill		defeated 1945
1945	1945–50	Attlee	Labour	re-elected 1950
1950	1950–1	Attlee	Labour	defeated 1951
1951	1951–5	Churchill	Conservative	retired aged 81 before 1955 election
1955	1955–7	Eden	Conservative	retired ill 1957
1959	1957–63	Macmillan	Conservative	retired ill 1963
	1963–4	Douglas-Home	Conservative	defeated 1964
1964	1964–6	Wilson	Labour	re-elected 1966
1966	1966–70	Wilson	Labour	defeated 1970
1970	1970–4	Heath	Conservative	defeated 1974
1974	1974–6	Wilson	Labour	retired aged 60 1976
	1976–9	Callaghan	Labour	defeated 1979
1979	1979–83	Thatcher	Conservative	re-elected 1983
1983	1983–6	Thatcher	Conservative	re-elected 1986
1986	1986–?	Thatcher	Conservative	

Item 8.10 The UK's post-war Prime Ministers: top Attlee, Churchill, Eden, middle Macmillan, Douglas-Home, Wilson, bottom Heath, Callaghan, Thatcher

be divided into three categories:

personal: education; health and welfare;
environmental: planning, housing and roads; and
protectional: weights and measures, the police and
fire services.

There are several sources of income to meet the
costs of local government. More than a third of the
revenue comes from government grants, a quarter
from the rates, another quarter from loans, and the
rest is made up from services that councils provide
and charge for, such as car parking. Education
accounts for half of local government spending.

Although so much of our daily lives is affected by
the decisions taken in local council chambers, very
few people seem to take much interest in local
politics and government. The average percentage of
the local population voting for the councillors, who
serve for four years, is between 30 and 40 per cent: in
some places it falls as low as ten per cent. Compare
this with France, where three quarters of the electorate of Paris often vote in their local elections. A
survey conducted for the Committee on Management of Local Government found that a quarter of
the electorate were unable to name just one service
provided by their local authority!

ACTIVITIES 6

1 Find out as much as you can about the rates,
spending and services of your own local authority.
If you write to your town hall or council offices,
you should find your council are willing to send
you, free of charge, information about their income and expenditure in a year.

2 Write a short, open-ended questionnaire and complete a survey of local residents or your neighbours
to discover how much they know about the council
services, income and expenditure.

Lack of interest in local affairs is coupled with a
lack of knowledge about local government. The
better informed may be aware of the functions of
local government but may feel that all the real
decisions taken in government are made in Whitehall
and not their local town hall. A healthy democracy
requires that there is public interest and participation
in all levels of government, both national and local.
Later units in this chapter look at different ways of
participating in politics.

▶ UNIT 29 Participation in UK politics

29.1 Political parties, beliefs and policies

ACTIVITIES 7

1 Make a list of party policies with three headings,
Labour, Conservative and the centre parties such
as the Social and Liberal Democrats and the Social
Democratic Party. Under each heading list the
kind of things you think each party wants and
the values you think it holds, when it comes to
education, defence, employment, trade unions, the
economy, law and order and so on. Even though
you may not be sure of the facts, put in your list
the impressions you have got from television,
newspapers and discussions with friends and
family.

2 Now look at Item 8.11 which shows the difference
between the parties and their different values and
policies. These differences stem from their different
beliefs and philosophies, so the table continues to
apply although it was drawn up to reflect positions
in 1983. (You will find this hard, so select just a few
of the headings.)

The cartoons in Item 8.12 on page 140 illustrate
how most people are unaware of party issues and
philosophies and are more interested in their own
immediate worries and problems.

Item 8.11 Values, policies and the political spectrum: positions in 1983

	Labour		SDP–Liberal	Conservative	
	Left	Right	Alliance	'Wet'	Right wing

Values

1. *Human nature*

Optimistic view of human nature in socialist context. Selfishness and other faults reflection of capitalist system.	Man both selfish and altruistic. Social and economic changes can produce limited improvement.			Man self-seeking but responds to certain changes in environment. Opposed to 'social engineering'	Pessimistic view of human nature in general and sceptical of possibilities for change

2. *Equality and liberty*

Equality the major political goal. Less concerned with 'liberties' which enable the strong to exploit the weak.	Pro-equality but not at expense of basic democratic values	Reduce inequalities where possible but not at expense of basic liberties		Equality a desirable goal but some inequality inevitable and liberty a more precious value	Inequality inevitable and to some extent desirable. Individual liberties sacrosanct, especially the economic ones

3. *Authority*

Anti-authority, privileged elites and excessive patriotism	Anti-privilege but accept 'establishment' institutions			Pro: authority, elites, family, traditional institutions and patriotism	

4. *Change*

Radical change possible and essential	Radical economic change possibly desirable but only gradual change possible or advisable	Some radical non-economic changes necessary and possible but in general gradual change best		Radical change to right or left not desirable or possible. Gradual evolutionary change best	Radical change desirable and necessary in some respects

Policies

5. *Economy*

Neo-Marxist Extension of State control to reduce (and ultimately eliminate) private sector. Vigorous intervention to stimulate growth. Workers' control at all levels. Free collective bargaining. No incomes policy	*Modified Keynesianism* Mixed economy with government planning of developments. Some control if money supply. Minimal further nationalisation. Centralised incomes policy to prevent inflation and facilitate growth.	*Keynesianism* Mixed economy, economic planning on decentralised basis. SDP pro-growth but Libs more concerned with post-industrial society. Emphasis on worker participation. Long-term incomes policy essential.		*Modified Keynesianism* Mixed economy, with intervention only where absolutely necessary. Encourage private sector in every way. Incomes policy to keep inflation in check	*Monetarist* Ideally a market economy unfettered by government controls. Tight control of money supply. Denationalisation where possible. Free collective bargaining, as incomes policies penalise the efficient and productive

6. *Employment*

Full employment through stimulated economy, with extensive training schemes. Import controls to protect ailing industries from foreign competition	Acceptance of some unemployment as inevitable product of poor economic performance but, as Heath said in 1981, 3 million unemployed is 'morally unacceptable'. Training and job creation measures to supplement government-led expansion of the economy. Selective import controls only, for fear of provoking retaliation by other countries.				Acceptance of unemployment for present as aid to 'realistic' wage demands; inevitable prerequisite for move towards low inflation, competitive and expanding economy. Government scheme to alleviate hardship. No import controls. '

7. *Trade unions*

No legal restrictions on activities. Government to consult closely on wide range of policies.	Some legal restrictions on trade union activities. Close co-operation when in government	New consensus with employers and unions, but union reform a priority: legal framework giving statutory rights to trade unions in exchange for defined limits on industrial action		Some legal restraints but emphasis on voluntary agreements and building of consensus	Tough legislation to restrict picketing, ban closed shop, remove trade union immunities and weaken link with Labour Party

| Labour | | SDP–Liberal Alliance | Conservative | |
Left	Right		'Wet'	Right wing
8. *Taxation* High taxes on rich, including wealth tax on personal fortunes	Reasonable taxes which do not destroy incentives. Wealth tax desirable, too difficult to implement	Reasonable taxes compatible with economic prosperity	Reduce taxes to level compatible with current levels of economic prosperity	Low taxes to give work incentives. Low public spending to help control money supply and encourage private sector
9. *Social services* High spending on social services. Increase benefits and index-link them to inflation	High spending on social services but cut if economy declines. Increase benefits: index-link to inflation	High spending on social services as far as economic prosperity allows	Favour private welfare sector (e.g. 'pay beds') but support efficient welfare state	Encouragement of private welfare schemes as possible substitute for State system but in favour of welfare 'safety net'. Oppose index linkage. Unemployment pay too high in some cases
10. *Education* Abolish private sector. Universal comprehensive education	In theory against private sector but in practice reluctant to move against it. Pro-comprehensive	Withdraw support for private sector but not abolish. (Shirley Williams favours abolition.) Reform exam system	Anti-comprehensive but will not abolish. Pro-private sector	Staunch defenders of private sector and maintenance of 'excellence' in educational system
11. *Law and order and civil rights* Opposed to extension of police powers. Pro-civil rights. Tendency to see criminal as victim. Anti-immigration controls	Cautious about police powers but firm on need for order. In favour of some immigration controls	Cautious about police powers, liberal on penal reform. Pro-individual liberties	Favour strong police force – see society as criminal's victim. Some controls on immigration	Very pro-police and anti-criminal. In favour of harsh sentences. Not so sympathetic to race relations legislation, in favour of controls on immigration if not repatriation
12. *EEC* Urge withdrawal from 'capitalist club' of EEC	In favour of staying in EEC, but with some doubts	Strongly pro-Europe: favours some form of EEC institutions. Liberals favour federal Europe	Pro-EEC: in favour of reform of budget structure, particularly Common Agricultural Policy	Pro-EEC, with some doubts and some outright opponents
13. *Defence* Low spending: unilateral nuclear disarmament. Anti-NATO and US foreign policy. Neutralist	Maintain current levels of defence spending. Multilateral disarmament. Pro-NATO. Opposed to Trident missiles	Maintain defence spending. Multilateral disarmament. Pro-NATO, anti-Trident. Unilateral disarmament lobby in both parts of Alliance	Increase spending if possible. Pro-NATO and Trident missiles. Multilateral disarmament	High spending. Very firm stance against Soviet Union. Very pro-NATO
14. *Structure of Government* Strong centralised institutions combined with open government, greater participation and accountability at all levels. Abolish House of Lords. Anti-PR [proportional representation] in general	More favourable to devolution. More elitist than left and tolerant of existing bureaucratic procedures. Reform but not abolish Lords. Anti-PR but some support	Decentralisation. Devolved regional authorities. Elected House of Lords. Open government. Very pro-PR. More power to local government: 'community' politics	Centralised elitist tradition. Lukewarm on devolution. Reform House of Lords. Some support for PR. Reform rates system	Elitist tradition. Opposed to devolution and elected House of Lords. Anti-PR

from Bill Jones & Dennis Kavanagh eds, *British Politics Today: a student's guide* (Manchester University Press, 1983)

Item 8.12   Taking politics to the people

From *SDP Birmingham Newsletter*, August 1986

29.2 Membership of political parties

Most of the constituency parties' business is concerned with local politics. At election time, party officials called *agents* and volunteers try to persuade the voters to come to the polls in support of their party. (Agents are often full time and paid in marginal constituencies, that is, constituencies without a clear majority for any one party.)

Each of the political parties holds an annual national conference, usually in the autumn, to debate issues of national policy. The *parliamentary party* – the party's MPs – has a considerable influence on party policy as most of the leading politicians in a party are MPs or members of the government. Yet the parliamentary parties cannot really afford to ignore the wishes of the ordinary constituency members on too many issues. The candidate is selected by the local organisation, and must pay some attention to the party workers in his or her constituency to keep their enthusiasm and support. The candidate must also look after all of the people in the constituency, whether or not they voted for him or her.

29.3 Politics outside the parties

Interest groups

Outside party politics, certain groups can exercise an influence on government and society. These groups are sometimes known as *pressure groups* or *interest groups*.

Interest groups can play an important part in society. Some examples of interest groups are: trade unions, the RSPCA (Royal Society for Prevention of Cruelty to Animals), the AA (Automobile Association), the NCCL (National Council for Civil Liberties), Shelter and the CBI (Confederation of British Industries). Almost every adult is a member of one interest group or another.

ACTIVITIES 8

1 To which interest groups might the following belong? You might list more than one.
   a motorists
   b consumers
   c ornithologists

2 Choose any one interest group or pressure group. Find out its address and send a large stamped self-addressed envelope asking for details and copies of any free literature which might be available.

3 Write a short piece, in the style of an article for your local newspaper or school magazine, about your chosen interest group or pressure group. Explain their ideas and why you have chosen your particular group for your article.

When a government is preparing a bill to put before Parliament it often consults the interest groups whose members may be affected by the measures contained in the bill. For example, the government may discuss proposals for new traffic legislation with such groups as the AA, the RAC (Royal Automobile Club), ROSPA (Royal Society for the Prevention of Accidents), and the Motor Manufacturers' Association. Interest groups may choose a variety of methods to win support. They may make direct appeals to MPs by writing to them and inviting them to attend functions where the interest groups will put their cases. Sometimes such groups try to win over public opinion by placing advertisements in newspapers or by writing to the press. Demonstrations and marches are another means of gaining publicity.

There are two kinds of interest group: those who act defensively to protect their members' interests if

these appear threatened, and those that try to promote a cause. The *protective* groups are trade unions, professional associations, and groups that may seek to protect individuals unable to look after themselves (for example, the NSPCC was created to prevent cruelty to children). *Promotional* groups are more concerned with getting things done, to promote or amend legislation which they feel will benefit society, or more directly themselves. Broadly, therefore, protective groups are concerned with the interests of individuals, and promotional groups seek a wider appeal for their causes.

Checklist

Interest groups can be of two kinds:

1 *protective groups* which aim to defend and safeguard their members, such as trade unions.

2 *promotional groups* which attempt to push the interest of particular groups and gain support for particular ideas or causes, such as CND (the Campaign for Nuclear Disarmament).

As in the political parties, members of interest groups may be drawn from many different walks of life. The main difference between interest groups and political parties is that interest groups have limited aims and do not seek power at Westminster.

Item 8.13   An interest group in action

A criticism of interest groups is that they may be undemocratic. Protective groups do not claim to represent anyone but their own members, and an interest group which is well organised and well financed is more likely to be successful than one which is poorly led and has a small budget. This means that various interests are not equally represented. For example, the motorists are well represented, but pedestrians, who are in the majority, are not able to exercise as much influence on governments. A strong trade union in a key sector of the economy may be able to make its strength felt, but old age pensioners have no industrial action at their disposal.

On the other hand, in an age of mass media and a developed technology and bureaucracy, interest groups may be able to inform governments of matters and issues which might otherwise have escaped their attention. We could therefore say interest groups are participating in and contributing to the wider democratic process. Electors do not vote specifically for each item on a political party's manifesto, so it may be that membership of an interest group looks after people's specific concerns and enables them to press for action on matters which were not covered in the election manifesto.

29.4 The resort to violence

ACTIVITIES 9

Read the account in Item 8.14 of newspapers' reactions to violence in politics.

1 What does the writer say all newspapers and both the BBC and IBA have in common?

2 What does it mean to say certain organisations are 'beyond the pale'?

3 What does Terry Ann Knopf mean when she says 'both the general public and the media prefer the myth of orderly peaceful change'?

ACTIVITIES 10

Read Item 8.15 and answer the questions that follow.

1 What does the writer mean when he says that in war 'you recognise the legitimacy of your opponent'?

Beyond the pale?

Whichever newspaper you read, there is one important strand which is common to all in their coverage of political news; they share an unswerving belief in parliamentary democracy as the only legitimate channel for effecting social and political change in the UK. It is a commitment which transcends their different political orientations and is also shared by both BBC and IBA networks. This is not to say that all other expressions of dissent are routinely ruled out of court, however. The ideology of the media is sufficiently liberal to recognize that many views and opinions exist over many issues and that these may be legitimately expressed outside parliament through; for example, peaceful campaigns. In other words, while certain newspapers may not agree with the views of CND or civil rights demonstrators they respect the rights of those marchers as long as they, themselves, respect the sovereignty of the rule of law and the democratic processes which it underwrites. Once dissent takes on a violent face, however, and the demonstrators begin to take direct political action then, quite regardless of the legitimacy of the grievance, those people and their organizations are declared as being 'beyond the pale'. Terry Ann Knopf makes a similar point:

> Both the general public and the media share the same dislike of protestors: both are unable to understand violence as an expression of protest against oppressive conditions: both prefer the myth of orderly, peaceful change, extolling the virtues of private property and peaceful decorum. People are expected to behave in a certain way; they just don't go around yelling or cursing or throwing rocks (1970, p. 858).

The most vivid and dramatic example of this process is provided by the media's coverage of the IRA: having taken the law into its own hands and embarked on a strategy of 'indiscriminate' bombing, the organization is unanimously condemned in the media; discussion of the legitimacy, or otherwise, of the IRA's grievances is firmly subordinated to a consideration of how the organization can be repressed.

from Ellis E. Cashmore and Barry Troyna, *Introduction to Race Relations* (Routledge & Kegan Paul, 1983)

Item 8.14 Newspapers' reactions to violence in politics

2 Use the passage to explain why the resort to terrorism might be condemned as illegitimate as well as immoral.

3 How might terrorist guerrillas see themselves?

4 Do you believe there can ever be an acceptable 'resort to violence'?

War may be an extremely nasty affair but it is also oddly reassuring, even chivalrous. You recognize the legitimacy or sovereignty of your opponent; you declare war at a certain moment in time and you declare the cessation of hostilities at another moment in time; you conduct military operations with due regard to the treaties, conventions and tacit understandings concerning the wearing of uniforms and insignia, the treatment of prisoners of war, the taking of hostages, the suitability of certain weapons and the unsuitability of others. But there are not – and can never be – conventions regulating the conduct of terrorism. It would be like trying to formulate rules telling us the proper and improper ways of committing murder or robbery with violence. However hard the terrorist seeks to invoke all manner of political grievances to justify murders, bombings and hijackings, the courts that try and sentence him will take his actions to be straightforward homicide or whatever. He wears the uniform of no state, he is the emissary of no state, he is a combatant in a non-existent war – he is regarded as a psychopath.

The self-proclaimed guerrilla will of course reject such a designation. He is fighting an occupying power, an oppressive state; he may not have the sophisticated weaponry or organization of his opponents but he has the support of the masses behind him; he is not indiscriminate in his choice of targets: he attacks the police, the military, the lines of supply and communications of his enemy; he demoralizes his opponents by raising questions in his mind about the legitimacy of his occupation or whatever.

from 'Combatants in non-existent wars' by George Szamvely, in *The Times Educational Supplement*, 5.12.1986

Item 8.15   War or terrorism?

▶ UNIT 30 Political socialisation

Political socialisation means the element of the general process of socialisation which relates particularly to a person's learning about power and politics. People can acquire basic attitudes about political matters at a very young age. All the agencies of socialisation make a contribution to political socialisation, but the family and the mass media have specific roles to play.

30.1 The family and political socialisation

Sociologists have found that even young children have a keen sense of political awareness. This may not be an understanding of political issues and arguments, but it certainly involves broad ideas and values, and judgements on people, personalities and political parties. Indeed, political preference is often passed on from parent to children in an unseen process of political learning.

30.2 The mass media and political socialisation

The mass media, both broadcasting and the press, are important agencies of socialisation in all its aspects; but they are particularly important in political socialisation because people, it is argued, take their opinions from the media, or at least base their opinions on the selection of facts they are presented with by the media. In this topic we will pay particular attention to newspapers, but the analysis would be similar for other forms of the press and for broadcasting.

Sociologists argue that most newspapers support the status quo – the order of things – against radical change. In general, this means most of the press support the Conservative party, so it might be assumed that the media influence people towards the right. It has also been argued, however, that newspapers simply reinforce opinions people already hold, because people buy newspapers that support their views (for example, Conservatives take the *Daily Telegraph*). This argument suggests that newspapers do not help to form the political opinions of their readers. Two sociologists called Trenaman and McQuail did research which seemed to support this side of the argument. They found that 89 per cent of Conservative voters read a newspaper which supported the Conservative party and 67 per cent of Labour voters read a newspaper which supported the Labour party (although the range of newspapers supporting the left is much smaller).

ACTIVITIES 12

Look at Item 8.16 and answer the questions that follow.

1 What effect do you think these front pages will have on the opinions and votes of their readership?

2 Look again at the circulation figures for each newspaper given in Item 7.3. What is the circulation for each of the newspapers in Item 8.16?

3 Using recent copies of both newspapers (the *Sun* and *Daily Mirror*) see if you can find examples of their current political preferences.

Item 8.16   Are newspapers politically biased?

UNIT 31   Voting behaviour

31.1 The electorate

The people entitled to vote in UK parliamentary and local government elections now are subjects of the UK who are resident in the UK, over the age of 18, are not serving prison sentences, have not been certified as insane, and are not Members of the House of Lords. Over the past 150 years the right to vote (the *franchise*) has been gradually extended, from a few male property holders before the Reform Act of 1832, to the present electorate. The electorate in Britain at the time of the general election in June 1983 consisted of approximately 42 million people. Nearly 72 per cent of this total electorate voted, and on average since 1945, three quarters of the electorate have cast their vote in general elections, as Item 8.17 shows.

The percentage of people who have voted in Britain at general elections is quite high compared with that of many other parliamentary democracies. A certain percentage of voters, though, deliberately choose to stay away from the polling stations on election day. They are *positive abstainers*. Those electors who made no deliberate choice to abstain but who fail to vote are known as *negative abstainers*.

	5 July 1945	23 Feb 1950	25 Oct 1951	26 May 1955	8 Oct 1959	15 Oct 1964	31 Mar 1966	18 June 1970[1]	28 Feb 1974	10 Oct 1974	3 May 1979	9 June 1983
United Kingdom												Thousands
Number of electors	33 240	34 412	34 919	34 852	35 397	35 894	35 957	39 615	40 256	40 256	41 573	42 704
Average – electors per seat	51.9	55.1	55.9	55.3	56.2	57.0	57.1	62.9	63.4	63.4	65.5	65.7
Number of votes cast	25 095	28 771	28 597	26 760	27 863	27 657	27 265	28 345	31 340	28 189	31 221	30 671
As percentage of electorate	75.5	83.6	81.9	76.8	78.7	77.1	75.8	71.5	77.9	72.5	75.1	71.8
Number of Members of Parliament elected:	640	625	625	630	630	630	630	630	635	635	635	650
Conservative	212	297	320	344	364	303	253	330	296	276	339	396
Labour	393	315	295	277	258	317	363	287	301	319	268	209
Liberal	12	9	6	6	6	9	12	6	14	13	11	17
Social Democratic Party	–	–	–	–	–	–	–	–	–	–	–	6
Scottish National Party	–	–	–	–	–	–	–	1	7	11	2	2
Plaid Cymru	–	–	–	–	–	–	–	–	2	3	2	2
Other[2]	22	4	4	3	2	1	2	6	15	13	13	18

1 The Representation of the Peoples Act 1969 lowered the minimum voting age from 21 to 18 years with effect from 16 February 1970.
2 The Speaker is included in Other.

Sources: Home Office: Scottish Home and Health Department; Northern Ireland Office

from *Annual Abstract of Statistics: 1986* (HMSO, 1986)

Item 8.17   Parliamentary elections, 1945–83

ACTIVITIES 13

Look at Item 8.17 and answer the following questions.

1 Why does the number of electors change each year?

2 Why was there a sudden jump in the number of electors in the election on 18 June 1970? What difference might this have made to the result?

3 Draw a histogram or bar chart for each election since 1970 showing the number of MPs elected for each of the main parties. (Include SDP MPs elected in 1983 with the Liberal MPs.)

31.2 Abstentionism

Positive abstainers are thought to be a smaller group than negative abstainers. The positive abstainer may choose deliberately not to vote for a number of reasons. These usually are:

1 Voters may not be able to vote for the party of their choice in their constituency (for example, a Liberal party supporter where there were only Labour and Conservative candidates).

2 Voters may have personal dislike for a candidate standing for their preferred party.

3 There may be some aspect of their preferred party's policy voters have considerable disagreement with.

4 Voters may think that the result is a foregone conclusion anyway, particularly in a safe seat (one where there has been a clear majority for one party in previous elections).

Negative abstainers, who are perhaps more numerous, tend to be the least interested and least informed about political matters. They are usually found amongst the youngest, oldest and poorest members of the community. they may also have practical reasons for abstaining. If the polling stations are in remote places as in some rural areas, if a mother cannot leave her very young children to vote, or possibly if someone is ill and has not got a postal vote, then abstentionism is inevitable.

If 25 per cent of the electorate fail to vote, between five and eight per cent (of the total) will not be true abstainers. These are people who have died since the electoral register was compiled; people who are on holiday or away on business at the time of the election, or people who have moved out of the constituency and have not obtained a postal vote. This leaves a real abstention rate of just under 20 per cent on average in general elections since World War II.

The *floating voters*, who change their allegiance from one election to another, and who are thought to number about 15 per cent of the electorate, are similar to negative abstainers in that they tend to be among the least politically minded and are easily swayed by election propaganda. Psephologists (people who study voting behaviour) say that the outcome of a general election in the UK is usually decided by the rate of abstentionism and the floating voter, who may be unaware of the serious issues involved.

31.3 The voters

Clearly, it is not just the parties' policies that make people decide to vote for them or not. Labour's image tends to be 'for the working class' and 'for the trade unions' while the Conservative image seems to be 'for the middle and upper classes' and 'for big business'. Voters are not as strongly rooted in their voting habits as they have been in the past. The electorate is much more volatile or changeable than it has been. What, then, influences voting behaviour?

Sex

Jean Blondel, a sociologist who has studied voting behaviour and party politics in the UK, suggests that women tend to vote Conservative more than men, in a ratio of about 60:40. In the 1983 election, for example, Labour only attracted around 25 per cent of the female vote. Robins, Brennan and Sutton, three sociologists who have studied politics in Britain recently, say that the main reason for the Conservative bias of women in general may be that they are less influenced by industrial conditions and trade union activity. Robbins et al. suggest that this may happen because more women than men do not go out to work, or because women, who often work in offices, do not experience conflicts of the kind found on the factory floor so much.

Age

Another factor linked to voting behaviour is that of age. On the whole, the young tend to be more radical in outlook and the old more conservative. This may be because the young are more idealistic. Young people, however, and particularly young couples with small children, are more likely to have problems establishing themselves economically. This too may make them tend to seek more immediate solutions for their problems in political changes.

Religion

Religion plays very little part generally in the UK's politics. The tragic exception is Northern Ireland, where people's votes are strongly influenced by whether they are Catholic or Protestant. Northern Irish Catholics have traditionally supported union with the Irish Republic, while Protestantism is traditionally tied to support for union with Britain.

Region

On the result of previous voting figures, if Scotland and Wales had their own parliaments Labour would have held power in those countries for half a century. In England, where most of the population is concentrated in the southern half of the country, the Conservatives usually have the support of the majority, except in the heart of industrial towns and cities.

Class

The strongest determining factor of voting behaviour is the social class of the elector. In simple terms, the higher up the social scale someone is, the more likely he or she is to vote Conservative. Three quarters of the middle class vote Conservative, and two thirds of the working class vote Labour. More than seven eighths of all voters identify a class-interest with either Labour or Conservative. There are, of course, exceptions: working-class Conservative voters have sustained the Conservative Party since World War II. The working class is greater than the middle class numerically, so the working-class Conservative vote is important. Most working-class Conservatives are found in the more prosperous middle-class areas and regions of England, such as the Midlands and the South East. In the predominantly working-class industrial towns and conurbations of the North East there is a more solid Labour vote.

The sociologist Nordlinger offers two explanations to account for the large conservative working-class vote. He refers to the *deferential* and the *pragmatic* voter:

1 Deferential working-class Conservative voters consider that the country is best run by those who were born to it and who have received the best education.

2 Pragmatic working-class Conservative voters admire someone who has achieved a position of

power through his or her own efforts and ability. Like the deferential voters they have a good deal of respect for political leaders of high social status.

ACTIVITIES 14: Play-reading

Read the play-reading and answer the questions that follow.

(Ray and Bert are watching a football match and discussing politics.)

Ray It gets me though – look at this channel tunnel business – we don't get asked if we want it. No discussion – they just decide and that's it!

Bert Yeah, but these politicians know what they're doing. They look at everything and weigh it up – *(suddenly shouting)* Oi! That's offside, ref! Blow your whistle! *(to Ray)* Y'know I don't think he knows what that shiny thing round his neck's for – probably think's it's jewellery.

Ray The point is politicians are supposed to do what we say – we elect them.

Bert They've got degrees and things, Ray – they're better informed – *(shouting)* A penalty??! Why don't you wear one of their jerseys and have done with it!! *(to Ray)* A chimpanzee would referee this game better.

Ray They do refereeing exams, you know.

Bert Yeah yeah – I bet he cheated to pass those. Two minutes to go.

Ray Anyway, look, politicians are supposed to carry out our wishes – not tell us what to do.

Bert People can never agree on anything. There's always someone moaning about something or other. People have to be told or nothing'd ever get done – we need leading.

Ray They're not God, though – ah, that's it – final whistle.

Bert Right – David's meeting us at the car at five o'clock. We'd better hurry – we're giving him a lift.

Ray Your son passed his motorbike test, though, didn't he? Two weeks ago?

Bert He went though the lights on amber last week and got caught. He's leaving the bike alone for a bit – serves him right. Come on then.

(Bert and Ray arrive at the car where they meet David, Bert's 18-year-old son, and a policeman who looks about the same age.)

Bert What's he done now, officer?

Policeman This is your car, I believe, sir? It's illegally parked I'm afraid. That's a ticket, sir. *(Hands it to him)* I'm sure you know double yellow lines aren't for decoration – good afternoon, sir. *(goes)*

Bert Just my luck! Look at him – I bet his chin's never seen a razor. These youngsters get a uniform on and they think they're God – well come on, let's get home.

David I think I'll walk, Dad – I don't want to associate with criminals.

Bert Very funny, very funny! Go on, jump in, Barry Sheene!

1 'The point is politicians are supposed to do what we say – we elect them.' Discuss this statement, saying whether you think it is true or not. Give reasons for your answers.

2 What attitude did Bert have toward:
a the referee?
b the policeman?

3 In what ways was Bert's attitude towards politicians different from his attitude towards both the referee and the policeman?

4 What kind of approach to politics would you say Bert seemed to have? Explain your answer by reference to the text.

5 Do you think this kind of approach to politics is common? What consequences might we see if everyone took Bert's attitude towards politics?

▶ UNIT 32 The electoral system

32.1 First past the post

The present system of organising elections is called the *simple majority* system, or *first past the post*. The winning party is the one that gets the most votes – even just one more than the nearest rival and even if it is less than half of all votes cast. In fact, no party has won more than half the votes cast since 1935 and over the past 25 years, until the election of 1983, the margin between the major parties has been narrow.

Under the UK system of election, therefore, the candidate who gains a simple majority wins even if the combined votes of his or her opponents total more. For example, suppose we have three candidates, Smith, Brown and Jones, and on election day the results are: Smith, 12 000; Brown, 11 750; Jones, 11 500. Smith wins with a majority of 250 even though Brown and Jones have a combined anti-Smith total of 23 250. The Alliance argued that this system was the reason they had only a small number of MPs after the 1983 election even though nationally they polled only 675 000 votes fewer than Labour (out of over 30 million!). To take another example, in 1951 more Conservative MPs were returned than Labour, although the Labour party polled nationally 231 000 more votes than the Conservatives. The same thing happened to Labour in 1974, and this precipitated the need for a second election the same year.

The lack of proportion between number of votes polled nationally and number of seats in Parliament is explained by the differences in size of majorities obtained in the constituencies. If a candidate gets only one more vote than his or her nearest opponent he or she is still elected and the party gets one seat just as happens when the majority is hundreds or thousands. Where the majorities are below four figures the seats are said to be marginal and it is in these constituencies

that a small swing in votes can unseat the sitting member. Psephologists usually concentrate their studies on these marginal constituencies.

ACTIVITIES 15

Item 8.18 shows again the distribution of seats in the House of Commons which resulted from the 1987 election. It also shows the percentage of votes cast for each party. Study it, and answer the questions that follow.

1 Using the table draw a histogram or bar chart to show for each party:
 a the percentage of votes cast.
 b the number of MPs elected.

2 Comment on the results.

3 Can you explain the differences you see?

The five major alternatives to the present system are briefly described in the checklist.

Checklist

1 *Second ballot* Two elections are held, one a week after the other, allowing losing candidates to withdraw. This system is used in France.

2 *Alternative vote* Losing candidates are eliminated and their voters' *second* preferences are then passed on to the remaining candidates. This method is used in Australia.

3 *Proportional representation by lists* Candidates are simply taken from party lists in proportion to the number of votes cast for each party.

Party	% votes cast	Party	Number of seats in Commons
Conservative	42.3	Conservative	376 (including the Speaker)
Labour	30.8	Labour	229
Liberal–Social Democratic Alliance	22.6	Liberal	17
		Social Democratic	3
Others	4.3	Others	23

adapted from *Britain 1988: An Official Handbook* (HMSO, 1988)

Item 8.18 Percentage of votes cast and members elected in the 1987 general election

4 *Additional members system*   The 'first past the post' system still operates but with extra seats allocated to each party in proportion to votes cast.

5 *Single transferable vote*   Candidates are listed by voters in order of preference. Once a candidate has achieved a minimum number of votes to win, any 'surplus' votes are transferred to voters' second and third choices, so no votes are 'wasted' and the election result reflects as closely as possible the actual votes cast. This system is used in the Irish Republic and is the system advocated by the Social and Liberal Democrats and the Social Democratic Party in Britain.

32.2 Electoral reform

It is figures like those in Item 8.18 that have led to calls for a reform of the electoral system. The first past the post system does not seem to allow fair expression to the wishes and voting preferences of the electorate, although there is considerable argument about the merits and disadvantages of the present system when compared to the alternatives. The alternative systems for organising elections could be referred to collectively as systems of *proportional representation*. They seek to produce a result (in terms of numbers of MPs elected to Parliament) which represents reasonably closely the proportions of the actual vote given to each party.

ACTIVITIES 16

Devise a questionnaire on electoral reform and find out the opinions of a sample of people drawn from your school or community. If you are able to conduct interviews instead of using a mail questionnaire you might show your respondents the statistics in Item 8.18 *after* they have answered your questions to see if they then change their views.

► UNIT **33** Political opinion polls

The purpose of political opinion polls is to discover the opinions and attitudes of the electorate – those entitled to vote. These polls give particular attention to people's voting intentions at times when an election is near, but at other times may ask questions about particular issues, policies or personalities. They aim to be accurate, systematic and scientific in their research, although they began as journalistic features in newspapers with little idea of proper research procedures.

33.1 How accurate are opinion polls?

ACTIVITIES 17

Read Item 8.19 and answer the questions that follow it.

Public opinion polls were first used in the USA. In one famous case, an opinion poll made a big mistake in predicting the winner of the 1936 presidential election. The *Literary Digest* magazine sent over 10 000 000 questionnaires to people whose names were taken from telephone directories or car registration lists. The result predicted by the poll was that Republican Alf Landon would become America's next President. George Gallup, who set up the American Institute of Public Opinion, interviewed only 3000 people and correctly predicted that the Democrat Franklin D. Roosevelt would remain President. How could a survey of 10 million be less accurate than one of three thousand?

from L. Robins, T. Brennan and J. Sutton, *People and Politics in Britain* (Macmillan, 1985)

Item 8.19   How accurate are opinion polls? (1)

1 What kind of people did the *Literary Digest* send its questionnaires to? (Look again at Chapter 2, on research methods and sampling.)

2 How *could* a survey of ten million be less accurate than one of three thousand?

3 Now read Item 8.20.

In fact, political opinion polls attempting to forecast how people will vote in elections have usually been accurate. Two noted exceptions to this are the 1984 election in the USA and the 1970 election in the UK. The polls predicted an easy win for Labour in 1970, when in the event the Conservatives won, led by Edward Heath.

33.2 Methods of research for political opinion polls

Opinion polls use the methods of social scientific survey research. (You should refer again to the units in Chapter 2 on survey research, sampling, questionnaires and pre-coded questions.) Political opinion polls may use random, stratified or quota sampling techniques. For the practical reasons of cost and speed, political opinion polls often use quota sampling techniques and may interview people either door-to-door or in a busy shopping centre. If they use random sampling the electoral register, of course, can act as an ideal sampling frame, but the interviewer then has to find the particular named individuals drawn in the sample.

If a political opinion poll aims to interview 2000 people in 100 constituencies, then there will have to be 20 interviews in each constituency. The quotas required might be as shown in Item 8.21.

ACTIVITIES 18

You should be able to conduct a political opinion poll in your own school. You might wish to choose a particular political issue which is currently in the news. You might alternatively try to find out which of the present party leaders your school's pupils think would make the best prime minister. Try to find out what qualities they look for in forming their opinion.

The *Literary Digest*'s sample was biased. Since it was based on people who owned telephones or cars, it reflected the opinions of the more wealthy individuals. The views of poorer people who were less likely to have phones or cars were not included. But poorer people would, of course, be voting in the election. Gallup's sample was small but it was representative. In other words, the 3000 people interviewed by Gallup was a fair cross-section of the whole electorate. It included rich as well as poor voters. Because Gallup's sample was representative, it did not matter that it was small.

from L. Robins, T. Brennan and J. Sutton, *People and Politics in Britain* (Macmillan Education, 1985)

Item 8.20 How accurate are opinion polls? (2)

	Men	Women	Total
Age of elector			
18–44	4	5	9
45 and over	5	6	11
	9	11	20
Social class of elector			
Clerical/executive	3	4	7
Manual	9	7	13
	9	11	20

from F. Teer and J. D. Spence, *Political Opinion Polls*, (Hutchinson University Library, 1973)

Item 8.21 Simple quota of interviews to be achieved

1 Draw up a few simple pre-coded questions. Make sure your questions are fair and do not 'prompt' an answer which would lead to· a particular response.

2 Decide what kind of sample to use, and then select the sample. Remember to use either random sampling techniques or a quota sample. If you decide to use a quota method you could send your interviewers out to the playground or dinner hall to do the survey. If you decide to draw a random sample of particular named pupils you may have to send the questionnaire out using the school registers.

3 Collect your questionnaires in, count up the results and send a published report to your headteacher and perhaps to all the forms in the school. If your school has a magazine you could write a short report for publication.

33.3 The influence of political opinion polls

Political opinion polls may influence the very opinions they are attempting to measure. In some countries political opinions polls are banned in the run up to an election. In the UK, poll results may be published on the very eve of the election itself.

Teer and Spencer (1973) argue that there are four things which opinion polls might influence:

actual voting behaviour;
government decisions;
party policy; and
political reporting.

Polls and voting behaviour

Polls are conducted for their news value, but Teer and Spencer argue that they may influence voting behaviour in two ways:

The bandwagon effect
By showing which party is likely to win an election the polls may encourage voters to climb on the winning party's bandwagon, and vote for it. People like to be on the winning side.

The boomerang effect
By showing which party is on top, the polls may encourage voters to change sides to support the underdog. At the same time, people who think their party is leading in the polls and is going to win may decide they need not bother to vote. By encouraging complacent abstention like this, polls may adversely influence the leading party.

Polls and government

Governments in a democracy must listen to public opinion, and polls give expression to public opinion. However, like all of us, politicians find themselves able to ignore results they disagree with. One politician has been quoted as saying 'I am only com-

pletely convinced of the findings of the polls when they confirm my own impression of what the public is thinking'. Indeed Harold Wilson (Prime Minister 1964–70 and 1974–6) has said 'A government cannot govern, and should not seek to govern, by relating its policies to public opinion polls' results.'

Polls and party policy

Polls are used by political parties to decide how policies should best be presented. Teer and Spence suggest there are three ways polls affect political parties:

a They can identify groups of voters who might be potential supporters, and who might best be the target of an election campaign.
b They can influence the morale of ordinary party workers in the constituencies.
c They can influence the popularity of party leaders.

Polls and political reporting

As we have said, polls are conducted for their news value and are used by the media to report political events. Newspaper coverage of elections always features poll results, and by improving the awareness politicians have of public opinion their results do contribute to political discussion and debate.

ACTIVITIES 19

1 Do you think the bandwagon effect or the boomerang effect is the stronger? Give reasons.

2 Should governments base their decisions on the findings of political opinion polls? Examine critically.

3 What use could opinion polls be to parties trying to win an election?

4 What problems do polls produce for politicians?

REVIEW

If you have studied and understood this chapter you should be able to ...

- explain the different ways by which a person can have power.
- distinguish clearly between power and authority.

- explain, with examples of your own, the three kinds of authority outlined by the sociologist Max Weber.
- describe briefly the stages an idea has to go through before it becomes a law.
- define or explain the following terms:
  a the executive,
  b the legislature, and
  c the judiciary.
- distinguish between those services central government provides and those services provided by local government.
- explain the difference between protective interest groups and promotional interest groups.
- outline the role in the process of political socialisation of:
  a the family, and
  b the mass media.
- outline, in only a few sentences for each, how the following factors might affect voting behaviour:
  a sex,
  b age,
  c religion,
  d region, and
  e social class.
- outline, again in only a few sentences for each, the ways in which political opinions polls affect:
  a voting behaviour,
  b government decision-making,
  c party policy, and
  d political reporting.

COURSEWORK SUGGESTION

Try to demonstrate different electoral systems by organising an 'election' in your own class or school. Write a report on your results. You might also include in your report results of a survey of your school or community on the need for electoral reform.

You can hold the 'election' with just your own class. Provide each 'voter' with a ballot paper with six names. These names could be fictitious and voting preferences could be entirely random. You only need voting patterns and no real issue needs to be involved. You should ask each 'voter' to put the candidates in order of preference by simply putting 1, 2, 3 and so on next to each name. When all the votes are collected in you can count up the votes in different ways to demonstrate different electoral systems.

1 *Alternative voting*
a Count all the votes. Any candidate getting over 50 per cent of the votes is the winner. If this does not happen on the first count then ...
b Sort out the losing candidate's ballot papers. The losing candidate is eliminated from the poll and the *second* choices of the voters who supported that candidate are then allocated to the other candidates. Losing candidates' votes are transferred like this until one candidate has over 50 per cent of the vote. Under the simple majority system these second choices are not counted and voting for a losing candidate might be regarded as a 'wasted' vote.

This system can still be used when only *one* person is to be elected, but then it is not really true proportional representation since the supporters of the losing candidates are still not represented.

2 *Single transferable vote for proportional representation*
Suppose you want to elect two candidates and suppose there are 30 'voters' in your class. We can say (and this is to simplify the actual figures used) that a candidate needs a minimum of 11 votes to be elected. This makes sense because *only two* candidates can get 11 votes each out of 30 votes – if the minimum were ten votes or fewer, three or more candidates could get an equal number of votes. This minimum number of votes is worked out as follows:

$$\text{minimum number of votes required} = \frac{\text{number of voters} + \text{one}}{\text{number of vacancies} + \text{one}}$$

The result is rounded up to the next whole number.

Now you know the minimum number of votes required by each candidate you can look at the total number of votes received by each candidate. Any candidate receiving 11 votes is immediately elected, if two candidates are not elected on this first count, once again the losing candidate is eliminated and the second choices of the voters who supported him or her are allocated.

This procedure is repeated until two candidates collect 11 or more votes each.

This system seems complicated even when explained simply, but you should be able to see the way these systems produce different results.

ASSESSMENT QUESTION

The mark allocations to sections of the question are shown in the right hand margin.

Parliamentary by-elections

	May 1979 –June 1983	Previous* General Election May 1979
Number of by-elections	20	
Votes recorded by party (*percentages*)		
Conservative	23.8	33.7
Labour	25.7	35.2
Liberal	9.0	8.0
Social Democratic Party	14.2	
Plaid Cymru	0.5	0.4
Scottish National Party	1.7	1.4
Other	25.1	21.2
Total votes recorded (= 100%) (thousands)	715	852

* Votes recorded in the same seats in the previous General Election.

(Adapted from *Social Trends 15* 1985)

a How many by-elections were held in the United Kingdom between May 1979 and June 1983? (1)

b How many votes were recorded in these constituencies in the General Election May 1979? (1)

c What change took place in the percentage of votes recorded for:
i the Labour Party; (1)
ii the Liberal Party (1)
in the by-elections compared with General Election May 1979?

d Name the Nationalist parties mentioned in the chart. (2)

e i Explain why no votes were recorded for the Social Democratic Party in the General Election May 1979. (1)
ii Which party would replace the Liberal party on the above table now? (1)

f Name **two** different types of pressure group. Give an example of each. (4)

g Give **four** methods used by pressure groups by which they hope to influence government policy and/or public opinion. (4)

h Identify and explain **two** reasons why the results of a poll on voting intentions taken one month before an election may not accurately reflect the actual result of the election. (4)

Adapted from the *Southern Examining Group*

9 *Work*

AIMS

At the end of this chapter you should be able to:

- describe the occupational structure of the UK.
- describe the social composition of the 'economically active' in terms of age, sex and ethnic origin.
- appreciate the merits of, and problems caused by, the division of labour.
- explain and evaluate the role of trade unions and employers in industrial relations.
- evaluate and critically assess the impact of technology and automation on the nature of work and organisations.
- show a critical awareness of the problems posed by unemployment both for individuals and for society.
- understand the relationship between work and non-work.
- appreciate the social importance of 'retirement' from work in different societies.

UNIT 34 The occupational structure of the UK

34.1 The changing occupational structure

The working population may conveniently be divided into three sectors:

1 The *primary sector* , in which workers are engaged in the first stages of production such as agriculture, mining and fishing. Industries in this sector are also referred to as *extractive industries* as the jobs involve taking raw materials from the earth and sea to use in production.

2 The *secondary sector*, in which workers mostly work in manufacturing industries transforming the raw materials into something which can be used (for example, transforming wood into furniture).

3 The *tertiary section*, in which workers provide services. In a modern affluent society this may make more than half the work force. In the UK, for example, over six million people are engaged in professional, financial, scientific and miscellaneous services, apart from those working in the distributive trades, in transport or for the government.

The relative importance of these sectors as providers of jobs in the UK economy has changed over the last 50 years. Item 9.2 on page 156 shows the division of employment between these three sectors for each census year since 1931.

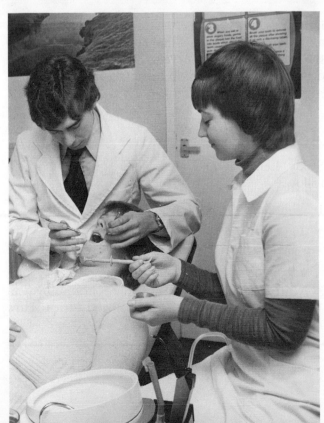

Item 9.1   Which sector of production is each of these
workers engaged in?

There are three groups of people who do not work for one reason or another or whose work is unpaid. These groups are excluded from the definition of the *working population*. They are:

children of pre-school age and those undergoing full-time education.
those who stay at home, perhaps to look after children or care for dependent adults.
retired people: usually women over the age of 60 and men over the age of 65.

There is, however, a further group of people who do not work – *the unemployed*. There may be those who are unemployed because they are physically or mentally handicapped, but there are also those who are fully fit and able-bodied but who are still unable to get a job or find employment. This last group of unemployed people are included in the definition of the working population because they are available for work and looking for work. The unemployed, however, are not included amongst the *economically active* members of the population.

Unemployment in Britain has increased rapidly in recent years, officially standing at 13.4 per cent of the working population or 3.2 million people in July 1985. Some believe that official figures underestimate the real extent of unemployment, because only those who can and do register as unemployed are counted. This does not include some people who may be available for work (for example, married women whose husbands are employed but who do not have a paid job themselves). Others, however, believe that counting everyone who registers actually overestimates the number unemployed.

ACTIVITIES 1

There have been substantial changes in the occupational structure of the UK over recent decades. The most marked change has been a shift from manufacturing to service industries:

– between 1955 and 1984 the proportion of employees in service industries rose from 45 per cent to 65 per cent.
– in 1955 manufacturing industry accounted for 40 per cent of all employees but in 1984 the proportion had fallen to 26 per cent.

Show these comparisons on a bar chart.
One of the main reasons for the growth in service

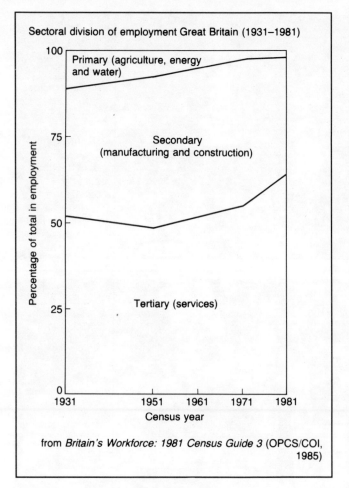

Item 9.2   Sectoral division of employment, Britain, 1931–81

industries has been the development of technology and computers. The fact that new technology reduces the demand for labour also partially explains the decline of employment in manufacturing.

ACTIVITIES 2

Study Item 9.3 and answer the questions which follow.

1 What does the term 'primary sector' mean?

2 What sector of production would you call:
a manufacturing and construction?
b the service industries?

3 Nearly 65 per cent of all employees in employment in 1984 worked in the service industries. How many employees was this?

Item 9.3   Employees in employment

Industry or service (1980 Standard Industrial Classification)	Thousands (as at June)				Per cent (1984)
	1976	1980	1983	1984	
Primary sector	**1,113**	**1,087**	**1,008**	**970**	**4.6**
Agriculture, forestry and fishing	393	361	349	340	1.6
Energy and water supply	720	726	659	630	3.0
Manufacturing*	**7,281**	**6,940**	**5,605**	**5,516**	**26.1**
Construction	**1,252**	**1,252**	**1,012**	**983**	**4.6**
Services	**12,889**	**13,690**	**13,430**	**13,685**	**64.7**
Wholesale distribution and repairs	1,039	1,163	1,147	1,174	5.5
Retail distribution	2,061	2,175	2,060	2,136	10.1
Hotel and catering	864	978	964	1,013	4.8
Transport	1,025	1,046	894	876	4.1
Postal services and communications	431	437	430	426	2.0
Banking, finance and insurance	1,494	1,697	1,822	1,881	8.9
Public administration	1,990	1,985	1,875	1,864	8.8
Education	1,618	1,628	1,583	1,586	7.5
Health	1,174	1,254	1,331	1,339	6.3
Other services	1,193	1,327	1,323	1,390	6.6
Employees in employment	**22,543**	**22,972**	**21,053**	**21,156**	**100.0**

* In June 1984 employment in the main sectors of manufacturing industry included 837,000 in office machinery, electrical engineering and instruments, 779,000 in mechanical engineering, 631,000 in food, drink and tobacco, 553,000 in textiles, leather, footwear and clothing, 187,000 in paper products, printing and publishing, 458,000 in timber, wooden furniture, rubber and plastics, 345,000 in chemicals and man-made fibres, and 293,000 in motor vehicles and parts.
Note: Differences between totals and the sums of their component parts are due to rounding for 1976. The difference also reflects the inclusion in the total number of some employers whose industrial classification could not be ascertained.
Sources: Department of Employment and Northern Ireland Department of Economic Development.

from *Britain 1986: An Official Handbook* (HMSO, 1987)

4 Which of the service industries have not seen a rise in the numbers employed? (You should name four.)

5 Which service industry has experienced the largest rise in numbers employed since 1976?

Not everybody in society is able to work, as we have seen. We have looked here at changes among those people in employment. Unemployment is dealt with more fully later.

Key terms

- primary sector
- secondary sector
- tertiary sector
- working population
- economically active
- unemployed

34.2 The impact on social differentiation

As our society becomes better qualified there is a tendency for the percentage of workers in the professional, managerial and skilled classes to increase, and the less skilled to decrease. The two main reasons for these changes are the improved educational opportunities available, and the greater demand for more skilled workers in an affluent modern society with a large service sector.

▶ UNIT 35 Social composition of occupations

35.1 Gender

There has been a considerable rise in the number of women in paid work. With some change in social attitudes towards women working outside the home, an increased cost of living, and increased male redundancy and unemployment, many families now rely on women's earnings as an essential part of their income. There have been a number of reasons put forward to explain this trend including later marriage, the greater availability of effective birth control, a decline in family size and equal opportunities legislation. Since World War II the proportion of married women in the British labour force has grown. Only four per cent of the labour force were female in 1921. The civilian labour force in Britain increased by 1½ million between 1971 and 1984 entirely because of an increase in the number of women in paid work – a rise from 37 to 40 per cent of the labour force. However, the unequal social position of women is reflected in the social composition of the professions. These overwhelmingly recruit males, as Item 9.4 shows.

ACTIVITIES 3

1 Using the lists in Item 9.4 as a starting point, list the sex of the members of your own family and neighbours and the work they do. Also ask members of your family and your neighbours the sex of their doctor, bank manager, dentist and solicitor.

2 When all members of your class have completed this exercise, put all your results together and comment on your findings. You should present your data in a bar chart, or a table like the one in Item 9.4.

The causes and consequences of the increased employment of married women are of great interest to the sociologist, because they are part of an important change in society. Some of the possible effects are given in Item 9.5. You should be able to add to the ideas suggested.

Nevertheless a higher proportion of men than women are economically active – 75 per cent of men compared to 49 per cent of women, according to the government's Labour Force Survey of 1985.

a

Profession	% Men	% Women
Bank Managers	99	1
Directors	Over 99	Well below 1
Chartered accountants	96	4
Cost and management accountants	96	4
Civil engineers	Over 99	Well below 1
Electrical engineers	Over 99	Well below 1
Mechanical engineers	Over 99	Well below 1
Electrical and electronic technician engineers	99	1
Dentists	83	17
General practitioners	84	16
Surgeons	Over 99	Below 1
Paediatricians	84	16
Barristers	90	10
Solicitors	92	8
Chartered surveyors	Over 99	Below 1
Surveying technicians	Over 99	Below 1
Architects	95	5
University professors	98	2
Advertising account executives	83	17
Air traffic control officers	97	3
Driving examiners	Over 99	Well below 1
Local authority chief executives	Over 99	Well below 1

Source: Figures obtained in 1980 from the professional organisations concerned. In general these apply to England and Wales only. Published in the 1981 Edition of 'Equal Opportunities: A Careers Guide for Women and Men', by Ruth Miller, (Penguin).
from The Sex Discrimination Act and Advertising (EOC, undated pamphlet, c.1984)

b

82% of electrical assembly workers ARE WOMEN
86% of winders/reelers in textiles ARE WOMEN
97% of hand machinists in textiles ARE WOMEN
83% of telephone operators ARE WOMEN
99% of typists and secretaries ARE WOMEN
82% of shop assistants ARE WOMEN
91% of office cleaners ARE WOMEN
92% of nurses ARE WOMEN
11.5% of managers ARE WOMEN

Source: 1971 Census of Population

from The Sex Discrimination Act and Advertising (EOC, undated pamphlet, c. 1984)

Item 9.4 Professionals: men and women, 1980 'Woman's work'

Causes	Likely Consequences
Emancipation of women	Struggle for equal pay
Increased demand for female labour	Less home care for children
	More women trade unionists
Nursery education for under-fives	Less time spent in looking after the home
More female career opportunities	
Time-saving domestic gadgets	Delinquency amongst children who return to an empty house
Inflation erodes the husband's pay	
Smaller families	Husband helps wife with the domestic chores
Desire for 'pin-money' to supplement the family income	Family dependent on joint income

Item 9.5   Increased employment of married women

35.2 Ethnic origin

The Race Relations Act (1976) makes it illegal to discriminate in employment and training on grounds of colour, race or ethnic or national origin. In spite of this, members of ethnic minorities still suffer disproportionately from unemployment and still suffer discrimination in employment. Economists Metcalf and Richardson report that other things being equal (age, experience, weeks worked, years of schooling, marital status, etc.) non-white males earn around 17 per cent less than equivalent white males. (Statistics relating work to ethnic origin are available only for men.) They report that the extent of this discrimination is greater for men of Asian ethnic origin than for men of West Indian origin. This discrimination is not attributable to unequal pay for equal work, say Metcalf and Richardson, but to the fact that black workers do not seem able to gain access to the higher-paying occupations. Metcalf and Richardson go on to say: 'while 58 per cent of Pakistani males and 32 per cent of West Indian males working in Britain are un-skilled or semi-skilled, the corresponding figure for whites is 18 per cent. Further, almost no whites with degree-level qualifications do manual work but around one-fifth of such men from minorities do manual work and members of ethnic minorities are much less likely than whites to be in professional and management occupations' (in A.R. Prest and D.J. Coppock, *The UK Economy: 10th Edition*, Weidenfeld and Nicolson, 1986).

35.3 Age

The Office of Population Censuses and Surveys (OPCS) note that there is some movement to a higher social class among the economically active as people get older and qualifications or experience are gained.

ACTIVITIES 4

Read Item 9.6 and answer the questions that follow.

1 What term would sociologists use to describe 'movement to a higher social class'?

2 What factors contribute to this movement, according to the writer of the passage?

Age differentials
There is some movement to a higher social class among the economically active as people get older and qualifications or experience are gained. Among 16–24 year-old men, the proportions in both Social Class I and Social Class II were less than half the proportion for men of all ages; whereas the proportions of the 25–34 year-olds and 35–44 year-olds were above it. The proportion then dropped for the 45–64 age-group – possibly because retirement before age 65 is commoner for Social Classes I and II. For women these age patterns are different. The 16–24 year-old group of women also had a below-average proportion in Social Class I and II; but unlike men of this age, there was also a much below-average proportion in Social Class V (unskilled occupations). This latter proportion rose for each successive age-group, because of a higher proportion of older women in manual occupations, from 2 per cent of 16–24 year-old women to 10 per cent of the 45–59 year-old women. Among the 25–34 year-olds the non-manual: manual split was 70/30; among the 45–59 year-olds it was 55/45. This changing pattern may be due to women taking manual jobs when returning to work in middle age; or it may reflect differing propensities to work among women with different job skills; or a difference between the skills of successive generations. The Census alone cannot provide an explanation, although following a sample of individuals over time – as in the OPCS Longitudinal Study – would be revealing.

from 'Britain's Workforce' in *OPS Census Guide 3: 1981 Census* (HMSO, 1985)

Item 9.6   Age and employment

3 What occupations are included in the the Registrar General's Social Class I and Social Class II categories? (You may need to refer again to Chapter 3, on social differences.)

4 For Social Class I and Social Class II, which age group:
a had higher proportions of men than in the population as a whole?
b had less than half the proportion of men compared to the population as a whole?

5 Why did the number of men in the 45–64 age-group in Social Classes I and II fall?

6 The figures show that a higher proportion of older women are found in manual than non-manual occupations. How does the writer explain this changing pattern of women's employment as women get older?

UNIT 36   Work organisation and technology

Item 9.7   Arkwright's cotton spinning factory

36.1 The division of labour

The more numerous a group of people is, the more specialised their tasks. A commune in China or a kibbutz in Israel may be almost self-sufficient, although goods from outside the community will be required if living standards are to be comparable with other societies – for example, the group would need new seeds, fertilisers, farm implements and more complex machinery. The *division of labour* is concerned with each worker concentrating upon one task or perhaps a few tasks.

It was in eighteenth-century Britain that the division of labour was introduced in an industrial setting. Workers specialised in some small part of the productive process. This industrial division of labour began in workshops that used some means of mechanical power.

The credit for organising factory production based on the division of labour is usually given to Richard Arkwright and Jedediah Strutt, who set up the first cotton spinning factory at Cromford in 1771. Their workers were assisted by water power. The factory on the river Derwent still remains as a fine example of industrial archaeology.

In *The Wealth of Nations*, Adam Smith described an eighteenth-century pin factory where ten people manufactured 48 000 pins a day. Smith wrote that if the workers had 'all wrought separately and independently, and without any of them being educated to this peculiar business, they certainly could not each of them have made twenty, perhaps not one pin a day'. Mass production by the conveyor belt system has resulted in the division of labour being operated so intensively that a worker's task may take only a matter of seconds. Production of the famous Ford Model T motorcar was divided into 7882 different pieces of work. Henry Ford wrote that the simplicity of each job was such that '670 jobs could be filled by legless men, 2638 by one-legged men, two by armless men, 715 by one-armed men and ten by blind men.'

ACTIVITIES 5

1 How might the principle of division of labour help you and your friends get your homework done faster?

2 What might be the benefits to the employer or producer of the division of labour?

3 What might be the disadvantages to the employee or worker of the division of labour?

4 Apart from the production of motorcars, list other things which are produced using the division of labour.

5 Ask your family or neighbours about their work and find out how many are working in a system of division of labour. Find out as much as you can from them about their particular role, and about its contribution to the final product.

It has been said that most of the advantages of the division of labour are economic, whereas most of the disadvantages are social. It is true that the division of labour has the great economic advantage of enabling output to be increased, but some of the advantages are also social. Some of the advantages that are at least partly social are listed below:

Workers quickly acquire a satisfying skill at a particular task.

Working with others on a conveyor belt system or an assembly line may bring a worthwhile feeling of co-operation at work.

Workers learn their task quickly and get on with the job of production.

Workers find a job that suits their particular talents.

Workers can be moved from one task to another so that they do not become bored.

Workers are saved the bother of setting aside one tool while they select another tool for the next task.

Goods which would be expensive were it not for the decreased costs made possible by division of labour are more widely available.

36.2   Alienation and deskilling

The division of labour and the grim industrial conditions of the nineteenth century led Karl Marx to develop his idea that the individual's or the class relationship to the means of production influenced and determined all other relationships within society.

The concept of *alienation* was developed by Marx to describe a worker's attitude and sense of frustra-

Item 9.8   Karl Marx

tion with a purely repetitive part in the industrial work process. Alienation means a separation of the individual from the process he or she is engaged in as it becomes meaningless to him or her. He or she may also become separated or cut off from fellow workers. An alienated worker has almost no interest in the work that he or she is doing, and views the job purely as means of earning money. To perform a routine task for many hours each day in a factory means that the worker is little more than an appendage to the machine. As workers have no economic resources to sell other than their labour, Marx said they are simply 'wage slaves'.

Car workers in particular have been the focus of attention for many sociologists possibly because of the monotony of the assembly line, which Henry Ford invented in 1910. Assembly–line work increases alienation. The high incidence of strikes, particularly unofficial strikes, in the motor industry is often thought to be caused primarily by this work situation.

The sociologist R. Blauner identifies four elements to alienation:

powerlessness – decisions are made over which the worker has no control;

meaninglessness – workers see only their own small part of the manufacturing process and not the whole, so there is little or no sense of purpose other than the weekly wage packet;

isolation – a sense of community is absent in a large factory with a high labour turnover and frequent job switching, and friendships become harder to form (there is neither the time for conversation nor is it often possible to speak without shouting above the noise);

self-estrangement – there can be no personal expression put into assembly-line work, as there can into something individually crafted, and there is no satisfaction in the task to be done.

Strikes are not the only symptom of alienation; other industrial problems such as absenteeism, lateness, labour turnover and even accidents are often much higher in those jobs where alienation is most apparent.

Key terms

- division of labour
- alienation
- wage slave
- powerlessness
- meaninglessness
- isolation
- self-estrangement

Item 9.9 Car workers on an assembly line

There are serious social disadvantages, then, to the division of labour:

There is a loss of job satisfaction because the worker is not involved with all processes that lead to the finished product.

The work is so repetitive that it is difficult to take much pride in the task itself, and the worker may rarely see the finished article.

Boring work may destroy creative abilities, so that even non-work time is spent passively and the employee is unable or unwilling to express any individuality in leisure activities.

Monotonous work leads to fatigue.

There has been a decline in individual craftsmanship and many unskilled factory hands have no opportunities for displaying any artistic talents or merit at work.

Standardisation can lead to dull uniformity both of products and producers.

Workers may have an increased risk of unemployment, because they may be replaced by automated modern machinery, or a large work-force may be laid off if a few key workers come out on strike.

ACTIVITIES 6: Play-reading

Read the play-reading and answer the questions which follow.

(Sausage factory canteen, Long-time factory hand Jean talks to new worker, Mike.)

Jean So you worked at the car factory?

Mike Yeah, I served four years, with time off for good behaviour.

Jean The pay's good though, isn't it? From what I've heard . . .

Mike If you're prepared to work, can be better than here.

Jean So why . . .?

Mike Well, they were bringing in new technology –

Jean What? Replace you with a robot, did they?

Mike Huh! I was one anyway by then. No, it's just I didn't think they could make the job any more boring than it was – but they did. The day before I handed in my notice, the supervisor told me I'd been daydreaming too much. 'Think about what you're doing!' he said. Well, that's the last thing you want to do – anything else but, you know –

but anyway, me and the other lads were on a collective bonus – the others were a bit cheesed off with me working at less than lightning speed.

Jean So, seeking excitement and thrills you've come to a sausage factory.

Mike Anywhere's better than there. We used to drop a loose screw into the door panel so the lucky owner would get driven mad wondering what that worrying rattle was. What's your solution to braindeath?

Jean We put meat in the sausages. Anyway, I'm glad I don't drive one of your cars. There must've been perks, though. I bet you got a big discount on all their models.

Mike I prefer other makes. If you knew how they were made . . . well, I bet you can't stand their sausages, eh?

Jean I'm a vegetarian.

Mike I rest my case! What's the time? Ah, three hours to the weekend. Bliss!

Jean Doing anything special?

Mike I'm stripping down a car engine, and putting it back together – my hobby.

Jean You can't be serious! Haven't you had enough of engines? Are you a masochist? I mean, you're not getting paid and you don't even have to do it!

Mike That's the point! Forget the money – work is what you've got to do. And what you don't have to do, that's done for enjoyment and satisfaction, and, well . . . cars are a part of my life really, except when I was at work!

1 What did Mike really mean when he said 'I served four years, with time off for good behaviour'?

2 What happened at the car factory to make Mike hand in his notice?

3 Why did the car workers drop loose screws into the door panels? Explain your answer fully.

4 What is Mike going to do at the weekend, and why was Jean so surprised?

5 How does Mike explain his liking for his hobby?

6 Referring to Blauner's four elements of alienation (powerlessness, meaninglessness, isolation and self-estrangement), explain, with reference to the text, how and why Mike felt alienated at the car factory.

36.3 The impact of technology

Information technology, resulting from the application of computing to telecommunications, has greatly speeded the pace of technological change. The use of personal computers in offices is now common. New technology is changing the face of banking, retailing and indeed many other areas – this sociology textbook was prepared on a word processor.

ACTIVITIES 7

1 List all those things, places and jobs you can think of which have changed because of advances in technology and computing. Use four headings for your lists: at home; leisure; at work; shopping.

2 For a few of your examples in each list you should now note the advantages computerisation has brought.

3 You should also note any disadvantages and problems which may have accompanied the changes.

Britain has one of the largest computer industries outside the USA. It is one of the world's leading

Item 9.10 High technology industry

Item 9.11 Robots on a production line

nations in the production and use of computers and in the provision of computing systems and services. The use of computerised controls is becoming widespread in steel mills, coal mines, oil refineries and chemical plants. Britain, too, was the world's sixth largest user of industrial robots by the end of 1984.

A French sociologist called Touraine listed three stages of the impact technology had on work:

1 *deskilling* or the disintegration of a worker's skill (for example, by division of labour);

2 the *mechanisation* of productive techniques and the development of an integrated system of production; and

3 the advent of *automation* – the worker merely controls and superintends

Automation may be considered as the reversal of the division of labour. Instead of dividing up work into many parts to be performed by a large work-force, automation involves the use of complex machinery which performs many tasks with the minimum workforce. The social consequences of automation will depend on the extent of the automatic processes but certain general social gains and losses are inevitable.

Key terms

- computerisation
- information technology
- robots
- deskilling
- mechanisation
- automation

The social advantages of automation may include:

the lessening of the soulless nature of work that is so much a cause of alienation.

more time available for leisure pursuits.

more economic goods available so that the standard of living can be raised.

an expansion of service industries (such as catering, holiday agencies, entertainment and sport), especially as less work-time will be spent in manufacturing and people will look for new ways in which to spend their increased leisure time.

a shorter working week and longer holidays in which to relax.

more resources available to keep the sick and the aged.

Some of the unfortunate social consequences of automation are likely to be:

an even greater gap between the rich and the poor because the means of production will be controlled by the wealthy technocrats.

a large increase in the number of unemployed in the short run, especially among less qualified workers who will be faced with redundancy.

an inability of trade unions to protect members who are unskilled.

shortage of purchasing power for those who cannot find work.

over-production of goods, consequent upon underconsumption by the employed.

white-collar workers gaining at the expense of the rest of society, with subsequent trade union quarrels.

Technological advances are bringing radical changes to our society. There is a continual trend towards increased industrialisation and urban living, together with a decline in rural activities. The workforce is becoming more skilled and mobile; the occupation structure is inevitably altering. Changes are far more rapid than they have ever been before.

36.4 The collapse of work

Clive Jenkins and Barrie Sherman, in *The Collapse of Work*, argue that industrialised societies will not in

---

As the first report of the Advisory Council for Applied Research and Development ('The Applications of Semi-Conductor Technology', September 1978) put it: 'This is the most influential technology of the twentieth century because: (i) it both extends and displaces a wide range of intellectual or intuitive skills; (ii) it is all pervasive; (iii) it is still advancing rapidly; (iv) it is very cheap and getting cheaper; (v) it will become abundantly available from international sources and (vi) it has exceptional reliability.' The Prime Minister stated it more simply at the December 1978 meeting of the National Economic Development Office when he described micro-electronics as 'the most rapid industrial change in history'.

from Clive Jenkins and Barrie Sherman, *The Collapse of Work* (Eyre Methuen, 1979)

Item 9.12   The most rapid industrial change in history

---

the future be able to provide work for all. They also argue that the impact of information technology on the world of work amounts to an industrial revolution – 'the most rapid industrial change in history'.

ACTIVITIES 8

Read Item 9.13 and answer the questions that follow.

1 The writers suggest that the digital watch has now become the standard lower cost conventional watch. What advantages do digital watches seem to offer consumers?

2 If 49 per cent of the world production of watches uses electronics and quartz, what kind of mechanism does the 'traditional' watch industry use?

3 As a result of the impact of new technology on the watch industry in Switzerland, what loss in employment and foreign trade did it suffer?

4 Do a quick survey on your class, or perhaps even on a full year of pupils and find out the proportion of people who have watches powered by electronics or quartz.
   Remember: an electronic or quartz watch can still have an analogue face (traditional face with hands that go round) as well as the more obvious digital display.

Jenkins and Sherman go on to discuss *technological unemployment* – unemployment caused by the introduction of new technology. Technological unemployment may occur in any country; in France people receive special redundancy compensation in such cases. Jenkins and Sherman are concerned that technological unemployment in Britain will rise over time to a high level. They argue that the world is not suffering from a lack of jobs, but rather from a lack of a political will to keep unemployment down. They suggest that policies in the communist countries of the Eastern European bloc are quite different from those which operate in Britain:

The Eastern European bloc has managed to keep unemployment to a minimum as a result of deliberate policy. The right to work is written into the constitution of the Soviet Union. They deliberately overman certain industries so as to employ more people. This leads to strange labour-creating situations. A multi-storey hotel was built with 'magic-eye' automatic door opening mechanisms, yet this hotel has a lady sitting near the lift door with a converted table-tennis bat which she waves in front of the beam in the event of people approaching. (adapted from *The Collapse of Work* pp. 81–2).

Is it better to run a society in a deliberately inefficient way to provide work for all or is it better to have an efficient society, where work is not regarded as so important?

The most visible signs of this new technology are, quite appropriately, those that the public at large can recognize. At present there are two major and two minor uses. The digital watch has swept all before it. Within the last 5 years it has completely changed an industry that had remained virtually unaltered since the invention of the balance wheel. From being a gimmick and a high cost one at that, the digital watch has now become the standard lower cost conventional watch. To the consumer it is cheaper, more reliable, more durable and, given consumer fickleness, more fashionable. The scale of impact has administered a severe shock to an international industry which had complacently watched its profits automatically mount. The public often associates this novel form of watch with a digital display (the fashionable aspect), but this type of drive also features in conventional watches with ordinary hands. In less than 10 years 49 per cent of the world production of watches has switched over to electronics and quartz and the technical development is by no means at an end.

The conventional watch industry was totally unprepared for the challenge and in great measure it succumbed. The Lip factory workers' work-in and co-operative in France foundered on the rocks of the new technology, not on its day-to-day managerial expertise. The Swiss watch industry, vital to the national balance of payments as well as a major employer, lost at least 25 per cent of its labour force and saw a 'turnaround' in its balance of payments to the extent of £125 million per year.

from Clive Jenkins and Barrie Sherman, *The Collapse of Work* (Eyre Methuen, 1979)

Item 9.13   Changes in the watch industry

ACTIVITIES 9

1 Give your opinions about the Eastern European policies described for keeping people in jobs.

2 What are the advantages and disadvantages of the two alternative approaches posed in the final paragraph? Try to give a reasoned opinion in answer to this question.

ACTIVITIES 10

Read Item 9.14 and answer the questions that follow.

1 Give examples of the mismatches the writer talks about between 'old skills and new needs'.

2 Explain in your own words what Shirley Williams might mean when she says that the move from one kind of society to another, based on information technology, is like a 'quantum leap'. What kind of change is she suggesting will happen?

> The scale of the mismatch between old skills and new needs shows that the industrial world is moving towards a second Industrial Revolution, a revolution based on information technology. The movement from one kind of industrial society to another is not a steady progression, but a quantum leap, like the change from feudal agriculture to manufacturing industry concentrated in the cities. The relics of feudal Britain, the half-timbered houses, the cathedrals and castles, remind us of a vanished society. The empty factories of Merseyside and the desolate mills of Yorkshire and Lancashire are, similarly, monuments to a fast-disappearing industrial past.
>
> from Shirley Williams, *A Job to Live* (Penguin, 1985)

Item 9.14 A second Industrial Revolution

3 What kind of society does it seem Shirley Williams is envisaging for our future?

UNIT 37 Industrial relations

The system of industrial relations in Britain is based on the organisation of employees and employers into trade unions and employers' associations.

37.1 Trade unions

Nearly all industries and occupations have trade unions which workers may join. Even though rising unemployment has led to a decline in recent years in union membership, at the end of 1983 the total membership of British trade unions was about 11.3 million. There are about 400 different trade unions in Britain. Among the largest are:

Union	Number of members
Transport and General Workers Union	1 500 000
Amalgamated Union of Engineering Workers	1 200 000
Municipal Boilermakers and Allied Trades Union	780 000
National Union of Public Employees	689 000

The national organisation of the trade union movement is the Trades Union Congress (TUC).

The main functions of trade unions are:

1 to improve the standard of living and increase the *real earnings* of their members. (Real earnings are not just monetary earnings, but rather the goods and services that can be bought with money earned.)

2 to work for better fringe benefits such as higher overtime rates, piecework rates and bonuses.

3 to strive for better conditions of work such as shorter working hours, longer holidays and workers' amenities.

4 to attempt to safeguard the jobs of their members, especially where redundancies can be avoided.

5 to work for the reform of industrial legislation possibly by participating indirectly in political matters (for example, by contributing to the finances of the Labour party).

6 to co-operate with employers and the government in the establishment of effective bargaining machinery.

ACTIVITIES 11

1 Devise a short open-ended questionnaire or interview schedule to find out why individual people belong to a trade union in the first place and what they then expect the union to do for them.

2 Ask members of your family and family friends to answer your questions and then report your findings to your class.

Relationships between employer and employee depend to a considerable extent upon the type of trade union to which employees belong. There are five main types of trade union in Britain today:

1 *General unions* are the largest unions representing workers in a number of jobs. The general unions have considerable financial strength, but their power is often not as great as their membership would suggest because their members are engaged in different occupations.

2 *Industrial unions* represent workers in one industry and their power derives from the common interest of their members.

3 *White-collar unions* are becoming increasingly important as the service industries expand and more people work in the sphere of administration, finance, government, science and the professions.

4 *Craft unions* are the oldest and most numerous unions, but their membership figures are decreasing. (Over half the 1983 total number of unions had under 1000 members.)

5 *Confederations of unions* are organisations of unions that join in a loose way to give workers the strength that comes with unity. Their main importance, as far as the relationships between employers and employees are concerned, is that they enable workers to face the large confederations of employers with something approaching equal strength.

37.2 The CBI

The CBI (Confederation of British Industry) is the central employers' organisation in Britain. It represents 250 000 businesses which together employ about half the working population.

The CBI was formed in 1965. It was granted a Royal Charter which required it to act as a national point of reference for those seeking industry's views. It was also, among other things, to provide advice, information and services to British industry. The CBI has an Information Directorate whose task is to make known CBI policies. CBI National Conferences, which are televised in the same way as annual political party conferences, have been held since 1977 in order to present employers' views to a wider audience. The CBI also has a Parliamentary Department which lobbies MPs in order to inform them of employers' views about topics which may be debated in Parliament.

37.3 Industrial disputes

The interests of employers and employees may be at odds if the employers are preoccupied with maximising profit without regard for the welfare of their workers. But even in a *mixed economy* such as that found in Britain, strikes and other forms of unrest still occur as well in the public-sector industries that are controlled by the state, and in which profit is not the main motivating influence. Some of the reasons for industrial strife include:

employers attempting to secure cheap labour.

workers believing that they are not securing their fair share either of the industrial organisation's initial profit or of extra profit brought by increased productivity.

some workers believing that they are a special case and are not receiving a just reward for their labour.

day-by-day frictions which arise when communications break down and one side of industry does not fully consider the other side's point of view.

demarcation disputes over who should do a particular job.

a lack of effective *negotiating machinery*, so that causes of dissatisfaction cannot be adequately discussed and eradicated.

income differentials for skill and responsibility becoming eroded.

ACTIVITIES 12

Using secondary sources, such as newspaper articles, comment on one particular current industrial dispute. You should cut out the newspaper articles and include them in your work. In your work try to answer some of the following questions:

1 What is the main central cause of the dispute?

2 What is the role of the trade unions in this dispute?

3 What steps have so far been taken to resolve the dispute, and what are the remaining problems as far as you can see?

4 Which side appears to you to have:
  a the strongest case?
  b the strongest bargaining position?

5 How do you expect this dispute to end? Explain your ideas with reference to your sources of information.

Bargaining machinery in Britain may be considered in three stages. Each stage is of a slightly more serious nature, although strikes may occur at any stage if bargaining procedures break down. The stage at which bargaining between employer and employee may cease to operate depends upon the industrial climate and the amount of goodwill, or lack of goodwill, that exists between the two parties. The three stages are:

1 *negotiations* by employers and unions to secure a settlement to a dispute without calling upon outside help.

2 *conciliation* by Department of Employment officers in an effort to draw the parties closer together.

3 *arbitration* by a third party that gives an independent decision, although employers and unions may not agree to be bound by the results of the arbitration.

Economists Metcalf and Richardson suggest the significance of strikes can be measured by:

the number of stoppages that occur;
the numbers of workers involved in the stoppages;
the number of working days lost through stoppages.

Strike action is usually the last resort by a trade union. Even in a society that provides reasonable social security benefits, workers are likely to suffer most from a strike; employers may lose business,

goodwill and profit while shareholders may suffer from a loss of dividends, but it is unlikely that they will have to cut down on foodstuffs. Before strike action takes place, trade unions are likely to use other bargaining weapons. Workers may deliberately *go slow*, or *work to rule* by rigidly adhering to an employer's rule-book. The Royal Commission on Trade Unions and Employers' Associations (in the Donovan Report, 1968) drew attention to the fact that, although Britain's number of days lost through breakdowns in relations between employers and employees was not excessive (compared with countries such as Australia, Canada, Italy and the USA, which had far worse records), up to about 95 per cent of strikes in Britain were unofficial. These *wildcat strikes* were to some extent caused by a double system of industrial bargaining. The informal system of negotiation between individual employers and shop stewards often clashed with the formal system of official associations of employers and workers.

The Industrial Relations Act (1971) tried to eliminate the double system of bargaining, but it was unsuccessful because of conflict between the government and the unions. This culminated in the Trades Union Congress advising unions affiliated to the TUC not to register under the Act. The 1971 Act was so unsuccessful that in 1972 there were a record 24 million workdays lost through strikes. The 1971 Act was replaced by the Labour government's Trade Union and Labour Relations Act (1974) which restored the pre-1971 privileges of the unions. Further Labour legislation followed which seemed to strengthen the position of the unions: the Employment Protection Act (1975), the Health and Safety at Work Act (1975) and the Industry Act (1975). Then the Conservative government, elected in 1979, introduced Employment Acts in 1980 and 1982 and their Trade Union Act in 1984. Metcalf and Richardson argue these Acts did a number of things:

they narrowed the limits of legal picketing;
they reduced the scope of legal immunities applying to industrial action;
they regulated the closed shop; and
they extended the requirement for secret ballots.

The union leaders believed their movement was being attacked by these measures.

Some would say that the most successful industrial relationships are where employers and employees negotiate freely without the government attempting to force industrial co-operation by legislation.

▶ UNIT 38   Unemployment

38.1 Types of unemployment

Eight causes of unemployment which arise from the economic system itself are given in Item 9.15.

38.2 The social incidence of unemployment

In this section we shall attempt to show just who in our society has joined the ranks of the unemployed. Unemployment does not threaten everyone equally. As item 9.16 shows, those who are young, from the manual social classes and not white are much more likely than others to be affected by unemployment.

ACTIVITIES 13

1 Using Item 9.16 draw three bar charts or histograms showing what percentage of each of the three groups (age, colour and socio-economic) have had one spell of unemployment. These histograms will show you the social incidence of unemployment very clearly. Remember to label your charts fully.

2 See if you can suggest any reasons to explain the patterns that appear.

In mid 1987 there were about 3.2 million people claiming unemployment benefit. This represents an unemployment rate of 13.4 per cent of the working population. This underestimates the true picture of unemployment, however, by perhaps as much as the 700 thousand (0.7 million) who do not register themselves as unemployed.

Economists Metcalf and Richardson point out that in any one year, only three per cent of the labour force account for 70 per cent of the total weeks of unemployment. This group, who seem to bear the burden of unemployment, are those who are towards the bottom of the pay scales, work in the most risky occupations and suffer a high incidence of ill health. Such disadvantages in the labour market seem to have a snowball effect, all increasing the problems of the same sections of the work-force. In this topic we

Type of unemployment	Main cause
1 Casual	Employment offered cannot always be steady and some workers are unspecific, such as manual labourers who move from one unskilled job to another.
2 Cyclical	Trade cycles have brought mass unemployment, eg. about 3 million in Britain from 1931–3; these cycles have largely been replaced by milder yet still serious recessions.
3 Frictional	Unemployment is caused by workers with a special skill not being able to get work in one area, but a shortage of the same type of worker existing in another area.
4 International	Unemployment can spread between countries as was seen after the Wall Street crash of 1929. About 20 million workers were out of work in the USA and the effect of their decreased purchasing power on imports caused unemployment to spread throughout the world.
5 Regional	Workers in some regions, such as NE England, suffer from long-standing unemployment because of the decay of old stable industries upon which they had come to place complete reliance; they are loath to move to another area or learn another job.
6 Residual	There will always be a hard core of people who are unable to work: even laziness may be regarded as a disability, especially if it is caused by some deep-rooted psychological upset.
7 Seasonal	A man may find work at a seaside resort in the summer and at a sugar beet factory in winter, but unemployment will be caused by the lag between these seasonal jobs.
8 Structural	Unemployment is caused by the changes in demand for products, eg more people might decide to travel by air, with a consequent increase in unemployment in the shipbuilding industry.

Item 9.15   Types and main causes of unemployment

Male unemployment[1] in the previous 12 months[2]

Great Britain   Percentages and numbers

	No spells of unemployment	1 spell of unemployment	2 or more spells of unemployment	Sample size (= 100%) (numbers)
Males[3] aged *(percentages)*:				
18–24	65	28	7	1,167
25–39	84	14	2	2,554
40–59	88	11	1	2,664
60–64	83	16	1	602
All males aged 18–64	82	15	2	6,987
Colour *(percentages)*				
White	83	15	2	6,289
Coloured	71	28	1	272
Socio-economic group *(percentages)*				
Professional/employers and managers	94	5	1	1,546
Intermediate/junior non-manual	89	9	1	1,101
All non-manual	92	7	1	2,647
Skilled manual	83	15	2	2,749
Semi-skilled/unskilled manual	68	28	4	1,468
All manual	77	20	3	4,217

[1]Excludes periods of voluntary waiting to take up a job and periods of inability to look for work owing to temporary sickness and periods of unemployment experienced while a person was a full-time student or on a government training scheme.

[2]In the 12 months before interview.
[3]Excludes full-time students and those permanently unable to work.

Source: General Household Survey, 1983

from *Social Trends 16* (HMSO, 1986)

Item 9.16 Male unemployment over 12 months: by age, colour and socio-economic group

	Numbers (m)
1983 unemployment (average)	3.1
Add unregistered unemployment	0.7
Subtract claimants not actively seeking work	–0.4
TOTAL	**3.4**

from *Prest and Coppock's The UK Economy: 11th Edition*, ed M.J. Artis (Weidenfeld and Nicholson, 1986)

Item 9.17 Composition of the unemployed

United Kingdom   Percentages and thousands

	Duration of unemployment (weeks)						Total (= 100%) (thousands)
	Up to 2	Over 2, up to 8	Over 8, up to 26	Over 26, up to 52	Over 52, up to 104	Over 104	
Males aged:							
16–19	9.5	17.6	28.4	24.3	15.3	4.9	212.5
20–24	11.0	14.3	21.9	18.2	15.7	18.8	390.8
25–34	5.2	9.8	18.8	16.8	17.0	32.4	491.2
35–49	4.0	7.8	16.3	14.4	15.7	41.7	479.1
50–59	2.8	5.3	14.0	14.3	17.4	46.2	369.2
60 or over	5.6	10.2	26.3	32.2	13.6	12.2	65.8
All males aged 16 or over	6.1	10.2	19.2	17.4	16.2	30.9	2,008.5
Females aged:							
16–19	10.6	17.2	26.5	25.3	15.3	4.9	151.4
20–24	14.7	16.1	23.5	20.0	11.7	14.0	220.7
25–34	7.4	13.6	28.3	26.6	12.3	11.7	220.6
35–49	7.0	11.3	22.8	19.8	16.9	22.2	172.0
50 or over	3.1	5.6	13.3	15.2	17.4	45.5	133.2
All females aged 16 or over	9.0	13.2	23.6	21.8	14.3	18.1	898.0

Source: Department of Employment

from *Social Trends 18* (HMSO, 1988)

Item 9.18   Unemployment: by age and sex

shall study the social incidence of unemployment, looking particularly at age (and youth unemployment), sex, marital status, social class and region.

Age, sex and unemployment

Item 9.18 on page 171 shows unemployment rates by age and sex. Young workers are more likely to become unemployed than other groups, but other statistics reveal that, although older workers are less likely to become unemployed, once they are unemployed they are likely to remain unemployed for a long time.

The unemployment rate for males under 20 has doubled in the last decade. When firms are in trouble one of the easiest economies is to reduce recruitment.

Marital status and unemployment

Single men experience unemployment rates double those of married men of the same age and social class. Metcalf and Richardson suggest this may be due to the quality of labour offered by these two groups, and to the fact that single men have less pressure to take another job.

Social class and unemployment

The likelihood of a period of unemployment for manual workers is over twice that for non-manual workers. In June 1982 there was one registered vacancy to every 200 unemployed general labourers.

Regional unemployment

Unemployment affects the different regions to different degrees. See Item 9.20.

An equally pressing problem is the high rates of unemployment in cities. The male unemployment rates given by the 1981 census for the inner areas and outer areas of four majors towns are shown in Item 9.21.

38.3 Unemployment as an individual problem

Since World War II there has been a remarkable change in the employment situation in Britain. In 1931, unemployment was 21 per cent and until the outbreak of the war in 1939 the percentage of unemployment was nearly always over ten per cent.

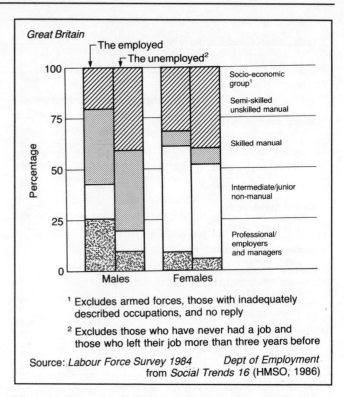

[1] Excludes armed forces, those with inadequately described occupations, and no reply

[2] Excludes those who have never had a job and those who left their job more than three years before

Source: *Labour Force Survey 1984* *Dept of Employment* from *Social Trends 16* (HMSO, 1986)

Item 9.19 Unemployment: by socio-economic group

	Unemployment %		
	1966	1975	1983
N. Ireland	5.3	7.9	21.0
Scotland	2.7	5.2	15.0
North	2.5	5.9	17.3
North West	1.4	5.3	15.7
Wales	2.8	5.6	16.1
West Midlands	0.8	4.1	15.7
Yorks & Humberside	1.1	4.0	14.1
East Anglia	1.4	3.4	10.6
South West	1.7	4.7	11.3
East Midlands	1.0	3.6	11.7
South East	0.9	2.8	9.5
UK	1.4	4.1	13.0

from *Prest and Coppock's The UK Economy: 11th edition,* ed. M.J. Artis (Weidenfeld and Nicholson, 1986)

Item 9.20 Regional unemployment

%	Inner area	Outer area
Birmingham	25	17
Liverpool	31	21
London	14	8
Manchester	28	18

from *Prest and Coppock's The UK Economy: 11th edition,* ed. M.J. Artis (Weidenfeld and Nicholson, 1986)

Item 9.21 Unemployment in the city

A government white paper entitled *Employment Policy* was published in 1944 and successive governments succeeded in maintaining a state of full employment (using this term to mean that more than 97 per cent of those registered for jobs are employed) until 1972, when the unemployed numbered over one million for the first time since the war. The total unemployed rose to 1.6 million in 1978. Unemployment has continued to rise since and stood at nearly four million by the end of 1986.

Unemployment for whatever reason is bad for an individual and long-term mass unemployment is far worse than temporary unemployment from casual or seasonal causes. Long-term unemployment can lead to a feeling of inadequacy and, if widespread, can result in social unrest. Mass unemployment before World War II led to misery and despair in those without a job, and the mass unemployment of the 1980s is no different in that respect.

ACTIVITIES 14

Read Item 9.22 and answer the questions that follow.

1 What kind of attitude did Kate have to unemployment when she was at school?

2 How similar to or different from your own attitude to unemployment is Kate's?

3 What are Kate's plans now?

4 Explain briefly in your own words the kind of impact the experience of unemployment has had on Kate.

In *The Unemployment Handbook*, Dauncey suggests that a job gives people important personal support in five basic ways:
a purpose and direction
b daily routine
c self-respect and identity
d friendship
e money.
When a person loses his or her job, or just doesn't have one, he or she may also lose these important supports.

ACTIVITIES 15

Using the five main areas of support listed above draw up a questionnsive for someone who is working. Find out whether their job provides these supports and if so, in what ways.

38.4 The social impact of unemployment

McKee and Bell studied unemployment in Kidderminster. Kidderminster had a population of just over 50 000 at the 1981 census and an unemployment rate of just under 12 per cent the same year. It is a small industrial town in the West Midlands – a region McKee and Bell noted was, at the time of their study, experiencing the highest rate of increase in unemployment in the UK. McKee and Bell's study aimed to draw conclusions about the impact of unemployment on family and marital relations.

When I was at school, I didn't take unemployment seriously. We talked about it a bit in some of the lessons, from about the third or fourth form. And in my last year we had some games and exercises to do as projects. One of them was pretending to run your own business. I ended up broke after the first week, so it's just as well I haven't run my own business since. We had some lessons about modern history and we had to write about the causes of unemployment. I just wrote 'unemployment is 'cos there aren't enough jobs'. When I left school I had a careers session and got given information and an advice pack. It had lots in it about how to look for jobs and training and how to sign on, but I just when down to the dole office with a friend and that was it. At school, unemployment sounded like the summer holidays, though they'd try and frighten you with it to make you behave in class. I'd had part-time jobs, and I thought I'd just carry on like that. With a bit of extra from dole like pocket money. I live part at home, part in squat, part round my friend's. I'm too busy to look for a job really, what with trying to get the squat sorted out and helping my friend and I'm going on holiday soon anyway, to France. You can get jobs picking grapes of washing up in hotels and just sleep on the beach. Just sit in the sun.

from 'Kate Barber – unemployed' in *Using Unemployment* (Channel 4, 1986)

Item 9.22   Unemployment – a personal view

As far as I can see there's nothing in Kiddy [Kidderminster] for us or the kids, there's nothing, although there's plenty of factories. They started building all these new places, and you think you'd get work but you just can't get hold of one.... All the work's gone in Kiddy. There's nothing you can do.

... there's half the town lay empty.

They're closin' down factories every day.

Kiddy's a ghost town ain't it? At one time every one of my mates was at work. I bet you I can't even name one that's at work now.... round Kidderminster ... all they're concerned about is how many cars can we park in so and so car park. They've built an enormous ring road, they don't think about the small shops they've cut off. Multi-storey car parks and one-way streets that's all they're interested in. There's a carpet warehouse and a picture house and tobacconists next to it, they've closed them off to build a bloody supermarket – Asda Superstores – and all the jobs have gone. All the jobs have gone and they haven't even cleared the site yet.

from S. Allen *et al., The Experience of Unemployment* (Macmillan, 1986)

Item 9.23   Unemployment in Kidderminster

Some of their respondents described Kidderminister in the ways given in Item 9.23.

ACTIVITIES 16

McKee and Bell began their study of unemployment and family life with certain *hypotheses* or expectations. We shall go on to see what these are, but before that, how would *you* expect male unemployment to affect family life and the roles of husbands and wives? List the problems (and possibly the pleasures) that male unemployment may bring to families.

McKee and Bell suggest that through their 'imaginative viewfinder' they supposed they might see 'moving pictures of unwaged men collecting the children from school and preparing family meals'; in other words, they thought they might see the social life and roles of men and women draw closer together as a result of male unemployment.

ACTIVITIES 17

Read the accounts and quotations in Item 9.24, taken from McKee and Bell's study of unemployed males, and comment on them. What impact does male unemployment actually seem to have had on the roles men and women see for themselves and each other?

McKee and Bell describe what they observed as a 'collision of male and female social worlds'. In Item 9.25 (overleaf) they describe a process of *double isolation*, with *wives'* social contacts being curtailed as a consequence of the *husband's* job loss.

ACTIVITIES 18

Read Item 9.25 and answer the questions that follow it.

1 What do McKee and Bell mean when they talk about 'the restricted social world of unemployed individuals'? Try to give examples to illustrate your answer.

2 Explain in your own words the 'increasing privatisation of wives' lives' referred to in Item 9.25.

3 How might the impact of *female* unemployment affect family life?

4 How would the impact of *female* unemployment on family life differ from the impact of *male* unemployment? Give reasons for your answer.

[1] No, no I can't sign on, 'im bein' out of work. It's a waste of time. I won't get nothin' see.

[2] (I was working) . . . part-time so I packed that in 'cause it wasn't worth me working now. They'd have taken it off what he was getting. (Worked as barmaid part-time)

[3] That's the problem. You try to build yourself up and they all stop it right away. I think I was allowed to earn £4. I mean, by the time I had me bus fare out of that it didn't add up to nothing, you know, we just couldn't manage. (Worked as cleaner part-time)

[4] Any job I get, even part-time, Derek's social security would be cut to the equivalent so therefore I think I'm not going to do anything that I don't like . . . to do a grotty job and have our money cut, I think well what the hell! (Former tax officer)

[5] I'd have the feeling as if people would be staring behind my back, my missus keeping me, she's paying for all the food, the clothes, the roof over our heads, paying for me to go out and have a drink . . . If she just worked alone I'd probably go round the bend.

[6] I think there's two different situations. As Roy says, he likes to be the breadwinner and that's hard on a man, but the hardest bit on a woman is like *managing on unemployment* . . . that's the biggest problem. 'Cause, to me, being unem-ployed, I know it sounds daft, but you've got to work at being unemployed if you want to survive. (Wife).

[7] I couldn't live off a woman . . . I think I'd leave before I'd live off her. That is the way I am.

[8] . . . the man he is, is like a he-man. 'I'll keep my family and nobody else.' That's Bill's attitude anyway. Nobody else keeps his family, he's very old-fashioned that way. He don't believe in this Women's Lib or nothing like that. He says women are equal to men in some ways, but he says men will always be the breadwinners. He says he's been the breadwinner for years and he'll be the breadwinner for another few years.

[9] I'm not going to slave myself to death while he sits at home all day on his backside doing nothing. (Wife)

[10] *Husband* (unemployed bricklayer): There's been lots of times we've had £150 come in . . . and I've ended up with about £10 or £15 and you've had the rest.
Wife (former secretary): But it's like I keep telling you it's not *me* who has it. He thinks when he got £150 he'd want a bit of it and I have the rest. And he seems to think it's me who's having it, but it's not me. I spend it on paying the bills, buying food, clothes things like that. But he seems to get the idea that it's me who's having it. Whereas with him, when he has his cut, it's *him* who's having it, it's being spent on him!

from S. Allen *et al., The Experience of Unemployment* (Macmillan, 1986)

Item 9.24   Kidderminster men and their wives talking about unemployment

The collison between, rather than the harmonisation of, male and female social worlds was a constant theme raised by our respondents. Women could find their social contacts controlled and observed by their menfolk while the men themselves often found the private domain unwelcoming and confining. The restricted social world of unemployed individuals has been well-documented by many studies of the unemployed ... The unique contribution made by our research is to highlight the differential impact this can exact on members of the family unit. We found evidence of *double isolation* with the contacts and social ties of women being dramatically curtailed in response to husbands' job loss....Our findings suggest that it was not just unemployed men who had to respond to a reduction of social contacts. So too did their partners. This has the effect not just of dividing off the unemployed from the employed but it separated a wide range of those associated with the employed (wives, children, even parents) from those associated with the unemployed.

Our respondents often explained this increasing privatisation of wives' lives either as a consequence of husbands directly or indirectly discouraging women's outside links *or* because of withdrawal of contacts by others. The privacy of homes was stressed by the male's presence and often marital primacy was alluded to. One woman reported 'Mind you I don't like going anywhere where husbands are.' The theme of some husbands having *control over wives' social lives* could be detected in the language used. Wives talked about being 'allowed' to keep in touch with friends, to go out socially, and permissive husbands were praised: 'He's very good like that.' In a few cases the impression was also given that husbands *control use of domestic space*, visitors come only with *his* approval even if they are *her* friends. Friends who stay away may just be respectful of marital privacy *or* may be deferring to perceptions of the husband's 'mastery' of his home.

from S. Allen *et al., The Experience of Unemployment* (Macmillan, 1986)

Item 9.25   His unemployment: her problem

39.1 The relationship between work and non-work

There are close relationships between occupations and the way in which non-work time is spent. One piece of research on these relationships, *Coal is our Life*, was first published in 1956 and has become a classic community study. The focus of the study is a Yorkshire community which the authors called 'Ashton'. They spent two years studying various aspects of the miners' life there.

Ashton had a population of 14 000 and lay in the centre of the Yorkshire coalfield. The dominant feature of the landscape was the slag heaps which were, say the authors, 'the physical symbol of work and life in Ashton'. For the average male inhabitant of Ashton, coal was the means of gaining a living. Item 9.26 shows the profound influence the miners' work had on their leisure.

ACTIVITIES 19

Read Item 9.26 and answer the questions that follow it.

1 Using the first paragraph of the passage, but in your own words, described the kind of leisure pursued by the coal miners in Ashton.

2 The writers of this passage describe six factors which they suggest determine the leisure patterns of coal miners in Ashton. List these factors from the passage.

3 How do you spend your leisure?

4 How do you think your leisure time is affected or determined by what you have to do at school?

The pursuit of leisure in Ashton has two principal characteristics. It is vigorous and it is predominantly frivolous. Without wishing to enter into the question of which are 'better' or 'worse' ways of spending leisure time, it should be explained that the word frivolous is used in the sense of 'giving no thought for the morrow'. It is used in this way as a contrast to those forms of recreation which pursue a definite aim such as intellectual improvement by means of study in adult classes or discussion groups, or spiritual improvement through membership of a church.

Before considering in detail the content of the individual leisure activities, it is of some importance to appreciate why they should be of this generally frivolous nature. Briefly the hypothesis is this. The way in which the Ashton miner uses his leisure has been determined by a particular set of factors. These factors influence all miners but there are many other factors which are peculiar to particular groups of individuals, and finally, of course, there are variations of individual personality. In fact the consequences vary from behaviour based on extreme prudence to behaviour based on its opposite. What can be said, however, is that in the main the latter type of behaviour does predominate, and determines the texture of community life in Ashton. The former behaviour is found only among a minority.

Among the many factors at work a small number appear to exert the predominant influence. There is first insecurity arising from the danger of being killed at work – a danger which is more real to a miner than to a worker in almost any other industry. Secondly there is the insecurity of income based upon the miner's greater liability to injury as compared with other workers. Thirdly there is the fact that in the past the miner has lacked security of employment. Fourthly there is the insecurity based on the fact that the miner cannot be sure that he will spend his life in a well-paid job (even if he escapes injury): generally speaking, in his youth he works as a day-wage man, and returns to day-wage work in the fifties. In addition to these considerations, all of which are concerned with insecurity in one form or another, there is the fact that the people of Ashton not only work together but also live in the same neighbourhood. In this Ashton differs from large towns, where people working at the same place may live in widely separate places. Finally there is the influence of shift-work on social life.

from N. Dennis, F. Henriques and C. Slaughter, *Coal is Our Life* (Tavistock Publications, 1969)

Item 9.26 Leisure and insecurity

A sociologist called Parker has suggested that there are three ways in which work might influence leisure patterns. For coalminers, and others in very hard and demanding occupations (fishermen, car assembly workers, etc.) work and leisure will be *in opposition*; that is, work and leisure will be very different from each other with one compensating for the other. For people with more enjoyable jobs, which yield a lot of personal satisfaction and interest, more usually leisure will be an *extension* of their work – teachers may read in their spare time and nursery nurses may organise Brownies and Guides. Parker also suggested a third possibility, that work and leisure may not have any relationship to or effect on each other. Parker described this a *neutrality* pattern. In this case, people may be indifferent to their work, and feel able to pursue any kind of leisure without either need to 'recover' from their work, or desire to continue any work interest.

ACTIVITIES 20

1 Collect some information on work and leisure from your family and neighbours. If each member of your class collects information on their parents and neighbours you may be able to see some relationship emerging between the work people do and the way they spend their leisure.

2 Display your data in three columns – the first showing the respondents' occupation or work, the second showing the favourite or main leisure activities, and the third showing the kind of pattern (oppositional, extension or neutral) which you believe has been described. See if Parker's ideas are supported by your own research.

Although less time is spent at work than was the case 50 years ago (largely because of shorter hours and longer holidays) nevertheless the average person

Item 9.27 Work or leisure?

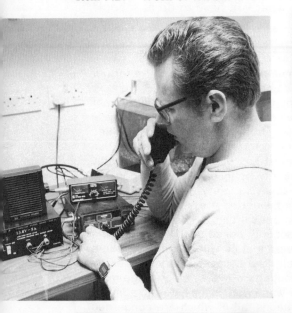

is more involved with his or her occupation than people were centuries ago. In 1978 the average number of hours worked was 44, but the average basic week in Britain was 40 hours. This is a longer working week than those of most continental countries, such as Germany and France. The average person is in many ways more occupationally orientated nowadays (that is, the job has more effect on their way of life).

Greater involvement in one's occupation means that it is increasingly difficult to distinguish between *work* and *non-work* activities. This is especially true of the professions and higher grades of work. A doctor may get great satisfaction from delivering a baby even though it may be late at night. A professional footballer might be very willing to enjoy a game and display his skills even if no pay were involved. Where does work stop and non-work begin in these occupations? In the economic world, though, we are concerned with occupations in market situations. People's places in society are governed not merely by their type of occupation but by the amount of goods and services they can command because of the money they receive for carrying out their occupations.

ACTIVITIES 21

Which of the photographs in Item 9.27 show people working?

Some of the occupations that have been the subject of special studies by sociologists have been jobs which have a great influence on those engaged in them. Jeremy Tunstall's study *The Fisherman* shows how a trawlerman sees himself as a member of a class drawn together by occupation so that 'he has indelibly printed on him certain habits, reflexes, patterns of spending, attitudes to life ...'. There are extracts from Tunstall's work in Items 9.28 and 9.29.

ACTIVITIES 22

Study Items 9.28 and 9.29 and answer the questions that follow.

1 After reading Item 9.28, return to Item 9.26 and the passage about coal miners in Ashton. How is the leisure of coal miners and deep-sea fishermen similar? How is it different?

2 'Giving away drinks buys a man status.' Explain in your own words what this statement means.

3 Why should such fishermen attempt to 'buy status' in this way?

At sea a fisherman suffers, but when ashore he has money to spare. He is unlikely to have any self-improving hobbies. His favourite relaxation is drinking, mainly with other fishermen, because only they are free all day when ashore, have the same attitude to life, and the same spare cash.

When fishermen drink they buy rounds compulsively. Giving away drinks buys a man status – even if only temporary. Some young lads when they get drunk start buying drinks for total strangers. In their sober moments, they will refer to such people as bums and scroungers, but for the moment the fisherman buys their deference and gains for himself the centre of the stage. When he throws his money away on drink, he is trying not only to shut out the thought of another trip to the Arctic, but also he is trying to forget his lowly position in society – an awareness of which originally contributed to his desire to go trawling.

A normal first day ashore might go like this: at ten a.m. the man goes down to the fish-dock to 'settle', to collect the poundage money which is due to him. At eleven a.m. he goes into a Hessle Road pub. Later with some pals he goes by taxi to another pub in the centre of Hull. At three o'clock a move is made again by taxi back to Hessle Road, and drinking continues in a club. This closes at five p.m. and the man goes home. He's out again for the evening session in one of the clubs, and after closing-time may well go to a party where there is more drinking. Fishermen don't drink draught bitter much, but draught mild, bottled beer, whisky, rum, and gin are all popular.

from Jeremy Tunstall, *The Fishermen* (MacGibbon and Kee, 1969)

Item 9.28   Life ashore

Item 9.29   Deep-sea fishermen

39.2 Leisure

A knowledge of the ways in which work and leisure are inter-related helps us to understand that the problems of leisure are not likely to be successfully tackled without consideration of the quality and meaning of working life (S. R. Parker, *The Sociology of Industry*, Allen & Unwin, 1981).

We have seen that there is a close connection between work and leisure. If two people are watching a cricket match they may be at work, at leisure or participating in both work and leisure. One might be paid for writing an account of the match for the press, or for scoring or umpiring. Another might write and describe the match to an absent friend, or might be very happy to score or umpire if asked, and might be quite willing to do these things voluntarily for pleasure. The difference between work and leisure in these cases is very difficult to distinguish. If the first person, who was being paid as a journalist, scorer or umpire, would rather have been doing something else such as sailing or gardening, then work becomes more clearly discernible from leisure. But is garden-ing work? It can be work or leisure depending upon the person, place and time. It is the opportunity to do what one wants to do, indulging in one's chosen pursuits, having free time at one's own disposal, that is the real substance of leisure. Parker has pointed out that we cannot comprehend the problems of leisure without considering a person's working life. For example, people who enjoy their work will want it to carry over into their spare time, whereas other people may wish to have a complete change of activity.

A sociologist called Abrams classified five ages of leisure. 'Young marrieds', for example, find it difficult to manage financially but they are wrapped up in each other, and young children give pleasure; the 35–45 year olds have time and money to spend outside the home, although they are probably still struggling to get 'established'; the 45–65 year olds have most to spend and fewer financial worries, but it is often a time of frustration and cynicism; the over 65s have more time for leisure after retirement, but usually have not then got the money to get the best from their spare time.

▶ UNIT 40 Retirement

40.1 The social institution of retirement

Parker points out that in the UK and the USA retirement was virtually unknown until the early nineteenth century. It started to grow in the years before World War II, but the shortage of labour during and just after the war meant that older workers were encouraged to remain in, or re-enter, the labour force. Parker goes on to say:

Fixed-age retirement and occupational pensions developed alongside bureaucrats and large companies and were spurred on by the belief that older workers were *slowing down overall productivity in increasingly competitive markets. Thus, in short, there were successive periods of rare retirement, discouraged retirement and encouraged retirement. A comparison of the economic situation and the prevailing 'official' attitudes to retirement during these successive periods strongly suggests that retirement practices and attitudes in modern industrial societies owe more to a concern with the 'needs' of the economy than the needs of individual men and women.* (S. R. Parker, *Work and Retirement*, Allen & Unwin, 1982).

Parker notes that retirement is rare outside modern industrial societies and in simpler societies there is generally more respect for, and status accorded to, the elderly because they have a more significant role to play in the life of the community. In many parts of the world today retirement is either rare or gradual, but hardly ever complete at a fixed age.

Parker tells us that the numbers of old people in Britain, along with most other industrial societies, are growing. Between 1961 and 1976 the numbers of people of pensionable age (65 for men, 60 for women) rose by 1.8 million to 9.4 million and they are expected to go on rising until at least 1991. Meanwhile, there are fewer people of pensionable age in some kind of paid employment. In 1931 more than half of the men over 65 were working; in 1951, 31 per cent; in 1971, 19 per cent; and in 1980, 12 per cent (and only ten per cent of women). Over the next few years Parker says the figures will almost certainly continue to go down even further.

He suggests that there are two ways of looking at work and retirement:

The *conservative* and *conformist* approach which demands that we have retirement policies based on the 'needs' of the economy, and argues that people lose their ability to work well as they get older. This approach is based on an assumption that work and leisure are separate.

The *radical* and *creative* approach which is based on the needs of people, and which encourages people to participate actively in preparation for retirement and to continue with previous life-styles. This approach is based on an assumption that work and leisure are integrated.

Parker lists the problems and achievements which have accompanied the development of retirement as a socially recognised institution. He suggests that retirement not only changes the lives of individuals but, more importantly perhaps for a sociologist, that retirement has led to changes in the norms and values of society.

Achievements

1 More people are living to a healthy old age in retirement.

2 There is now a better standard of living for the retired, absolutely, if not in comparison with other sections of the population.

For many years a few mostly unheeded voices have been advocating that old age should not be treated as a passive period of waiting for death, but should be seen as offering a new lease on life which, in optimum fulfilment, calls for new ways of living – ways possibly as different from those of mid-life as adolescence is from adulthood. The modern and radical expression of this point of view is the Gray Panther phenomenon in the USA, which advocates that people in their later years need not remain passive and impotent in the face of unacceptable roles. Maggie Kuhn, the leader of the Gray Panthers, disdains the activities of Golden Age Clubs as 'play-pens for the old' and has declared the 'we are not mellow, sweet old people. We have got to effect changes and we have nothing to lose.'

The increasing assertiveness, even militancy of at least some of the present generation of older people will in the long run necessitate appropriate responses from all sectors of society. In Britain, Len Murray, the trade union leader, has expressed his belief in a society in which retirement is regarded as a liberation, as an incentive to live actively and positively. We must not rely only on what the state and other bodies can do – there is a need for retired people themselves to take the initiative in creating the desired types of environments and attitudes for their lives in retirement.

The future of retirement is a matter, first, of understanding what are the various possible roles for older people in our society, and secondly of taking steps to see that individual choice is catered for as far as possible. The role possibilities are many, but they may be crudely dichotomised as (I) encourage retired people to live out their years in pursuit of time-filling hobbies, entertainments and in reflective vegetation, or (2) regard them as a rich source of energy, experience and wisdom, capable of attaining self-realisation and carrying, if they wish, important community responsibilities. The first alternative promises boredom, deterioration, dependency, conservatism, depression and institutionalisation. The second promises continued growth, preservation of vital functions, purposeful living, continued social usefulness and self-sufficiency.

from S.H. Parker *Work and Retirement* (Allen & Unwin, 1982)

Item 9.30   Work and retirement

3 The average age of retirement has come down and retirement is more often voluntary.

4 The retired population is getting younger, not only in age but also in life-style and outlook.

Problems

1 Population pressures such as the falling birthrate are tending to raise the age of retirement, while economic pressures are tending to lower it.

2 There are conflicts between the interests of the retired and the working population.

3 The old tend to be relegated to non-functional roles and lose their status and identity.

4 Sudden retirement can have bad effects on some people.

5 We are forcing many healthy older people into a retirement they do not want.

6 There are increasing difficulties in satisfying the needs of those older people who prefer work to retirement.

7 There is a lot of unfounded prejudice against the old, particularly relating to their ability to work satisfactorily.

8 Age has a low status in our society; we tend to devalue the past.

9 Retirement is seen as the end of life – it needs a new image.

10 We have not yet evolved acceptable norms for retired people.

40.2 Retirement in other societies

ACTIVITIES 23

Read Items 9.31 and 9.32 about retirement and answer the questions which follow.

Item 9.31

1 'There is less age-grading in rural societies.' Explain what you think this might mean by giving examples of 'age-grading' in your own culture, society or community.

There are several differences between rural and urban life, or between 'simpler' and industrialised societies, which influence both the incidence of retirement and the forms it takes. First, there is less age-grading in rural societies, chiefly because it is less pertinent to the main occupational roles. Secondly, there is more self-employment in rural societies, which means that the individual is more able to control whether he works or not and when he may give up work. Thirdly, because of the need to keep down the proportion of the dependent to working population, there is less tolerance of the non-work role. Fourthly, retirement is frequently associated with the transfer of property to children or younger relatives. Fifthly, a higher proportion of women also work, and so they share in the arrangements for retirement. Sixthly, more is expected to be done by children for their aged and retired parents, with whom living quarters are often share...

Although there is usually no formal retirement in pre-literate and simpler societies, the old men are not expected to keep on being hunters or warriors or farmers. They are commonly promoted to become elders, headmen or priests. In other words, they shift from roles requiring much physical exertion to sedentary, advisory or supervisory positions. Cessation of work in most pre-literate societies occurs only when the individual, regardless of age, has lost his physical or mental ability to engage in socially useful activities, or is so defined by his culture.

from S.R. Parker, *Work and Retirement* (Allen & Unwin, 1982)

Item 9.31   Retirement in 'simpler' rural societies

In the traditional Confucian family of China, once men and women became grandparents they could choose whether or not they wished to continue to manage households (in the case of women), or to operate family businesses or property or hold public office (in the case of men). Retirement did not mean loss of authority in decision-making: they were always consulted and had the final word in family councils. Withdrawal from some activities did not mean complete loss of other functions, such as scholarly pursuits and religious duties....To some extent these arrangements continue in modern China. The government programme stipulates that men can retire from the age of 55, women from 50. How completely an individual actually retires depends on his needs and health, and the needs of his community. The Chinese retiree plays an important role as a transmitter of skills and cultural heritage, although it must be remembered that about 80 per cent of older workers earn their living from the land.

from S.R. Parker, *Work and Retirement* (Allen & Unwin, 1982)

Item 9.32   Retirement in China

2 List six differences between rural and urban life which might affect attitudes toward retirement.

3 What role might 'old men' play in pre-literate and 'simple' societies? Compare and contrast this with the role 'old men' might play in your own community.

Item 9.32

4 'The Chinese retiree plays an important role as a transmitter of skills and cultural heritage.' Explain what this might mean.

5 In what ways are the retirement roles of older people similar in rural societies and the traditional Confucian families of China?

REVIEW

If you have studied and understood this chapter you should be able to . . .

- define or explain the meaning of the terms:
  a primary production,
  b secondary production, and
  c tertiary production.
- list those categories of people who are excluded from the working population.
- outline those factors which have led to an increased number of economically active women.
- describe the patterns of employment found in different ethnic groups and different age groups.
- give an account of the advantages and disadvantages of the division of labour.
- explain the relevance of the following terms to the concept of alienation:
  a powerlessness,
  b meaninglessness,
  c isolation, and
  d self-estrangement.
- give examples of the way technology has changed the organisation of work.
- outline the main causes of unemployment.
- suggest ways in which the work people do might affect the way they spend their leisure time.
- outline some of the problems posed for society by the social institution of retirement.

COURSEWORK SUGGESTION

The aim of this project on the meaning of retirement is to provide an opportunity to use, interpret, analyse and evaluate qualitative sociological data with reference to one aspect of the social implications of retirement and the meanings people attach to retirement. You will be presented with qualitative data in the form of quotations from both older workers and retired people who were asked what retirement meant to them. The data may also help to throw light on the nature of the changing roles the elderly are expected to occupy and the importance work has, for many, as a central life interest.

Research using the scientific method and quantitative or statistical data begins with ideas and theories about a topic. A hypothesis is *deduced* from these theories and tested against the data collected. The hypothesis is then either proved correct or in need of modification. This is called *positivistic* research. In this project, you will be taking an alternative approach to sociological research. You will begin with qualitative data and, by a process of *induction*, will attempt to make sense of that data. You will point out patterns and common themes in the data. Your theories and ideas about retirement will come from your collection of data rather than the other way round. Sociologists Glaser and Strauss argue that ideas which are developed from data like this are much more likely to make sense. They call such ideas *grounded theories* because they are grounded or based on data and the real world. Grounded theories do not force data into categories thought up by the research; rather, they use the categories which the people being studied themselves use to make sense of their experiences.

Parker completed a national survey of older workers and retired people in 1980 to find out what meanings people attached to retirement. For some it was happiness, fulfilment, freedom and novelty, while for others it was misery, frustration and boredom.

Look at the responses in Item 9.33 from Parker's study of retirement. For each one you should say whether you think it is a positive(P) or negative(N) feeling about retirement.

You should then attempt to put the answers into different categories or groups depending upon what kind of thing they refer to – freedom and escape, hobbies, relaxation, poor health, old age, enjoyment, loss of money, etc. In this way you may be able to discover patterns or common themes in the responses people give and thus the meanings they attach to retirement. Do this before you read Parker's own conclusions.

When I've reached 65 I won't feel terribly happy about it. I don't feel I want to retire. If I wasn't well, that would be different altogether. I don't want to be old and useless and not be able to do anything. I want to be active. (Male bus driver, 62)

I think it's great, you can mix pleasure and work – a bit of work and a lot of pleasure. (Ex-engineer, aged 71)

I hate it because I was never an idle person in my life – I've taken it badly being at home. (Ex-salesman, aged 72)

Retirement is the finest thing that ever happened. If every man retired at 65, their health would improve and they would live much longer. (Ex-boilerman, aged 68)

I can't say I'm happy – there's so much that I'd like to do that I'm unable to do ... I can't do much because of my state of health. (Ex-housekeeper, aged 64)

Retirement means loss of income – when you have to live on a third of what you've been living on for the past 25 years. (Ex-ambulance driver, aged 70)

It means escape from work. I think I've done enough work to get retirement. Time to open up a few years of leisure. (Fitter's mate, aged 64)

I don't like the time on my hands. (Ex-nurse, aged 68)

I haven't come to accept it yet. I keep hoping a miracle will come along and I'll be able to get another job (Ex-foreman, aged 63)

I'm living a new life, meeting different people, relaxing more and seeing more of my friends. (Ex-catering manageress, aged 62)

I can spend my time with my flowers in the garden. I hope to do a bit more travelling ... (Man, aged 61, compositor)

Having a damned good rest. I've never had a rest in my life. I've worked hard all my life. I've never had anyone to spoil me. (Woman, aged 59, presser)

I'm retired compulsorily – it hit me hard, but I've learned to live with it. I've always worked and would love to have worked. (Ex-foreman, aged 66)

Your life's centred on the home then. Instead of getting up to work you do what you want: dress-making, decorating or gardening. (Manageress, aged 54)

I have no garden and no hobbies. There are times when I get fed up – I feel I'd like to go back to work. (Ex-market trader, aged 64)

When you retire it leaves a sudden gap in your life. One minute you're busy and the next your're on the shelf — In my job I met a lot of people, getting to know them. In retirement I miss this ... (Ex-insurance man, aged 66)

It's blinking monotonous. Life is tedious when you can't do anything ... time goes slow, you get fed up with it. (Ex-stock keeper, aged 71)

You come to the age when you have to retire and you just accept that ... you wonder how you will spend your time, but honestly I'm so busy now that I sometimes wonder how I managed to find the time to go to work. (Ex-typist, aged 68)

A tragedy. I can't bear the anger of being unable to go around. I hate the thought of being an old-age pensioner – I've always been active. I hate the thought of it. (Ex-truck driver, aged 64)

It means you've got to start on something different altogether and adjust to not doing as much. I've got hobbies and it doesn't bother me now. (Ex-blacksmith, aged 70)

It's the firm's idea, not mine. They think you're too old to go on working. (Ex-lorry driver, aged 69)

from S.R. Parker, *Work and Retirement* (Allen & Unwin, 1982)

Item 9.33 Attitudes to retirement

Parker's conclusions

Parker found that two fifths of older workers were looking forward to retirement and had positive feelings toward it, about one in eight were definitely not happy about the prospect and had negative feelings about it, and the rest had mixed feelings. However, those with 'mixed feelings' seemed to express a mixture that was on balance negative. Parker concluded with the suggestion that negative feelings and experiences tended to outweigh the positive, and that for a lot of people retirement meant a reduced quality of life compared with when they were still working.

From quotations such as those in Item 9.33 Parker derived the following different categories of meanings attached to retirement. Again, (N) designates a negative feeling and (P) designates a positive feeling.

1 For older workers he found the following common themes, in descending order of approximate frequency:
  a a feeling of freedom and being able to please yourself (P).
  b looking forward to more leisure time for hobbies (P).
  c the idea of getting old (N).
  d the end of working life (N).

2 For retired people, he found the following nine common themes in his responses, again in descending order of approximate frequency:
  a retirement means poor health (N).
  b a time to enjoy life (P).
  c something to adjust to and accept (P).
  d feeling the loss of money (N).
  e nothing to do, having time on your hands (N).
  f boredom, being fed up (N).
  g something to dislike, even hate (N).
  h loneliness (N).
  i wanting a job (N).

You might like to repeat this kind of research using a sample of retired people and older workers who live in your community. Look at the suggestions that follow before you start.

1 Would a quota sample be more practical than attempting to draw a random sample? Outline the problems with each method of sampling for this particular project.

2 Would your data be better collected using questionnaires or interviews? Explain the reasons for your choice of method of data collection.

3 What would you ask of your respondents? Apart from discovering the meaning they attach to retirement, are there any other sociological issues you could explore at the same time?

4 How will you present your final report?

ASSESSMENT QUESTIONS

The mark allocations to sections of the questions are shown in the right hand margin.

1

The unemployed (totals of thousands)

	1971	1973	1974	1975	1976	1977	1978
Men	660	515.2	513.8	777.1	1025.1	1069.2	1023.2
Women	126.4	103.6	101.4	200.5	332.5	414.2	405.1
Total	792.4	618.8	615.1	977.6	1357.6	1483.5	1428.3

(Source: *Sociology: An introductory course*, P. Selfe)

a From the figures given above, how many women were unemployed in 1973 and 1977? (2)

b From the above table, outline **two** trends in unemployment during the period 1971 to 1978. (2)

c Name **two** Welfare State services which may help the unemployed. (2)

d Name **three** groups of people other than the unemployed who are likely to be living in poverty in Britain today. (3)

e Voluntary organisations often try to help those who are poor. Name **one** of these organisations and state **two** ways in which it tries to help. (3)

f Give **four** social consequences of unemployment. (4)

g Construct a diagram to show what sociologists mean by the 'cycle of poverty'. (4)

Southern Examining Group

2

'People only work for money'

a Explain the meaning of the term 'work'. (2)

b List two occupations which can be considered work by some and leisure by others. (2)

c Outline four different ways in which work can affect leisure. (4)

d For what other reasons, apart from money, do people work? (7)

London & East Anglia Group for GCSE Examination

3 This question carries 15 marks.

'There is an increasing number of professional sportswomen and sportsmen in this country. This reflects a society with more money and leisure.'

Write an essay about leisure. Your answer could include reference to the following:

the differences between work and leisure;
changing patterns of spending;
the influence of the mass media on leisure activities;
changes in employment patterns;
consequences for employment of a growth in leisure activities.

Credit will be given for any other relevant information.

Northern Examining Association

10 *Social order, crime and deviance*

AIMS

At the end of this chapter you should be able to:

- recognise the way social order is maintained by informal and formal methods of social control.
- understand the relationship between customs and values and between morality and the law.
- recognise and describe the role of the police in Britain and the structure of the law courts.
- identify the problems associated with the interpretation of official criminal statistics.
- outline and discuss different explanations for crime and delinquency in society, including the process of 'labelling'.
- show appreciation of the role of the media in both the creation of stereotypes of crime and deviance, and the process of 'deviancy amplification'.
- show awareness of the social problems caused by abuse of drugs, solvents, alcohol and tobacco.
- appreciate the social problems caused by un-employment.

Social life is carried on according to rules, rather like a game of chess. For instance, the player decides how he or she will move the chess pieces but every move must obey the rules for the game. The match can be played because each player knows and understands these rules; this allows both of them to plan their game with the objective of winning the match. If a player were suddenly to invent his or he own rules, the opponent would be confused and the game could not go on.

In the same way there are rules which control how we act in social groups and in society. If the rules are broken the situation becomes confusing, and social order can be threatened. Imagine what driving a car would be like if there were no rules of the road.

Item 10.1 What are the correct rules of behaviour in these situations?

►UNIT 41 Informal social control

41.1 Norms

Not all social rules are written down and there are many types of unwritten rule which exist in society. An unwritten rule such as this is called a *norm*. A norm tells people the way to act and behave. Individuals who break these rules do not necessarily get in trouble with the police or courts, and sociologists therefore refer to norms as *informal* social controls. A norm is part of the culture or a subculture of a society and is passed from one generation to the next through socialisation.

We are so familiar with the norms of the society we grow up in that they are almost second nature to us; we take them for granted, seldom thinking about them or questioning their importance.

ACTIVITIES 1

The way you behave and dress when you are with your friends is affected by such norms. List the things you could do that would make your friends fall out with you and those things you could do which would make them 'disown' you. You will be listing the sort of behaviour which breaks the unwritten rules or norms of your social group.

41.2 Norms and morality

Some norms are particularly important in society; for example, those that refer to the way we should behave towards one another, such as that we should treat each other justly and honestly. These norms have embedded in them the idea that it is *morally* wrong to treat people unjustly or to be dishonest. The sociologist calls such norms *mores*. Some of the most widely held mores in our society are concerned with respecting the lives and the property of other people.

Mores are important in society because of the moral values they maintain. For example, it is thought morally important not to steal, not to kill and not to injure deliberately. These values are part of the culture of society. Some values, such as the right of human beings to life and dignity, are widely accepted in many different cultures.

Item 10.2 Norms are passed on from one generation to another

Mores play an important part in maintaining social order and many have been written down and incorporated into our laws. The law, however, does not always reflect mores. Sometimes it is at variance with popular social mores and it may become acceptable to break certain laws rather than to observe them.

189

Theft by shoplifting is not an easy offence to quantify in moral terms. On the one hand, an act of shoplifting is an act of dishonesty, which breaks an accepted code of behaviour between buyer and seller. A shoplifter is a thief. But it is also apparent that an intention to acquire goods dishonestly is often not a suspect's main motive in carrying out an act of shoplifting. Some of those in my survey gave the following reasons for their actions:

'I have a serious drink problem. My 14-year-old daughter died four days ago and it's sort of been too much' – man aged 51, stole a bottle of Cinzano Bianco, price £2.79. Probation order made for twelve months.

'It's so stupid, but I've been feeling bad ever since my divorce two years ago and it just got too much' – man aged 32, stole a picture frame, price £1.99. Fined £25.

'Occasionally I get ideas to do things that are totally out of character, like today's incident. I knew it would happen' – man aged 30. Received a head injury in a road accident a year previously. Stole two LPS, price £4.48. Fined £25.

'I stole the blouse because I wanted to change clothes a bit so I couldn't be recognised; you see, I was thinking of running away from home, because I don't get on with my parents – young woman aged 18, stole a blouse, price £12.99. Fined £25.

All these have been convicted of theft because of their acts of shoplifting. Apart from the formal sentence of the court, a conviction for an offence of theft can have other consequences: a loss of employment, the break-up of domestic relationships, self-identification as thief. The effects may far outweigh the harm caused by the original offence. The decision to prosecute in such cases is not one that should be taken lightly.

from Robert Munday, 'Who are the shoplifters?', *New Society*, 14 Feburary 1986

Item 10.3 The motives for shoplifting

ACTIVITIES 2

Read Item 10.3 and answer the questions which follow.

1 We often think the main motive for shoplifting is to acquire goods dishonestly. Explain in your own words the reasons given for shoplifting by two of the people interviewed.

2 Were these people simply dishonest? Explain your answer.

3 What does the writer mean when he says that 'theft by shoplifting is not an easy offence to quantify in moral terms'?

4 Consider the following examples of behaviour which is against the law:
a under-age drinking.
b breaking the speed limit.
c not wearing a seat-belt.
How morally wrong do you consider these examples of behaviour to be?

41.3 How norms affect behaviour

Even though people cannot be made to obey norms in the same way that the threat of punishments may make us obey the law, norms do succeed in controlling what we do. How is it that they are effective? The reason is that we control each other. This can be seen if we think of someone learning a new role – as a student, a secretary, a wife, a motor vehicle mechanic, etc. In every case we are socialised into the role through the reactions of other people. For example, a shop assistant who gives a customer the wrong change learns from the agitation of the customer, or the manager, that it is part of the role to keep the money transactions in the shop accurate. Of course, most people already know something about a particular role because, besides being directly influenced by other people, we are also influenced indirectly through films, magazines and television.

We control one another's actions in other ways besides showing agitation: for instance, praise and reward encourage us to go on behaving as we are. Showing surprise, disappointment or disgust or completely ignoring someone are some of the other ways in which we bring people's actions in line with perceived social norms.

ACTIVITIES 3

If one of your friends is doing something you don't like – for example, something which might be embarrassing – how do you react? What can you do to make them stop?

41.4 Folkways

There is a norm in the UK that people should form a queue when waiting for the bus, but it is not usually taken so seriously that there are heavy penalties for ignoring it. This is for two reasons: first, standing in line when waiting for a bus has little to do with morally right behaviour, although we often feel it is the fairest way to cope with this problem; secondly, there is no widespread agreement that forming a queue is so important that people should be made to conform. This, then, is an example of a type of norm which the sociologist calls a *folkway*. Other examples include eating with a knife and fork, celebrating birthdays, and exchanging greeting cards at Christmas. Folkways are norms which are observed throughout society by particular social groups but the breaking of which is not considered to be morally wrong. Customs are folkways which have existed for a long time in society. The use of holly and mistletoe at Christmas is a custom. Remember, too, that norms and values are part of the culture of society and, like any other aspect of culture, they change. Nor are norms and values always the same for everyone in society. Different social groups have different norms and values. Talk about the 'generation gap' is often an observation that the different generations hold different values and norms.

ACTIVITIES 4: Play-reading

Read the play-reading and answer the questions that follow it.

(Punk rocker Jim is sitting on the bonnet of a Mercedes swigging a can of lager. Paul, the owner, is dressed in a suit and tie and returns to his car ...)

Paul   Excuse me. Could I get in my car, please?

Jim   Just keeping the sun off for you. Don't want the paint job to fade, do we?

Paul   Haven't you got anything better to do with your – ?

Jim   *(Interrupting)* No, as it happens – don't I know you?

Paul   I hardly think so.

Jim   You're Paul Jarvis! Well, well, well. Small world and other clichés. It's Jim Coombes.

Paul   Jim ... ? The fifth year at school?

Jim   Yeah yeah. What, must be three years eh? Gawd, look at you. What've you been doing, then, to earn this gleaming little status symbol?

Paul   Architect – well, nearly, I'm training. Company car.

Jim   Some company! Architect, eh? Yeah, you were good at drawing at school, weren't you?

Paul   What about you?

Jim   Scrounger. Well, nearly, I'm training.

Paul   Why, though? You were the star at school – top in English. A bit too adventurous with the illegal substances, as I remember.

Jim   Still am. That's why I'm unemployed.

Paul   How d'you mean?

Jim   Sniffed some glue, a year ago this was, and while under the influence you might say I was a naughty boy.

Paul   What? I mean, what did you do?

Jim   Borrowed a car – don't worry, it wasn't a Mercedes – er, had an argument with an unco-operative cigarette machine and had some fun with a credit card I found in a telephone box. Possessing an offensive haircut. And drugs.

Paul   Fun? I think you mean fraud.

Jim   It's only numbers on a computer. You sound like the magistrate.

Paul   So you were done, then, were you?

Jim   You're looking at the proud owner of a criminal record – but I don't give a monkey's.

Paul   You should. It's hard enough getting a job nowadays without having that against you. You seem to think it's a joke.

Jim   And you think I've been terribly antisocial, don't you?

Paul   Well, yes –

Jim   . . . a menace to society?

Paul   Yes, I do. It's not funny. I'm not stupid for believing in ... well –

Jim   Decency? Self-respect? Rule Britannia? Paying tax and having a mortgage? Clean socks every day?

Paul   Yes!

Jim   What's 'society' ever done for me? Self-respect isn't just wearing shiny shoes, Paul. Or driving one of these. I don't particularly want to be accepted by your society – bailiffs who turn up to batter down a family's door when they can't pay the rent are 'respectable'. What a nice job that is.

Paul   Someone has to do it,

Jim   Why? They need help, not punishment, a family with problems – it's bad enough having to live in that high-rise without paying for it. The architect who designed that should be put in prison – no! that's too pleasant. They should be made to live there! And you call me antisocial . . .

Paul   Well, I'm sorry you feel that way. I'll see you some time perhaps.

Jim   Yeah. Give my regards to the other success stories.

1 Give examples of the way the norms and values held by Jim and Paul differ.

2 'Fun? I think you mean fraud.' Discuss.

3 What does Jim mean when he says that bailiffs are 'respectable' and architects should be put in prison for designing high-rise blocks?

4 In what different ways have the systems of social control and socialisation affected both characters and their roles in society?

5 Try to think of ways in which norms have changed over the years. You should also be able to think of differences between different groups in society and between different cultures and societies. Begin by thinking of:
a the role of women in the home.
b the way we greet our friends.
c behaviour at meal times.

6 Copy out the chart in Item 10.4 and fill in more examples of your own.

Checklist

1 Norms are unwritten rules.
2 Norms supported by strong moral values are mores.
3 Norms of lesser importance are folkways.
4 Norms traditionally accepted are called customs.
5 Some norms are enforced by the law.

Item 10.4   Social control

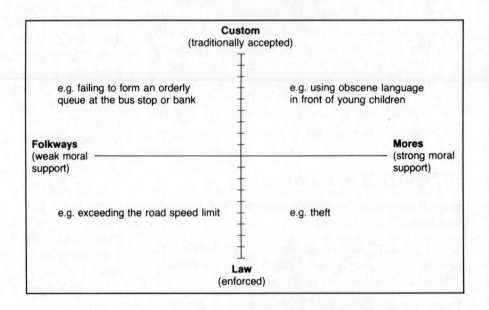

As we have seen, sociologists distinguish between several different types of rules. The most obvious rules in society are those which make up the law.

42.1 The law

There is a vast body of rules which is called the law and which applies to almost every aspect of social life. To ensure that everyone abides by these laws there are specific penalties, such as fines or imprisonment, for anyone found guilty of breaking the law. Breaches of the law are of two sorts: *civil offences*, which are offences against only the wronged *individuals*, and *crime*, in which an offence has been committed against *social order*. A civil offence would be letting your dog bite the postman; a criminal offence would be stealing the postman's registered letters. The authority of the law in society is backed up by a complex system of agencies such as the police, the courts, the legal profession and the prisons, which ensure that the law is enforced and that those who break the law are punished.

The law is a means of social control: by the threat of punishments it affects what people do. The sociologist refers to the law as a *formal social control*. Laws are set out in writing and specific penalties have been drawn up to punish people who break the law. The police and courts are dependent on the law being set out clearly, otherwise it would not be possible to enforce it. In the UK, laws have been formally drawn up and administered since Roman times although the accepted interpretation of the law is arrived at by High Court Judges. The main sources of the law in the UK are legislation, common law and European Community law. Legislation consists of formally passed Acts of Parliament and by-laws made by local government and other authorities. Common law is derived from custom and interpretation, and European Community law is derived from European Economic Community rulings and those given by the European Court of Justice.

42.2 Law and morality

We have already seen some points which are common to formal laws and informal social rules such as norms. Both are types of social control. We know also that important mores, such as those about deliberately injuring or killing someone, or stealing property, have been formalised and become laws, which are enforced by the threat of punishment. However, morality and the law do not always go hand in hand, as we have seen.

People's opinions about what is right and wrong change. The problem is that the law involves all sorts of procedures, so although it can be altered, often it is not quick to change and reflect the ideas current in society.

We have also seen that norms are not always the same for everyone in society. Sociologists point out that the law reflects the views of those people who have enough power in society to put their ideas into effect. For example, laws which punished by death anyone found guilty of stealing cattle were in existence in this country until 1832. We may be sure that it was the people who owned cattle and not the poor people who introduced that law! Before 1832 it was only male landowners who had the vote and who were therefore able to influence the law.

ACTIVITIES 5

It is not always easy to recognise what is lawful and what might be illegal, or what is acceptable and what is unacceptable. Read Item 10.5 and answer the questions which follow.

1 In what way might a 'gift' be thought to be a bribe?

2 Why might it be difficult to tell the difference between an acceptable and lawful 'gift' and a corrupt and illegal bribe?

3 What does the writer mean when he says 'the rules do not change with the time of year'?

4 What sort of 'rules' is he referring to? Are the rules he refers to written down?

5 Do you agree with the statement that 'you cannot be just a little dishonest'?

Unfortunately, everyone employed at any senior level by any local authority may need to know the rules on gifts and bribes. As industry and commerce bump along the bottom of the recession, so the incentive for making and for accepting special 'gifts' increases...

So consider: When is it lawful for you or for a person in your employment to give or to receive a present, in cash or in kind, and when is it criminal? When are you entitled to receive some special gift from, say, those who supply the necessities for your department or unit? And when may you give one to a valued client or customer or to his representative?

Commissions, incentive bonuses and premium promotions are lawful, whether the recipient is a member of the public induced to buy through some 'special offer' or gift; your employee, given a cash bonus or holiday or conference cruise (he should be so lucky!) by suppliers trying to increase sales against the blast of recession; or even you, as executive, manager or boss.

The transaction becomes illegal when it is 'corrupt'. This word is not defined in the statute but former Lord Chief Justice Goddard once said: 'Corruption is like a sausage – difficult to define, but easy enough to smell!'.

Call the payment a bribe, greasing the palm, slush or dash – the drop or dropsy, payola or anything else and it is instantly recognisable, by its secrecy. That which is done openly is seldom improper; but the difference between a public 'fronthander' and a dishonest 'backhander' is patently clear to all the parties concerned as well as to any court.

Note: The rules do not change with the time of the year. Christmas provides no licence for bribery, nor the New Year new liberty to corrupt. Nor is there any reality in the common belief that the legality of a gift depends upon its size – so that, for instance, the gift of one bottle of whisky is permitted while that of a crate is not.

True, the smaller the gift, the less likely it is that anyone will bother to intervene; and the larger its extent, the greater the perils for both giver and recipient, if there is any possibility of corruption. But as a judge once said in the context of theft: 'You cannot be just a little bit dishonest, any more than a woman can be a tiny bit pregnant!'

from Greville Janner, 'Knowing the rules on accepting gifts', *Municipal Journal*, 10 January 1986

Item 10.5   Gift or bribe?

42.3 The police and the courts

There are 52 police forces in Britain. Outside London most counties have their own force. London is policed by both the Metropolitan Police Force, with its headquarters at New Scotland Yard, and the City of London force.

The police force in Britain numbered 132 500 people at the end of 1983, 11 700 of them women. The size of individual police forces depends upon the area covered and the population served. The strength of the Metropolitan Police Force is at its highest ever at around 27 000. The ratio of police officers to the general population is roughly one officer to every 400 or so people.

Police work includes the protection of people and property, crime prevention, criminal investigation, the arresting of offenders and traffic control. The police also, of course, are often called upon to deal with social problems. Police forces all have both a uniformed department and a criminal investigation department (CID) as well as a traffic department and other specialised departments such as mounted and river police, dog handlers, etc.

Magistrates' courts deal with nearly all criminal cases in England and Wales and have preliminary hearings of serious cases to assess whether there is sufficient evidence to justify a trial with a jury at a Crown Court. The magistrates' courts are usually staffed by three unpaid *lay magistrates* or JPs (Justices of the Peace) who apply the law and pass sentence. This is called *summary jurisdiction*, since a jury is not required and the procedures are therefore speeded up. People convicted by such summary jurisdiction have the right to appeal to the *Crown Court* and a jury if they wish. The Crown Court is staffed by *High Court judges*, full-time *circuit judges* and part-time *recorders*, but the decision whether or not to convict is always made by a jury. A person convicted by the Crown Court may appeal to the Court of Appeal, and a person failing in the Court of Appeal may, in certain cases of public importance, take the appeal to the highest court in the land – the House of Lords. The Coroner's Court investigates violent or unnatural deaths or sudden deaths where the cause is unknown.

Courts which are concerned with civil offences

Many civil cases never reach the courts and are settled 'out of court' through the solicitors of the persons concerned.

A County courts

These are courts which deal with smaller civil offences. There are about 300 of them throughout the country, grouped in districts. The county courts deal with hire purchase and rent cases as well as race and sex discrimination.

B High Court and justice

Maritime and commercial law is the responsibility of the Queen's Bench and Division. The Chancery Division deals with wills and estates. The Family Division is concerned with all jurisdiction attending the family, e.g, adoption and guardianship.

Courts which are primarily concerned with criminal offences

A Magistrates' courts

There are more than 700 magistrates' courts in England and Wales. Magistrates' courts are able to send a case to be tried at a higher court. They hear nearly all criminal cases in England and Wales.

B Juvenile courts

Juvenile courts can deal with any criminal offences (except homicide) committed by young persons aged from 10 to 17. They also deal with children and young persons under 17 who are brought to the courts as in need of care, protection and control.

About 98 per cent of criminal cases are dealt with in the courts described above.

C Crown court

Crown courts have a number of full-time and some part-time judges who preside at the courts. More serious cases are passed from the magistrates' court to these courts; the maximum sentences which can be passed in these courts are longer than those that can be passed in the magistrates' courts.

D The Central Criminal Court

This is now a crown court; it is the special criminal court of London called 'the Old Bailey'.

Item 10.6   Courts concerned with civil and criminal offences

The courts concerned with civil and criminal offences are shown in Item 10.6.

Once a person is found guilty there are a range of ways in which the offender may be treated. For murder there is a compulsory penalty of life imprisonment. Life imprisonment is the maximum, but not the only, penalty which might be given for manslaughter, rape, robbery and arson. The death penalty is still available in the case of treason, but is no longer used. There are a range of non-custodial sentences, too, including fines, probation, community service orders and 'binding over' to keep the peace. A judge may also pass a 'suspended sentence', which means that the sentence is not served unless a further offence is committed.

ACTIVITIES 6

Write to your local police station and ask for information about the job of the police. It may be possible to visit your local station and have a look round, including a visit to the cells. You might like to invite a police officer or local magistrate in to your school and ask him or her about the procedures in court and the range of penalties which may be used if people are found guilty.

► UNIT 43   Official crime statistics

Crime statistics for England and Wales are published annually by the Home Office. Other information about crime trends can be found in the annual report of Her Majesty's Chief Inspector of Constabulary and the Commissioner of Police of the Metropolis (London). Item 10.7 shows the number of offences recorded by the police in 1986 in England and Wales. The total number of offences in 1986 was 3.8 million, of which 32 per cent were cleared up.

Criminal statistics are notoriously misleading and it is a good idea to see why this is so before jumping to any conclusions. Statistics always need careful interpretation.

For example, the statistics, of course, only record crimes known to the police and the numbers of persons found guilty. It must be clear to us all that some crimes go unreported. It has been suggested, too, that the police may not be equally interested in all groups of the population as suspects: on the whole middle-class law-breakers are less likely to be apprehended or detected and therefore do not appear so

Offence group	1986
Homicide	1
Violence against the person (excluding homicide)	250
Sexual offences	45
Burglary	1 876
Robbery	60
Theft and handling stolen goods	4 014
Fraud and forgery	267
Criminal damage*	794
Other offences	24

*Excluding 'other criminal damage' valued at £20 and under.
Source: Home Office.

from *Britain 1988: An Official Handbook* (HMSO, 1988)

Item 10.7   Notifiable offences recorded by the police per 100 000 population, England and Wales, 1986

often in criminal statistics. Changes in methods of detection can also affect the numbers of cases known to and cleared up by the police.

It is sometimes suggested that crime, although frequent, is a minor irritant, given the range of problems the city dweller has to contend with. The public, on this view, suffer from hysteria about crime. Panics abound – particularly about mugging, sexual assault and violence – which are out of touch with reality. These arguments are backed up by evidence from sources like the British Crime Survey, which says that the 'average' person can expect 'a robbery once every five centuries . . . a burglary every 40 years . . . and a very low rate for rape and other sexual offences.'

But the inner city dweller is not the average citizen. Our study, with its ability to focus in on the highly victimised, indicates the realism of their fears.

It is scarely odd that 46 per cent of people in Islington should admit to worrying 'a lot' about mugging, given that over 40 per cent of the borough's population actually know someone (including themselves and their family) who has been mugged in the last twelve months. Nor is it unrealistic to worry about burglary when its incidence in the borough runs at five times the national average.

from Trevor Jones and Jock Young, 'Crime, police and people', *New Society*, 24 January 1986

Item 10.8   Crime in the city

Item 10.9   Violence in the inner city

Criminal statistics therefore present only a partial picture of the extent of crime in society and their fluctuations over a short period are not necessarily a good guide as to whether crime is increasing or decreasing.

In 1983–4 the Home Office and the Scottish Home and Health Department published the British Crime Survey. This survey asked people directly about crimes they had experienced. The survey showed that the incidence of crime was much higher than the official statistics suggest. It showed that of the crimes previously unknown and unrecorded, many were serious crimes.

The Islington Crime Survey (1985) was another attempt to survey the real extent of crime, but, in this case, in a particular local inner city area. A random sample of 2000 households was selected for the study. It showed that crime had a substantial impact on the lives of people in the London borough of Islington. A third of all households in the survey had been touched by serious crimes such as burglaries, robbery or sexual assault. Of those interviewed, 28 per cent said they felt 'unsafe' in their own homes. Item 10.8 gives more information about the results of this survey.

▶ UNIT 44   Crime and delinquency

Crime is behaviour which breaks the criminal law. *Delinquency* is a term which describes law-breaking whether committed by an adult or young person. *Juvenile delinquency*, however, is considered as any violation of the law by someone less than 17 years old. The recorded crime rate for adolescents and young people is much higher than for other age groups in the population. If we are going to explain crime, then we have at least to account for its being more prevalent among young working-class males than among other groups in society. Over the years, many theories have been suggested to explain why people become criminals. These have ranged from the idea that criminals have certain characteristic physical features, to the suggestion that family background accounts for criminal behaviour. It is likely that there is no one clear and simple explanation of criminal behaviour.

We are now probably all certain to reject the very early explanations of crime which suggested that some people were born criminal – that criminality was biological in nature. A nineteenth-century scientist called Lombroso even went to the lengths of describing and illustrating the facial features of criminals – low forehead, eyes close together, thick neck and so on.

There may be social and economic factors which account for delinquency. The boy from a working-class home, for example, may be rejected by the middle-class school system early on in his school career; he may be no good at school work and therefore termed a failure. This is a humiliating experience and will leave him uninterested in school. Because of his lack of success at school he will take an unskilled or semiskilled job when he leaves school, which may be boring and monotonous. He has failed in the eyes of society to get a good job – he is, again, a failure. Under these circumstances his leisure time becomes his opportunity to find satisfaction and success. Youths, out for excitement and something to give them a sense of satisfaction and success, might well end up committing delinquent acts. After marriage, at an early age, the working-class youth might 'settle down'. This will in turn lead to a lowering of cautions by police for working-class males above their early twenties.

These kinds of idea were put forward by a criminologist called Downes in 1966 and similar ideas are often put forward today to explain crime.

The extract in Item 10.10 suggests that crime may also stem from unemployment. The writers studied a sample of 800 incidents of disorder recorded by

197

The apparent relation between unemployment and disorder is not straightforward. There is a suspicion that those arrested may claim to be unemployed in order to minimise their fine. Others may give their previous job to avoid being labelled as socially inadequate ...

Town centres contain lots of pubs, because at one time they were centres of population. Male workers spent much of their leisure in pubs. In the north east, they were places where working class adult males went to drink ale. Drinking groups were usually workmates, those living in the same neighbourhood, or friends or relatives. Drinkers went to the same pub for long sessions, and drank a lot. Drinkers saw themselves as competent adults only if they had learned to 'handle' drink. Finding out how much they could take, and of what sort, was learned in groups by men of all ages. Older members passed on the 'culture' of drinking. Drinking as a leisure pastime, therefore, was controlled and regulated by the rela-

tions between the generations – which were based on community and work roles. But it is precisely these relationships which have dramatically changed in the past ten years. In Sunderland, twelve out of the 14 shipyards have gone with the loss of 36 000 jobs, and the virtual disappearance of apprenticeship opportunities. Youth Training Schemes now provide a totally different kind of job experience, which few accept as a substitute for a 'real' job. Young men no longer have the same contacts with the adult world; and in any case, many adults are themselves unemployed. In some places, those with jobs are in a very small minority – and the 'black' or 'grey' economy of fiddles and fiddle jobs is accepted as normal.

The moral implications of this are profound: society clearly cannot offer either a reasonable standard of living or a decent self-image to many of the population. For a lot of people, the only routes to these involve breaking the rules.

from L. Gofton and S. Douglas, 'Drink and the city', *New Society*, 20 December 1985

Item 10.10 Drink and crime in the city

police in Sunderland town centre between 1984 and June 1985.

All sorts of other explanations have been put forward to explain why people turn to crime. None is wholly satisfactory nor complete. In the next section we will look at deviance. We will see that crime and

deviance may best be explained not with reference solely to the individual offender or 'deviant', but also with reference to the rest of society and the way in which our *reaction* to certain kinds of behaviour provides a context which may 'cause' or create deviance.

45.1 Legal and illegal deviance

Deviant behaviour can be of two sorts, legal and illegal. We have already seen how some norms and mores are supported by law, while others are simply folkways or customs. In this section we will look specifically at deviance rather than crime.

Deviance has always interested and fascinated people. Behaviour which is out-of-the-ordinary arouses the curiosity of people far more than normal, everyday behaviour. The mass media have recognised this for years. One way of trying to understand deviance has been presented by a sociologist called Merton. He recognised that society sets up certain goals (like living in a nice house, owning a car, and so on). He also recognised that societies present particular ways by which these goals can properly be achieved (working hard and saving, for example). Merton does not really explain *why* deviance occurs but he thought there were five ways members of a society could adjust to the fact that there were certain desirable 'ends' and only certain acceptable 'means' available. People might accept the ideas and values predominant in their society (and work hard for their money, for example). Others might reject either the ends or the means (or both!), or even substitute alternative values – people might, in other words, decide to 'drop out' of society in one way or another.

Merton formulated all of this in the table shown in Item 10.11.

ACTIVITIES 7

Study Item 10.11 and answer the questions that follow it.

Types of deviance	Means	Ends
Conformity	+	+
Innovation	+	–
Ritualism		–
Retreatism	–	–
Rebellion	Substitution of alternative values	

Item 10.11   Merton's typology of deviance

1 You should be able to give examples of your own of conformists, innovators, ritualists, retreatists and rebels. Redraw the table and add a fourth column headed 'Examples'.

2 In which category might the following people be placed?
  a a tramp
  b a teacher
  c a gypsy
  d a thief
  e a bureaucrat

3 Item 10.12 shows the great white shark of Headington. The 25-foot shark became a tourist attraction in the area in 1986, but its owner, Bill Heine, was told by the local planning committee to get rid of it. Would you describe Bill Heine as a deviant? Explain your answer.

Item 10.12   The great white shark of Headington

ACTIVITIES 8: Play-reading

Read the play-reading and answer the questions which follow.

(DHSS Office, 4.55 p.m., Friday. Clive Barnet, a claims officer, is putting away files, and is about to leave. A man enters.)

Barnett   I'm sorry, sir, we're closed.

Man   It's not gone five already, is it? I thought I'd just made it.

Barnett   If it's a query then perhaps I can help.

Man   Well, no, I've got to fill in some of your forms. I got the letter this morning telling me I'd got an appointment with you.

Barnett   We don't do these appointments in the afternoon, especially on a Friday. What's your name?

Man   Peters – David Peters. No, I know; the appointment was for yesterday morning but your letter must've been delayed in the post. It came this morning and –

Barnett   Couldn't you have got here sooner, then?

Peters   My wife was rushed to hospital this morning, really early. Appendix. I got back about 4.15 and found the letter and tore round here. I'll need to have a cheque early next week, you see. I'm nearly out of money. Just enough for the weekend. Only just.

Barnett   *(Thinks: 'Appendix – a likely story.')* Well sir, look at the clock. I can't do anything now.

Peters   It's one minute to. My watch says two minutes to, in fact, and I set it by the radio –

Barnett   You don't understand, sir. We stop signing people on at 4.45 p.m. It can take fifteen minutes to do the paperwork on one claim. If we kept the desk open till 5.00 p.m. we'd be kept here late. I should've locked the door earlier but I forgot.

Peters   Look, I'll really need a cheque on Monday. Can't you make an exception? Please!

Barnett   If we do it for one we have to do it for every –

Peters   I won't tell anyone.

Barnett   You might.

Peters   I won't, though, *Will I?!!*

Barnett   No need to shout, sir.

Peters   I'm sorry, but I'm desperate.

Barnett   In any case, you can only get a cheque three working days after filling in form XYZ 3000B.

Peters   Why don't you backdate it? Eh? Go, on, this is an emergency. Date it from last Wednesday.

Barnett   More than my job's worth, sir. Now if you come back Monday –

Peters   No! I'm in dire need. Me not being able to eat Monday and Tuesday and probably Wednesday is more important than you leaving your office ten minutes late.

Barnett   In any case, Mr Peters, your surname begins with P. We see people in the middle of the alphabet in the middle of the week.

Peters   I'm not leaving this office and neither are you till this is sorted out!

Barnett   I'm sorry you're being so uncooperative, Mr Peters. I may be forced to call the police if you carry on being unreasonable.

1   Which of these people is behaving reasonably?

2   Which of these people might be described as deviant?

3   Look again at Merton's types of deviance. How would you describe the deviance which is illustrated in this scene? Explain your answer with reference to Merton's typology of deviance.

▶ UNIT 46 Labelling

46.1 Labelling theory

Another way of trying to understand deviance is to look at the way members of a society label people deviant. As we have seen from Merton's ideas, deviance occurs when individual people or groups have different values from society at large. If this is true, deviance really depends upon your point of view. It is not a characteristic of the individual or even of their actions. What is thought of as deviance is the result of ideas we have in society and the times and circumstances we are in. A sociologist called Becker says that looking for biological or psychological characteristics of people who are deviant to explain deviance is wrong. This would be to assume that there is something about deviants as individuals which makes them deviant. Becker's explanation of his ideas is given in Item 10.13.

The central fact about deviance [is that] it is created by society. I do not mean this in the way it is ordinarily understood, in which the causes of deviance are located in the social situation of the deviant or in 'social factors' which prompt his action. I mean, rather, that *social groups create deviance by making the rules whose infraction constitutes deviance*, and by applying those rules to particular people and labelling them as outsiders. From this point of view, deviance is *not* a quality of the act the person commits, but rather a consequence of the application by others of rules and sanctions to an 'offender'. The deviant is one to whom that label has successfully been applied; deviant behaviour is behaviour that people so label.'

from Howard Becker, *Outsiders* (Free Press, 1963)

Item 10.13 'Deviance is created by society'

ACTIVITIES 9

1 List examples of behaviour which:
   a *were* deviant in the past but no longer are.
   b were not deviant in the past but would be *now*.
   c are deviant in *western* society but not in other societies or cultures.
   d are not deviant in western society but which *would* be in other societies or cultures.
   e are deviant in some circumstances but not in others.

To help you, here are a few ideas:

- a pupil who shouts and cheers may be considered a model of perfection at the school football match but the same behaviour will be considered inappropriate in school assembly. The action, however, is the same in both cases.
- in traditional western society, drinking alcohol is considered to be a pleasant way to pass the time with friends. In Moslem society, this is strictly forbidden. The deviant, in fact, would be the drinker rather than the teetotaller.
- in the early twentieth century a woman who smoked in public was regarded as immoral. Smoking now, although increasingly frowned on generally, is not considered particularly inappropriate for a woman.

2 a 'Social groups create deviance by making the rules.'
   b 'Deviance is *not* a quality of the act a person commits.'
   c 'The deviant is one to whom that label has successfully been applied.'

Explain in your own words, and with examples, each of these ideas of Becker's.

When we label some people in our society deviant we ought also look at how they have come to be put in this position. In other words, whose rules have been broken? For example, are these rules drawn up and enforced mainly by powerful middle-class groups in society? If so, these may not be the norms with which every group in society agrees.

Having called some actions deviant and the people who commit them deviants, we react to these people as being different from ourselves. We set the deviants apart from us, and get set ideas into our head about how they think, what they do or how they dress. We build up a fixed picture of, for example, what an alcoholic is like. These fixed pictures are stereotypes and they mould our ideas about deviants in society. (See Chapter 7, topic 25.4, and topic 46.2 below, on the mass media's creation of stereotypes.) Stereotypes are a bit like police identikit pictures: a composite of characteristics making up an overall picture. We have stereotypes with which to view every type of behaviour in society from that of police officers to that of punk rockers.

The attitudes that people hold about deviants do not go unnoticed by the deviants. When a homosexual, an unmarried mother or a Rastafarian is prevented from getting a job or somewhere to live, the individual begins to think of him or herself as being fundamentally different from other people. The results can be far-reaching, forcing these people into the stereotyped role society has given them. This process is known as *deviancy amplification* and is considered in more detail in the following topics.

46.2   Stereotypes and the media

As we have seen, using stereotypes we often label people as deviants. These labels are like the labels on a pot of marmalade – they give us immediate information about what to expect and we need not think any more about it. This can have unfortunate consequences for the people who are labelled.

While many people might never have even seen a punk rocker, glue sniffer or alcoholic in real life, they believe they are experts because they have 'seen it on the telly' or read about it in the newspapers. This means, of course, that the people who control the media are in a position to affect our definitions of what is deviant, and once a group is labelled as deviant the media can reinforce this with its reporting and pictures. And as we have seen in Chapter 7, not all groups have equal access to the media.

ACTIVITIES 10

1 Look through a local or national newspaper and try to spot articles which seem to label different groups as deviant.

2 Using the newspapers and from your own knowledge, list the stereotypical characteristics of:
   a muggers.
   b punk rockers.
   c gypsies.
   d stockbrokers.
   e ministers of religion.
   f old-age pensioners.

46.3   The amplification of deviance

A sociologist called Jock Young has looked at the way in which the media can create deviant behaviour and then go on to exaggerate and *amplify* the deviance. Young studied the way the police and the media react to drug-takers. He argues that the process involves changes in both the police and the drug-user as each reacts in turn to the other. Young suggests the process goes as follows:

1 The police act against the drug-users in terms of their stereotypes.

2 The drug-user group finds itself in a new situation, which it must interpret and adapt to in a changed manner.

3 The police react in a slightly different fashion to the changed group.

4 The drug-users interpret and adapt to this new situation.

5 The police react to these new changes; and so on.

The end result of this process is what has been called deviancy amplification. Young shows the way this process operates using the diagram in Item 10.14.

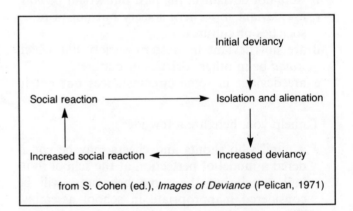

from S. Cohen (ed.), *Images of Deviance* (Pelican, 1971)

Item 10.14   The amplification of deviance

As a result of the isolation of deviants caused by the social reaction to the initial deviance, the deviants develop their own set of norms and values. Society perceives these are more deviant than before and reacts more forcefully – leading, of course, to increased isolation and increased deviancy. Jock Young talks about the 'spiral of deviancy amplification' which occurs as a result of this process.

46.4 Deviancy amplification and the media

Jock Young's account of the role of the media in deviancy amplification is given in Item 10.15.

ACTIVITIES 11

Read Item 10.15 and answer the questions that follow.

1 Give examples of the way in which we receive information about some social groups 'at second hand through the mass media'. You could again use newspapers as a source of examples and include copies of articles in support of your answer.

2 What does the writer mean when he says that the mass media portray information which is 'newsworthy'?

3 Describe your ideas of the 'over-typical hypothetical "man in the street"'.

4 What does the writer mean when he says that the 'moral conscience' of society is the popular newspaper?

5 Can you think of examples of deviancy amplification from your own experience? Think about:
   a family life, parents and children.
   b school, teachers and pupils.

The determining factor in our treatment of individuals is the type of information we receive about them. In modern urban societies there is extreme social segregation between different groups which leads to information being obtained at second hand through the mass media rather than directly by face-to-face contact. The type of information which the mass media portray is that which is 'newsworthy'. They select events which are *atypical*, present them in a *stereotypical* fashion and contrast them against a backcloth of normality which is *over-typical*.

The atypical is selected because the everyday or humdrum is not interesting to read or watch – it has little news value. As a result of this, if one has little face-to-face contact with young people one's total information about them would be in terms of extremes; drug-taking, sex and wanton violence on one hand and Voluntary Services Overseas and Outward Bound courses on the other. But the statistically unusual alone is not sufficient to make news. The mass-circulation newspapers in particular have discovered that people read avidly news which titillates their sensibilities and confirms their prejudices ... The stereotypical, distorted image of the deviant is then contrasted with the overtypical, hypothetical 'man in the street' ... Out of this, simple moral directives are produced demanding that something must be done about it: the solitary deviant faces the wrath of all society epitomized by its moral conscience, the popular newspaper.

from S. Cohen (ed.), *Images of Deviance* (Pelican, 1971)

Item 10.15 The role of the media in deviancy amplification

UNIT 47 Social problems

47.1 Drug dependency

When we think of drugs as a social problem we are not concerned with their use, under careful supervision, for healing the sick. The social problem is the compulsive use of drugs by people, not because they are ill, but because they want to experience the effects which drugs can produce or because they want to 'escape' their circumstances and immediate situation temporarily. Some drugs, after prolonged use, can have the effect of causing a person's body to become dependent on the drug. At this point the person has become *addicted*. For example, prolonged use of heroin results in a person becoming physically addicted and developing a compulsive need to take the drug.

There are other drugs which do not cause physical addiction. Instead, people may become dependent on the drug because they develop a state of mind where they want to continue using the drug, because it gives some satisfaction and pleasure. This is called *drug habituation*, and can occur, for example, with cannabis.

The terms addiction and habituation have often proved to be difficult to apply. This is because there are so many ways in which individual people are affected by various drugs that there is not always a hard and fast division between drug addiction and drug habituation. The term *drug dependency* might be a better way of referring to both these ideas.

We hear a lot about drugs in newspapers, in magazines and on television and this usually concerns the use of drugs such as heroin and cannabis. What is often overlooked is that in Britain there are large numbers of people who are dependent on other drugs such as barbiturates, and these are not the young people that the press tells us about: many of the people who depend on them are women in the 45–64 age group. However, here we will concentrate on cannabis and heroin, while bearing in mind that this is not the entire picture of drug-taking in Britain today.

Although cannabis (or marijuana) may lead to a psychological dependency rather than an addiction, many people worry that using cannabis can be an introduction to the more harmful drugs like heroin. Jock Young thinks that this happens in some cases not because of the drug itself but because of the way people react to deviants in our society. For instance, selling or being in possession of cannabis is illegal and this means the group who smoke it run a risk of arrest. This results in the cannabis smoker thinking of him or herself as different, and in an atmosphere where people see themselves as deviants the use of stronger drugs may creep in. The link between cannabis and heroin, therefore, might be partially explained by our earlier theories of labelling, stereotypes and deviancy amplification.

The slang term for a person who becomes addicted to heroin is a *junkie*. A person using heroin does not become addicted immediately, but gradually needs more doses to achieve the same effects. The body eventually becomes addicted to the drug. When this happens, the individual will be totally preoccupied with the next dose ('fix'). As soon as the effects of one dose have worn off an addict must start thinking about the next one. If he or she cannot get another dose, severe pains and complications set in ('cold turkey'). Addiction can lead to death. This may not result directly from the addiction but may be caused by careless hygiene, dirty needles and so on – dirty needles, for example, can spread serum hepatitis and AIDs, among other infections.

In addition to cannabis and heroin there is the growing problem of *solvent abuse* (such as glue sniffing) by young people. Item 10.16 shows the number of new addicts notified to the Home Office during the years from 1973 to 1986. Doctors are required to notify the Home Office of people whom they consider, or suspect, to be addicted to certain 'controlled' addictive drugs. As Item 10.16 shows, the age group with the greatest number of addicts has always been that from 20 to 24.

ACTIVITIES 12

Study Item 10.16 and answer the questions that follow.

1 Draw a bar chart to show the number of new addicts notified during 1984 by age and sex.

United Kingdom							Numbers
	Age						Total
	Under 20	20–24	25–29	30–34	35–49	50 or over	Not known	

Males

	Under 20	20–24	25–29	30–34	35–49	50 or over	Not known	Total
1973	149	334	89	23	20	24	5	644
1976	61	315	251	55	35	20	8	745
1981	141	544	511	269	78	15	49	1 607
1982	197	676	593	323	118	16	53	1 976
1983	402	1 011	766	440	192	38	130	2 979
1984	584	1 334	958	570	257	22	115	3 840
Females								
1973	41	79	20	7	8	8	0	163
1976	40	100	55	15	10	12	7	239
1981	91	225	186	84	18	14	23	641
1982	113	271	233	113	41	12	34	817
1983	170	446	315	150	59	18	49	1 207
1984	214	618	405	205	63	19	51	1 575

Source: Home Office

from *Social Trends 16* (HMSO, 1986)

Item 10.16   Narcotic drugs – total new addicts notified: by sex

2 Draw a bar chart to show how the total number of new addicts notified to the Home Office each year has grown since 1973.

According to the table in Item 10.16, there were 5415 notifications of new addicts in 1984. This is 30 per cent more than in 1983 and almost double the number in 1982. About 90 per cent of new addicts notified in 1984 claimed addiction to heroin. It should be recognised, of course, that the number of addicts is much greater than the number of notifications to the Home Office.

Explanations of illegal drug-taking

Illegal drug-taking is often very broadly explained by reference to the strains and stresses of a modern industrialised society. However, drug-taking is not a new problem in society and since not everyone turns to illegal drug-taking this is not a very good explanation. There are other ways in which people can legally relieve their frustrations; for example, by taking alcohol and smoking tobacco. People who drink in moderation or smoke tobacco are not looked on by society in the same way as people who use illegal drugs. Some portions of the mass media paint a picture of the illegal drug-taker as a depraved or weak individual unable to stand up to the realities of life. As we have seen, some sociologists think that this picture and the public's reponse to drug-takers contribute to changing them into the people the public thinks they are.

Key terms

- drug addiction
- drug habituation
- drug dependency
- solvent abuse

47.2 Alcohol and tobacco

Drug-taking in Britain is no new thing: alcohol and tobacco have been used in large quantities for years! Alcohol is a drug and, like heroin and cannabis, can lead to dependency. In the extreme case of alcoholism there is a physical addiction with associated withdrawal symptoms if alcohol is not available. Perhaps more often a habituation can develop where there is a strong desire to consume, and perhaps rely on, alcohol. In other words, alcohol can lead to physical addiction, but it does not always. Drinking alcohol is a social habit which, in moderation, is accepted and even encouraged by our society.

In our society there are norms about drinking

alcohol. For example, we have unwritten rules to the effect that a person should know when to stop drinking. It is acceptable to drink in moderation, but to drink regularly to the point of being drunk is generally not acceptable. In some groups, however, a male's drinking to excess is taken as a sign of being 'manly'. Clearly the social norms associated with the consumption of alcohol vary for different social groups. As we have already seen, they also can vary between different societies.

Who are alcoholics?

Because alcoholism is very often seen as being a sign of weakness and an inability to stand up to life, people go to some lengths to try to conceal their dependence on alcohol. The social stigma attached to alcoholism affects the life of the individual in many ways, leading to isolation from other people in society. The person who is dependent on alcohol is often middle-aged and male, but there has recently been an increase in the number of women and young people requiring treatment.

Alcoholism and smoking as social problems

One of the reasons why alcoholism and smoking are considered to be social problems is that they cost the country money. The group Action on Smoking and Health (ASH) suggests that the cost of smoking includes not only the expenses of treating diseases caused by smoking, but also other costs such as working days lost and social security payments. The Royal College of Physicians estimates that 50 million working days are lost every year due to smoking-induced illness, and the Department of Health and Social Security (DHSS) estimates the cost of treating diseases caused by smoking at £170 million a year. ASH also reports that 42 per cent of fatal casualties which occurred in accidental domestic fires were caused by smoking materials.

Alcohol causes similar problems for society. There are also reasons which cause alcoholism to be considered as a social, rather then an individual, problem: for example, prisons would be less overcrowded if it were possible to eliminate the problem of the drunkard who is arrested and ends up in gaol because of being unable to pay a fine. Drunken driving threatens not only the life of the person who has been drinking but also the lives of other people

Frequency of drinking	Number of units on a typical occasion		
	1–4	5–6	7+
Most days Three of four times a week Once or twice a week	FREQUENT LIGHT	MODERATE	HEAVIER
Once or twice a month	INFREQUENT LIGHT		MODERATE
Once or twice in six months Once or twice in the year	OCCASIONAL		

The sixth category was abstainers (those who had consumed no alcohol at all in the previous 12 months).

from *Social Trends 16* (HMSO, 1986)

Item 10.17 Categories of drinkers

on the road at the same time, so this too is cause for concern to society. People are also concerned about alcoholism as a social problem because it affects the lives and happiness of individuals and their families, often because of the social stigma which is attached to alcoholism in our society. The increased rate of alcohol-related problems is reflected in the growth in numbers belonging to Alcoholics Anonymous and Al-Anon Family Groups, which provide support for alcoholics' families.

Surveys designed to measure alcohol consumption consistently show lower levels of consumption than would be expected from statistics relating to the sale of alcohol! The government statistics, therefore, do not measure actual alcohol consumption. Instead they classify repondents into different *types* of drinker – abstainers, occasional, infrequent light drinkers, frequent light drinkers, moderate drinkers and heavier drinkers. The categories are shown in Item 10.17. ('Units' are amounts drunk which contain broadly similar amounts of alcohol. A standard unit is equivalent to half a pint of beer, a single measure of spirits or a glass of wine.) Item 10.18 shows how drinking habits changed between 1978 and 1982.

ACTIVITIES 13

Study Items 10.17 and 10.18 and answer the questions that follow.

Great Britain								Percentages and numbers
	Males				Females			
	1978	1980	1982	1984	1978	1980	1982	1984
Type of drinker* *(percentages)*								
Abstainer	5	5	6	7	11	12	12	13
Occasional	9	9	10	9	25	22	23	20
Infrequent light	11	12	12	12	19	19	20	19
Frequent light	34	37	37	38	39	41	40	42
Moderate	15	14	14	14	4	4	4	4
Heavier	25	23	21	20	2	2	1	2
Sample size (= 100%) (numbers)	10,015	9,959	8,780	8,070	11,650	11,557	10,185	9,430

*Persons aged 18 or over only.

Source: General Household Survey

from *Social Trends 18* (HMSO, 1988)

Item 10.18   Drinking habits: by sex, 1978 and 1982

Great Britain							Percentages and numbers	
	Socio-economic group							Average weekly cigarette consumption per smoker
	Professional	Employers and managers	Intermediate and junior non-manual	Skilled manual and own account non-professional	Semi-skilled manual and personal service	Unskilled manual	All persons	
Percentage smoking cigarettes								
Males								
1972	33	44	45	57	57	64	52	120
1976	25	38	40	51	53	58	46	129
1980	21	35	35	48	49	57	42	124
1982	20	29	30	42	47	49	38	121
1984	17	29	30	40	45	49	36	115
1984 Sample size (numbers)	448	1,413	1,384	3,063	1,350	478	8,417	
Females								
1972	33	38	38	47	42	42	42	87
1976	28	35	36	42	41	38	38	101
1980	21	33	34	43	39	41	37	102
1982	21	29	30	39	36	41	33	98
1984	15	29	28	37	37	36	32	96
1984 Sample size (numbers)	384	1,487	2,436	2,585	1,864	518	9,788	

Source: General Household Survey

from *Social Trends 18* (HMSO, 1988)

Item 10.19   Adult cigarette smoking: by sex and socio-economic group

1 Describe the trends in changing drinking habits evident from Item 10.17.

2 What percentage of men were moderate or heavy drinkers in 1984? Compare these figures with those for women.

3 What percentage of women are abstainers or drink only occasionally? What is the equivalent figure for men?

4 What changes have occurred in the period 1978–84 in the drinking habits of males and females?

ACTIVITIES 14

Item 10.19 shows that smoking is a habit which varies with both sex and social class.

1 Describe in your own words what has happened to the average weekly cigarette consumption per smoker between 1972 and 1984.

2 Describe in your own words what has happened to the actual numbers of persons smoking between 1972 and 1984.

3 Comment on any relationship there may be between cigarette smoking and a person's sex and socio-economic group.

Explanations for alcoholism

It is misleading to try and look for one way of explaining alcohol dependency. The range of backgrounds of people who are known to be alcohol dependent and the number of different circumstances in which they come to be dependent make it impossible even to talk of alcoholism as a single problem. It may be better, in fact, to talk of alcoholisms.

Some sociologists suggest that a person who does not know the norms which surround restrained drinking in the company of other people is more likely to become a compulsive drinker than someone who knows the rules of drinking socially. This would imply that someone brought up a teetotaller might be more likely to become a compulsive drinker than would someone brought up in a household where social drinking was the norm. However, we have at present no very satisfactory ideas explaining alcoholism. The only thing we do know about it is the way in which people tend to react to someone who has passed beyond the level of drinking which we look on as being acceptable. The stigma attached to someone in this condition is likely to have the effect of pushing the excessive drinker still further into the state of being dependent on alcohol.

REVIEW

If you have studied and understood this chapter you should be able to . . .

■ define or explain the following terms:
  a norms,
  b mores,
  c folkways,
  d customs, and
  e laws.
■ explain the difference between criminal offences and civil offences.
■ give an account of the reasons why official criminal statistics must be very carefully interpreted, including in your answer an account of the significance of the British Crime Survey and the Islington Crime Survey.
■ outline the way social and economic factors can lead to delinquency.
■ explain the differences between crime and deviance.
■ give an account of Merton's typology of deviance, explaining (in one or two sentences each) the four types of deviance.
■ explain what labelling theory is, and how it differs from other explanations of deviance.
■ explain in a paragraph the process of deviancy amplification.
■ give an account of the way both the police and the media can contribute to the process of deviancy amplification.
■ outline in what way alcohol and smoking may cause *social* problems.

COURSEWORK SUGGESTION

Do a survey of pupils in your school on smoking. Pupils at a school in Walsall, West Midlands, carried out a survey of smoking in their school. They distributed a questionnaire around the school using the form registers as a sample frame.

Pupils were asked two simple questions:

1 Have you ever tried a cigarette?

2 Do you smoke regularly?

The percentage of pupils who had said they had tried a cigarette at least once are shown in Item 10.20.

Year	%
1st	32
2nd	24
3rd	38
4th	60
5th	72
6th	78

from *The Imhoff Report* (Barr Beacon School, 1986)

Item 10.20   Pupils claiming to have tried a cigarette at least once

Year	%
1st	0
2nd	2
3rd	5
4th	13
5th	19
6th	37

from *The Imhoff Report* (Barr Beacon School, 1986)

Item 10.21   Pupils claiming to smoke 'regularly'

England & Wales (1982)		Percentages and numbers					
		Age					
		11	12	13	14	15	16
Percentage who:							
Have never smoked		74	62	45	36	28	26
Tried smoking once		18	25	27	24	22	28
Used to smoke		4	5	12	15	14	11
Smoke occasionally		4	6	9	9	11	8
Smoke regularly		–	1	7	16	25	26
Number of pupils							
(=100%)		479	574	607	589	600	121

Source: 'Smoking among secondary school children', J. Dobbs and A. Marsh, *Office of Population Censuses and Surveys*

from *Social Trends 16* (HMSO, 1986)

Item 10.22   Smoking behaviour among secondary school children: by age

The percentage of pupils who said they smoked 'regularly' are shown in Item 10.21.

Item 10.22 shows the results of a national survey for comparison. Comment on any conclusions you can draw by comparing the survey at this school and the results of a national survey. Say why such comparisons may not be reliable. Comment on why the surveys may have produced different results.

When you have completed your own survey you should try to answer the following questions:

1 How do your survey results differ from the results of the national survey?

2 What explanations are you able to provide for the pattern of smoking you have discovered in your own school?

3 What norms apply to smoking in your school? You should consider:
  a formal social control (such as school rules and the law).
  b informal social control.

ASSESSMENT QUESTIONS

The mark allocations to sections of the questions are shown in the right hand margin.

1

The Number of Certain Crimes in Birmingham in 1978 and 1981

	BIRMINGHAM	
	1978	1981
POPULATION	1 041 000	1 020 300
Murder	45	35
Rape	93	83
Robbery	1 060	1 543
Burglary	40 633	57 702

(Source: *Police Review*)

a According to the above information, how many cases of rape were there in Birmingham in 1978? (1)

b From the above information, give one example of a crime which has increased between 1978 and 1981. (1)

c What is the difference between legal and illegal deviancy? (4)

d Identify and explain **three** reasons why crime statistics do not necessarily show the true extent of crime in society. (6)

e What explanations have sociologists put forward to explain juvenile crime? (8)

Southern Examining Group

2

a What is the difference between criminal and
  non-criminal deviance?   (3)
b Give **two** examples of non-criminal deviance
  and explain why each is considered deviant.   (5)
c 'Laws vary from time to time and from
  place to place.' Why do laws change?   (7)

London & East Anglian Group for GCSE Examinations

3

a What is the difference between crime and
  deviance?   (2)
b How do the mass media influence the way
  that many people think about crime levels?   (3)
c Why might official statistics not be a good
  guide to the true level of criminal activity?   (4)
d By using examples, show how stereotyping
  and the idea of 'labelling' might help to
  explain the activities of the police and courts
  in dealing with crime.   (6)

Northern Examining Association

Acknowledgements

Lindsay Fursland (Head of Drama and Head of Year, Claremont School, Brent) wrote the original play–readings which appear as stimulus material in each chapter. The authors wish to thank him for his contribution.

The authors and publishers wish to acknowledge with thanks the following photographic sources: Aerofilms p. 131 top; The Arkwright Society/Ray Kenning p. 128 centre right; Associated Press pp. 128 centre right, 136 centre; Barnaby's Picture Library pp. 20, 98 left, 98 right; BBC Enterprises p. 121; John Bentley p. 199; Birmingham Daily News p. 37 bottom; Jim Brownbill pp. 14, 16, 19, 56 top left, top right, 89, 128 bottom right, 155 bottom left, 178 top; Camera Press pp. 35 bottom right, 37 top, 41, 52, 110, 123, 128 centre left, 136 top centre, 136 centre left, centre right, bottom right, 141, 161, 164, top; J. Allan Cash pp. 76, 83, 155 top left, 188 right, bottom, 189 top; Express Dairy Co. (London) Ltd p. 155 bottom right; Fords of Britain pp. 162, 164 bottom; Sally and Richard Greenhill pp. 35 centre, bottom left, 56 centre, bottom, 78, 85, 178 top right, 189 bottom; Hampshire County Council p. 18; John and Penny Hubley pp. 32, 60; Rodney Jennings pp. 128 top right, 178 bottom right; Keystone Collection pp. 77, 131 bottom; Mansell Collection pp. 35 top, 68; National Coal Board p. 155 centre right; Network p. 196; Paul Popper Ltd p. 179; Press Association pp. 136 top left, centre bottom; Syndication International p. 144; Zefa (UK) p. 188 top.

The authors and publishers wish to thank the following who have kindly given permission for the use of copyright material. Barr Beacon School for an extract from a report by M. Imhoff; Basil Blackwell Ltd for material from *Social Class Differences* by Ivan Reid, Grant McIntyre, 1981; BBC Enterprises Ltd for material from *BBC Annual Report and Handbooks 1986 and 1987* and *Annual Review of BBC Audience Research Findings*, No. 4, 1976/77; Benn Business Information Services Ltd for material from *Benn's Media Directory 1986*; Cambridge University Press for material from *The Affluent Worker in the Class Structure* by Goldthorpe et al., 1969; Chapman and Hall Ltd for material from *Social Analysis: Methods of Discovery* by J. A. Hughes, Nelson, 1976; Commission for Racial Equality for material from *Annual Report 1985*; Gower Publishing Company Ltd for material from *British Social Attitudes: The 1984 Report* by R. Jowell and C. Airey, 1984 and *Black and White Britain: The Third PSI Survey* by C. Brown, 1985; Grafton Books for material from *The Home and School* by J. W. B. Douglas, MacGibbon and Kee, 1964; The *Guardian* for material from issues 28.1.86 and 27.5.82; The Controller of Her Majesty's Stationery Office for Crown copyright material; Christopher Huhne for 'Share boom halts equality trend', *Guardian*, 28.9.86; Independent Broadcasting Authority for material from *Yearbook of Independent Broadcasting*, 1988; Independent Television Publications Ltd for material from *TV Times*, 19–25 April 1986; J.I.C.N.A.R.S. for material from *National Readership Survey*, 1987; Josephine Klein for material from *Samples of English Cultures*, Routledge & Kegan Paul, 1965; London & East Anglian Group, Northen Examining Association comprising Associated Lancashire Schools Examining Group, Joint Matriculation Board, North Regional Examinations Board, North West Regional Examinations Board and Yorkshire and Humberside Regional Examinations Board, and Southern Examining Group for specimin GCSE Sociology questions; Longman Group UK Ltd for material from *The Family* by R. J. Cootes, 1974, and *Class Antobiography* by R. Fielding, Longman Mirco Software, 1987; Manchester University Press for material from *British Politics Today* by B. Jones and D. Kavanagh, eds, 1983; Methuen, London for material from *The Collapse of Work* by Clive Jenkins and Barrie Sherman, 1979, and *Class* by Jilly Cooper, 1980; Macmillan Publishers for material from *People and Politics in Britain* by L. Robins, T. Brennan and J. Sutton, 1985, *Minority Families in Britain* by V. S. Khan, 1979, *Investigating Society: Talking to People* by R. Whitburn, 1979, *The Experience of Unemployment* by S. Allen *et al.*, 1986, and *Ethnicity & Education Achievement in British Schools* by G. K. Verma & B. Ashworth, 1986; Municipal Journal Ltd for material from 'Knowing the rules on accepting gifts' by Greville Janner, *Municipal Journal*, 10.1.86; John Murray Publishers Ltd for material from *Understanding Society* by C. H. Brown, 1979; National Council for One-Parent Families for material from *Information Sheet, No. 5*; The National Magazine Company Ltd for material from 'School's Out' by Caroline Western, *She*, 1980; Thomas Nelson and Sons Ltd for material from *Sociology: An Introductory Course* by P. L. Selfe, 1981; Maureen O'Connor for 'If you can beat them you should join them', *Guardian*, 28.1.86; Penguin Books Ltd for material from *Equal Opportunities: A Careers Guide* by Ruth Miller and Anna Alston, copyright © Ruth Miller, 1966, 1970, 1973, 1975, 1978, 1981, 1982, 1984, 1987, copyright © Anna Alston, 1984, and *Images of Deviance* by Stanley Cohen, Collection copyright © Penguin Books Ltd, 1971; Police Review Publishing Company Ltd for material from *Police Review*; *Social Science Teacher* for material from 'Teaching the Politics of Everyday Life' by Clive Harber, vol. 10, no. 2, 1980, and 'The Hidden Curriculum' by Roger Fielding and Lindsay Furland, vol. 14, no. 1, 1984; Tavistock Publications for material from *Coal is Our Life* by N. Dennis, F. Henriques and C. Slaughter, 1969; Times Newspapers Ltd for material from 'Combatants in non-existent wars' by George Szamvely, *The Times Educational Supplement*, 5.12.86; The Universities Central Council on Admissions for material from the *Statistical Supplement to the Twenty-fifth Report 1986–87*; Unwin Hyman for material from *Doing Sociological Research*, eds. C. Bell and H. Newby, Allen & Unwin, 1979 and *Work and Retirement* by S. R. Parker, Allen & Unwin, 1982; Vacation Work Publications for material from *The Kibbutz Volunteer* by John Bedford, 1986; George Weidenfeld & Nicholson Ltd for material from *The U. K. Economy* by Prest and Coppock, 1986; Wheaton Publishers Ltd for material from *A Sikh Family in Britain* by W. Owen Cole, Religious and Moral Education Press, 1973.

Every effort has been made to trace all the copyright holders but if any have been inadvertently overlooked the publishers will be pleased to make the necessary arrangement at the first opportunity.

Index